The Usefulness of Scripture

The Usefulness of Scripture

ESSAYS IN HONOR OF ROBERT W. WALL

Edited by
Daniel Castelo,
Sara M. Koenig, and
David R. Nienhuis

Eisenbrauns | University Park, Pennsylvania

Library of Congress Cataloging-in-Publication Data

Names: Castelo, Daniel, 1978– editor. | Koenig, Sara M., editor. | Nienhuis, David R.,
  1968– editor. | Wall, Robert W., honoree.
Title: The usefulness of scripture : essays in honor of Robert W. Wall / edited by Daniel
  Castelo, Sara M. Koenig, and David R. Nienhuis.
Description: University Park, Pennsylvania : Eisenbrauns, The Pennsylvania State
  University Press, [2018] | Includes bibliographical references and index.
Summary: "A collection of essays covering theology and methodology—emphasizing
  Wesleyan biblical hermeneutics, canonical perspectives, and the implications of
  these approaches for church life and work—as well as biblical texts/themes and
  the relationship of the study of Scripture to the life of the Christian"—Provided by
  publisher.
Identifiers: LCCN 2018002087 | ISBN 9781575069609 (cloth : alk. paper)
Subjects: LCSH: Bible—Criticism, interpretation, etc. | Bible—Canonical criticism. |
  Bible—Theology.
Classification: LCC BS511.3 .U84 2018 | DDC 220.6—dc23
LC record available at https://lccn.loc.gov/2018002087

Eisenbrauns is an imprint of The Pennsylvania State University Press.

The Pennsylvania State University Press is a member of the Association of American
University Presses.

It is the policy of The Pennsylvania State University Press to use acid-free paper.
Publications on uncoated stock satisfy the minimum requirements of American National
Standard for Information Sciences—Permanence of Paper for Printed Library Material,
ANSI Z39.48—1992.

Contents

Acknowledgments

We the editors would like to express our thanks to First Free Methodist Church of Seattle and its sometime pastor Blake Wood for their generous subvention that made this volume possible. Also, we would like to recognize the aid of our student worker Griffin Lamb, who helped in the tedious details of putting this book together. Our deep thanks to Jim Eisenbraun and the entire staff at Eisenbrauns for supporting this project. And finally, thank you to all who contributed to the volume itself. It was a wonderfully collaborative effort to organize this volume in recognition of Rob's witness and contributions.

Accolades

Rob Wall has the gift of convincing seminary students that critical scholarship matters — and that it matters precisely in the practicalities of pastoring. Thank you for holding things together and making us think!
  —*Revd. Canon Professor Loveday Alexander, Emeritus*
  Professor of Biblical Studies, University of Sheffield

***

When working on the Book of James a few years ago, I was often bored reading commentary after commentary. Too often exegetes did little more than repackage what others before them had written. Rob's *Community of the Wise* was, happily, a consistent exception. I always looked forward to opening it, knowing that I would find fresh suggestions and creative connections. And such is the hallmark of all of Rob's work: independence of mind and original insight.
  —*Dale Allison, Richard J. Dearborn Professor*
  of New Testament, Princeton Theological Seminary

***

Rob Wall's *capacity* amazes me. This book testifies to his capacious life as a biblical scholar. Those who know him beyond the academic world are aware of his keen interest and expertise in the arts, music, and literature. Above and beyond these many areas of expertise stands Rob's great capacity for friendship. For thirty-nine years I have witnessed Rob's enormous investment in collegial and mentoring relationships, including ours. My life is richer for it.
  —*Bob Drovdahl, Professor of Educational Ministry,*
  Seattle Pacific University and Seminary

***

In my line of work I get to know so many good scholars, teachers, and writers. Rob does all these things well, for which I am grateful. I am even more grateful for the compelling magnetism with which he brings and holds people together in conversation (which—of special interest to me—tends to produce both books and wise advice), for the determination and persistence with which he pursues theological reading of Scripture, and for his theological seriousness and passion. These things are very closely related; they are facets of the same thing: loyal friendship, Godward and usward. Rob, when I think of you and Carla, I thank God. You are a gift to so many.

    —*James D. Ernest, Vice President, Editor-in-Chief,*
    William B. Eerdmans Publishing

∗∗∗

Congratulations to Rob Wall on this fitting tribute from colleagues and students. We need more Rob Walls, scholars who venture bold proposals with enthusiasm, who encourage the work of others, who instill genuine interest in our texts, and who sit lightly with their own learning. Our corporate endeavor is enhanced by Rob Wall.

    —*Beverly Gaventa, Distinguished Professor*
    of New Testament Interpretation, Baylor University

∗∗∗

It now seems clear that at least one item on my lifetime wish list will go unfulfilled. Beginning with my earliest interactions with Rob Wall, I have hoped that, one day, we would serve on the same faculty. I am sure that much would be gained by this kind of proximity and partnership, but my primary motivation rests on the history of our conversations. Sharply put (as Rob would say), I seem always to come away from our interactions overtaken with more stimulating thoughts and proposals and what-if's than when we started. There is much to appreciate about this faithful friend, this guileless Wesleyan, this unrepentant scholar of the whole of Scripture, but this capacity to catalyze the theological imagination—this is what I celebrate most.

    —*Joel B. Green, Provost, Dean of the School of Theology, and Professor*
    of New Testament Interpretation at Fuller Theological Seminary

∗∗∗

For many years, Rob Wall has been out ahead of most of us in the field of New Testament studies. More clearly than the rest of us, he has seen the hermeneutical significance of the shaping of the canon of New Testament writings: beyond the question of which texts were included in the canon or excluded from it, Rob has taught us to think also about the *architecture* of the canonical collection. That question, in turn, has opened up interesting fresh perspectives, particularly on Acts and the Catholic Epistles—texts whose significance for early Christianity is often underestimated. I have come to know Rob as a gracious colleague, an asker of provocative and fruitful questions, and—perhaps most importantly—a fellow serious sports fan. Whether we are talking about canonical hermeneutics or the current fate of the Mariners, our conversations are always lively. Rob, on your seventieth birthday, thanks for your scholarship and your friendship.

—*Richard B. Hays, George Washington Ivey Professor*
of New Testament, Duke Divinity School

***

As a sophomore at SPU I would visit Rob's office. Peering at me between the stacks in his book-bedecked office, Rob asked me questions, and through that taught me how to read the Bible. I mean really read it, opening up worlds within worlds that I didn't know existed.

—*S. Brent Plate, Visiting Professor of Religion, Hamilton College*

***

I have known Robert Wall for nearly thirty years. More recently, when he's able, he joins our weekly pub gathering out on the Olympic Peninsula of Washington State. There a group of searching minds—the churched, unchurched, and post-churched—cordially discuss issues of the day and of the ages. This is an entirely different *Sitz im Leben* from the Seattle Pacific University classroom or SBL and SNTS meetings. But as a native of the Pacific Northwest, Rob fits right in. Here the person I know as a New Testament scholar who has made formative contributions to the theological interpretation of Scripture engages politics or history or evolution or anthropology or matters of faith over suds and peanuts. I take it as an example of flourishing where you are planted, in one region, one institution, one church, and one rule of faith.

—*Dan Reid, Editorial Director, IVP Academic*

***

Rob Wall changed my life. His deep love of God, of the church and of Scripture led me to new ways of understanding Scripture and what it means to be a Christian. His amazing intellectual ability disciplined by his faithfulness to God opened for me new ways of reading Scripture. From the first day I met him so many years ago he embraced me as his great friend, and I am deeply grateful for his brotherly love. So, we celebrate seventy years of Rob Wall who, thanks to CrossFit, doesn't look a day over sixty-nine.

—*Les Steele, Executive Vice President, Northwest Commission on Colleges and Universities*

***

Rob Wall taught me the single most important lesson I ever learned about being a teaching scholar: Students are more likely to learn to love you if you insist only that they respect you, than they are ever to respect you if you try too hard to make them love you. Of course, you don't "insist" that your students respect you by *telling* them to. That would never work, and would in any case be self-demeaning. Rather, you do it by your uncompromising adherence to the highest standards of classroom instruction, by your sincere reverence for and delight in your subject matter, and by your fierce demand that students come to class well prepared and turn in work that has been thoroughly researched, rigorously argued, elegantly written and carefully edited. And you do it by making no bones about your refusal to put up with anything less from them—through asking tough questions in class and covering their papers with red ink. This is Rob's approach, and many students initially find it intimidating. But the wise ones soon realize that it comes from his deep respect for them and for the craft of scholarship. They discover that he expects more of them than they ever expected of themselves, and that he sees more potential in them than they ever knew was there. Then it occurs to them that they must do their best to actualize that potential in order to show proper respect for themselves, for Scripture, and for the entire endeavor of Christian higher education. At which point they wake up to the fact that this formidable professor, who has made no effort whatsoever to be "lovable," is eminently worthy of their love.

—*Richard B. Steele, Professor of Moral and Historical*
Theology, Seattle Pacific University and Seminary

***

I was acquainted with Rob Wall by reputation for a long time prior to my knowing him well. His stature as the preeminent scholar of Wesleyan Biblical hermeneutics led me to respect him profoundly—though from afar, since we navigated in somewhat different theological guilds. But when—a decade ago—I became Rob's dean, and thereby had the privilege of working with him almost daily, I learned firsthand why he's revered by so many. In addition to being the quintessential model of a scholar who lives and breathes a theological interpretation of Scripture through a Wesleyan lens, Rob also exhibits other remarkable characteristics revealed to those of us who are his colleagues. Rob demands, for example, that Christian colleges expect the highest level of academic production from their faculty. He insists that rigorous scholarship among Christians can (and, at its best, must) be animated by a deep, prayerful piety. He is committed to the concept that one's best scholarly research grows out of one's teaching, and vice versa. He's continually open to hearing about, and—with sufficient evidence—changing his mind regarding, new ideas. And even though he's introverted, nonetheless he's the finest example I know of an academician who finds joy in thinking, writing, and teaching collaboratively. Rob has become a trusted friend and co-laborer in the Gospel work of being a professor—literally "one who professes" what he believes. For this, I give thanks to God.

—*Doug Strong, Dean, School of Theology,*
Seattle Pacific University and Seminary

***

Rob Wall is one of those colleagues who looks for the forest and does not stop at describing the trees. Using text observations he works in an admirable balance between critical historical thought and appreciation for the whole of the literary result. Few people have managed to steer up the consensus and lead the path to new pastures as Dr. Wall has done in his life's work. Thank you, Rob.

—*David Trobisch, Director of Collections,*
Museum of the Bible, Washington D.C.

***

> A CLERK from Dallas was there also,
> Who'd studied theology, now and then.
> As lean was his horse as is a rake,
> And he too was not fat, that I take,
> But he looked toned, moreover, soberly.
> Very worn off was his overcoat; for he
> Had no stock in fashion's worldly call,
> Nor was he greedy to pursue material goods,
> For he would rather have at his bed's head
> Some twenty books, all bound in black or red,
> Of Wesley and his thought
> Than rich robes, fiddle, or gourmet delights.
> He took utmost care and heed for his study.
> Not one word spoke he more than Facnet asked;
> And that was said with due formality
> And short and lively, and full of academic chops.
> Filled with moral virtue was his speech;
> And gladly would he learn and gladly teach.

With apologies to Chaucer and gratitude for Rob's
friendship and love of literature.

—*Susan VanZanten, Professor*
of English, Seattle Pacific University

***

On an impossibly rainy Friday night in the late fall of 1968, I called the play-by-play for a college football rivalry game. In the mud and flood, Valparaiso's middle linebacker, Rob Wall, set a school record for tackles. But the highly favored Crusaders of Valpo lost to my Wheaton Crusaders. Wheaton salvaged a miserable season by winning the coveted Crusader Shield.

I didn't actually meet the standout linebacker until nearly ten years later, when Rob joined me on the Seattle Pacific faculty. We became colleagues, teachers of each other, fellow faculty activists, deeply committed brothers. Our wives became fast friends; our children grew up together and remain close. And I can attest that Rob Wall has never lost that linebacker's grit. Still a contender, still a record setter, but now in the classroom and from the scholar's desk, he crusades for the church and her Scripture. He has taught me much, and I am grateful for four decades as his teammate.

As in those long ago days, my friend and colleague Rob Wall remains a team leader and a team player, still instructing and still inspiring those in the battle, on the bench, and yes, up in the booth.

—*William Woodward, Professor of History, Seattle Pacific University*

Introduction

David R. Nienhuis

From the stories I've heard over the years, most first encounters with Rob Wall are memorable. Mine certainly was: I met Rob in the autumn of 1986, right at the start of my freshman year at Seattle Pacific University. I was a gung-ho eighteen-year-old planning on a future in youth ministry, so of course I signed up for as many theology courses as I was allowed to take. Thus, at 7:30 a.m. every weekday morning, I made my way to Peterson Hall for Rob Wall's "Introduction to the New Testament" course.

I was enthralled. Confused, certainly, and frequently incredulous, but still I ate it up and found myself hungry for more. Then as now, Rob was a formidable presence in the classroom. With a lecture style that is part homily, part blitzkrieg, there are not many students brave enough to ask questions. I'm fairly certain I didn't raise my hand the entire quarter. But that did not keep me from earning an A on the mid-term exam, and with it, an invitation to join Rob one afternoon for a meeting in his office.

I have a mental image of that meeting imprinted on my consciousness. Indeed, every time an intimidated freshman sits down to meet with me, I recall that first one-on-one encounter with Rob. He was young then, just in his later thirties. I steeled myself as I entered the room expecting to meet the same imposing figure I'd come to know in class. Much to my surprise, the person I met instead was warm-toned, soft-spoken—almost introverted even—more concerned pastor than stern prophet. I remember he asked me questions about my life. He asked how class was going. He asked about the hopes I held for the future. When I told him I wanted to be a youth pastor, he paused and looked me in the eyes long and hard. This is the imprinted image in my mind, Rob staring at me, and it is accompanied by my recollection of the words he said next: "First quarter freshmen don't typically get A's on my exams. You obviously have all the necessary goods to be a theology major, but you should be thinking beyond your immediate course of study.

Any youth minister worth his salt will plan on going to seminary. We can advise you on what schools you should consider. . . ."

I'm sure he said more than that, but these empowering words were the ones that had a lasting impact. I was a first-generation college student, and had never before been told I was academically capable, much less that I should already be aiming toward graduate school. That one gracious meeting opened up a whole new vista of vocational insight and, indeed, when I trace the early development of my professional life as a teaching scholar, that meeting with Rob stands out. Afterward I headed downstairs to my work study job as an office assistant for Les Steele, and I must have had a rather giddy look on my face, because he flashed his trademark grin and asked, rather knowingly, "So, how was your meeting with Rob?" I responded breathlessly, "He told me I should be thinking about going to seminary!" Les chuckled in response and said, "And with this you have learned the true version of the first of the Four Spiritual Laws: God loves you, and Rob Wall has a wonderful plan for your life."

What most impressed me about Rob way back then turned out to be the very thing that continues to set people like Rob apart in the world of contemporary biblical scholarship. Somewhere between the general intellectual inheritance of Enlightenment modernity and the anti-intellectualism of my American evangelical upbringing, my eighteen-year-old self already took for granted that an academic career would force a wedge between scholarly discipline and Christian discipleship. Some served the academy, and others served the church— and I'd been repeatedly warned of the dangers the former held for a life of authentic faith.

Yet in Rob (and, indeed, most of the theology faculty I met at SPU) these distinctions were confused: here was one who produced rigorous, guild-shaping scholarship *as* an expression of his discipleship to Jesus; here was one who did not simply cultivate separate professional identities in the guild and the church but united them, truly, in his own person. At that time in my life I was not yet acquainted with Charles Wesley's prayer that children be trained to "*unite the pair so long disjoined, knowledge and vital piety: learning and holiness combined*"— but in the years since, I and countless others have witnessed the fruit of this union in Rob's life and work.

It seems clear that his upbringing and academic training combined to make this orientation an inevitability. I am not the one to tell that story in the detail it deserves, but anyone who has spent time with Rob will have heard him recall memories of his grandmother, the traveling holiness preacher and end-times theologian, along with stories of his beloved parents, who led the family in Scripture study each night after dinner and encouraged Rob's pursuit of academic excellence. One also hears Rob tell of the many years spent at Dallas Theological Seminary, which cemented in him an explicit and indissoluble connection between the intellectual practices of biblical studies and the spiritual habits of the life of faith. Indeed, it was not the school's dispensational hermeneutics but an intense focus on "learning and holiness combined" that Rob took from his years at DTS. In his own words: "The methodological stuff is pretty easy to change with new information and maturity; it's this connection between the mind and the heart that's much more difficult to cultivate and to keep. I've long ago given up on dispensationalism, but it's hard to forget holiness."

The unashamed binding of Scripture study to spiritual formation was, until relatively recently, a minority view in the mainstream, Society of Biblical Literature crowd—something confessed in private, perhaps, but not proclaimed from the lecture podium or the writing desk. And while there are of course those today who still insist on maintaining a sharp distinction between the etic and the emic pose, between the object of study and the subject doing the studying, it is now far more common to hear scholars affirm without reservation the sort of things Rob has insisted on from the beginning of his work: that this fascinating text we study is, first and foremost, a graceful provision of God for the benefit of the life and work of the church. According to one of Rob's recent formulations,

> the Bible is conceived as a particular and portable place, built over considerable time by the church under the direction of God's Spirit; and biblical interpretation is that worshipful activity of entering into a sacred place to gather with other readers across history and cultural settings to hear a pertinent word from God.[1]

Rob's persistent word is this: The Bible is not merely interesting, it is useful. Indeed, the Bible is Christian Scripture, a carefully constructed holy text, given by God through the work of human hands, for the express purpose

---

1. "The Canonical View," in *Biblical Hermeneutics: Five Views* (ed. Stanley E. Porter and Beth M. Stovell; Spectrum Multiview Books; Downers Grove: IVP Academic, 2012) 112.

of cultivating a people set apart to perform God's work in the world (2 Tim 3:15–17).

Hence, when Richard Hays observes, "For many years, Rob Wall has been out ahead of most of us in the field of New Testament studies," he's not simply speaking in his characteristically gracious manner; he's acknowledging a fact about the state of the field. The basic range of commitments now commonly accepted as mainstream among adherents of the so-called "theological interpretation of Scripture" have been upheld by Rob consistently through nearly forty years of faithful teaching and writing.

We are indebted to Rob for his creative, critical, and prescient work in leading us to a deeper appreciation of the usefulness of Scripture. It should come as no surprise, then, that a collection of essays gathered in his honor should strive to reflect the "learning and holiness combined" that characterize his life and work. Some of the chapters that follow are more doctrinal and methodological in focus, while others are more text-centered and exegetical in nature—but all of them approach the Bible as the church's Scripture. These essays are written by pastors, publishers, and professors alike. Five of us have collaborated with Rob on other book projects. Four of us are former students. Two were on the faculty when Rob was hired (and neither were in favor of his hire, it turns out— but alas, we all make mistakes now and again). All of us are colleagues who have learned from Rob and cherish his friendship.

So, in honor of Rob's seventieth birthday, and in celebration of his many contributions to the church, to the academy, and to Seattle Pacific University, we invite you to consider with us *The Usefulness of Scripture.*

Published Works by Robert W. Wall, 1973–2015

Stephen Z. Perisho

Books

Wall, Robert W. *Why the Church? Reframing New Testament Theology.* Nashville: Abingdon, 2015.

Wall, Robert W., and David R. Nienhuis. *Reading the Epistles of James, Peter, John, and Jude as Scripture: The Shaping and Shape of a Canonical Collection.* Grand Rapids: Eerdmans, 2013.

Wall, Robert W., with Richard B. Steele. *1 & 2 Timothy and Titus. Two Horizons New Testament Commentary.* Grand Rapids: Eerdmans, 2012.

Wall, Robert W., and Anthony B. Robinson. *Called to Lead: Paul's Letters to Timothy for a New Day.* Grand Rapids: Eerdmans, 2012.

Wall, Robert W., and Anthony B. Robinson. *Called to Be Church: The Book of Acts for a New Day.* Grand Rapids: Eerdmans, 2006.

Wall, Robert W., and Shannon Smythe. *Women with a Passion for Ministry: Catechism.* Seattle: Seattle Pacific University, 2004.

Wall, Robert W. *The Acts of the Apostles: Introduction, Commentary, and Reflections.* Pp. 1–368 in *The Acts of the Apostles, Introduction to Epistolary Literature, The Letter to the Romans, The First Letter to the Corinthians,* vol. 10 of *The New Interpreter's Bible: General Articles & Introduction, Commentary, & Reflections For Each Book of the Bible Including the Apocryphal/Deuterocanonical Books in Twelve Volumes.* Edited by Leander E. Keck. Nashville: Abingdon, 2002.

Wall, Robert W. *Community of the Wise: The Letter of James.* Valley Forge: Trinity Press International, 1997.

Wall, Robert W. *Colossians & Philemon.* IVP New Testament Commentary Series 12. Downers Grove: InterVarsity, 1993.

Wall, Robert W. *Revelation.* Peabody: Hendrickson, 1991.

Wall, Robert W. *Commentary on Romans.* Seattle: Seattle Pacific University, 1985.

Edited Collections

Wall, Robert W., and David R. Nienhuis, eds. *A Compact Guide to the Whole Bible: Learning to Read Scripture's Story.* Grand Rapids: Baker Academic, 2015.

Wall, Robert W., New Testament ed. *The Wesley Study Bible: CEB.* Edited by Joel B. Green and William H. Willimon. Nashville: Abingdon, 2012.

Wall, Robert W., and Karl-Wilhelm Niebuhr, eds. *The Catholic Epistles and Apostolic Tradition.* Waco: Baylor University Press, 2009.

Wall, Robert W., New Testament ed. *The Wesley Study Bible: NRSV.* Edited by Joel B. Green and William H. Willimon. Nashville: Abingdon, 2009.

Wall, Robert W., and Douglas Geivett, guest eds. *Jesus and the Academy. Christian Scholar's Review* 28.4 (Summer 1999).

Wall, Robert W., and Eugene E. Lemcio, eds. *The New Testament as Canon: A Reader in Canonical Criticism. Journal for the Study of the New Testament* Supplement Series 76. Sheffield: Sheffield Academic Press, 1992.

Wall, Robert W., ed. *Resources for the Church: Self-Esteem.* Seattle: Pacific Northwest Conference of the Free Methodist Church, 1986.

Wall, Robert W., ed. *Resources for the Church: The Family.* Seattle: Pacific Northwest Conference of the Free Methodist Church, 1984.

Essays

Wall, Robert W., and David R. Nienhuis. "Preface." Pp. 7–10 in *A Compact Guide to the Whole Bible: Learning to Read Scripture's Story.* Edited by Robert W. Wall and David R. Nienhuis. Grand Rapids: Baker Academic, 2015.

Wall, Robert W., and Daniel Castelo. "Reading the Bible as Scripture." Pp. 11–25 in *A Compact Guide to the Whole Bible: Learning to Read Scripture's Story.* Edited by Robert W. Wall and David R. Nienhuis. Grand Rapids: Baker Academic, 2015.

Wall, Robert W. "Epilogue." Pp. 149–60 in *A Compact Guide to the Whole Bible: Learning to Read Scripture's Story.* Edited by Robert W. Wall and David R. Nienhuis. Grand Rapids: Baker Academic, 2015.

Wall, Robert W. "Foreword." Pp. ix-xiii in *Women in Ministry: Questions and Answers in the Exploration of a Calling,* by Shannon Nicole Smythe. Eugene: Wipf and Stock, 2015.

Wall, Robert W. "1 John" (Introduction and Study Notes). Pp. 474(NT)–483(NT) in *The CEB Study Bible with Apocrypha*. Edited by Joel B. Green. Nashville: Common English Bible, 2013.

Wall, Robert W. "2 John" (Introduction and Study Notes). Pp. 485(NT)–487(NT) in *The CEB Study Bible with Apocrypha*. Edited by Joel B. Green. Nashville: Common English Bible, 2013.

Wall, Robert W. "3 John" (Introduction and Study Notes). Pp. 489(NT)–492(NT) in *The CEB Study Bible with Apocrypha*. Edited by Joel B. Green. Nashville: Common English Bible, 2013.

Wall, Robert W. "The First Letter of Paul to Timothy" (Introduction and Study Notes). Pp. 1515–21 in *The Wesley Study Bible: CEB*. Edited by Joel B. Green and William H. Willimon. Nashville: Abingdon, 2012.

Wall, Robert W. "The Second Letter of Paul to Timothy" (Introduction and Study Notes). Pp. 1522–27 in *The Wesley Study Bible: CEB*. Edited by Joel B. Green and William H. Willimon. Nashville: Abingdon, 2012.

Wall, Robert W. "The Letter of Paul to Titus" (Introduction and Study Notes). Pp. 1528–31 in *The Wesley Study Bible: CEB*. Edited by Joel B. Green and William H. Willimon. Nashville: Abingdon, 2012.

Wall, Robert W. "The Canonical View." Pp. 111–30 (Chap. 5) in *Biblical Hermeneutics: Five Views*. Edited by Stanley E. Porter and Beth M. Stovell. Spectrum Multiview Books. Downers Grove: IVP Academic, 2012.

Wall, Robert W. "The Canonical Response." Pp. 188–200 (Chap. 10) in *Biblical Hermeneutics: Five Views*. Edited by Stanley E. Porter and Beth M. Stovell. Spectrum Multiview Books. Downers Grove: IVP Academic, 2012.

Wall, Robert W. "Participatory Holiness: A New Testament Perspective." Pp. 40–49 (Chap. 5) in *Holiness as a Liberal Art*. Edited by Daniel Castelo. Eugene: Pickwick, 2012.

Wall, Robert W. "Reading Scripture, the Literal Sense, and the Analogy of Faith." Pp. 33–46 (Chap. 3) in *Wesley, Wesleyans, and Reading Bible as Scripture*. Edited by Joel B. Green and David F. Watson. Waco: Baylor University Press, 2012.

Wall, Robert W. "Salvation's Bath by the Spirit: A Study of Titus 3:5b–6 in Its Canonical Setting." Pp. 198–212 in *The Spirit of Christ in the New Testament and Christian Theology: Essays in Honor of Max Turner*. Edited by I. Howard Marshall, Volker Rabens, and Cornelius Bennema. Grand Rapids: Eerdmans, 2012.

Wall, Robert W. "A Canonical Approach to the Unity of Acts and Luke's Gospel." Pp. 172–91 in *Rethinking the Unity and Reception of Luke and Acts*. Edited by Andrew F. Gregory and C. Kavin Rowe. Columbia: University of South Carolina Press, 2010.

Wall, Robert W. "James" (Overview and Study Notes). Pp. 894–99 in *The New Interpreter's Bible One Volume Bible Commentary*. Edited by Beverly Roberts Gaventa and David Petersen. Nashville: Abingdon, 2010.

Wall, Robert W. "The New Testament Practice of Holiness." P. 14 in *Holiness: Eight Essays from the School of Theology at Seattle Pacific University*. Seattle: Seattle Pacific University, 2010.

Wall, Robert W. "Reading the New Testament in Canonical Context." Pp. 372–96 (Chap. 17) in *Hearing the New Testament: Strategies for Interpretation*. 2nd edition. Edited by Joel B. Green. Grand Rapids: Eerdmans, 2010.

Wall, Robert W. "Wesley as Biblical Interpreter." Pp. 113–28 in *The Cambridge Companion to John Wesley*. Edited by Randy L. Maddox and Jason E. Vickers. Cambridge: Cambridge University Press, 2010.

Wall, Robert W. "The SNTS Seminar on the Catholic Epistles (2001–2006)." Pp. 1–5 (Chap. 1) in *The Catholic Epistles and Apostolic Tradition*. Edited by Robert W. Wall and Karl-Wilhelm Niebuhr. Waco: Baylor University Press, 2009.

Wall, Robert W. "A Unifying Theology of the Catholic Epistles: A Canonical Approach." Pp. 13–40 (Chap. 2) in *The Catholic Epistles and Apostolic Tradition*. Edited by Robert W. Wall and Karl-Wilhelm Niebuhr. Waco: Baylor University Press, 2009.

Wall, Robert W. "Acts and James." Pp. 127–52 (Chap. 7) in *The Catholic Epistles and Apostolic Tradition*. Edited by Robert W. Wall and Karl-Wilhelm Niebuhr. Waco: Baylor University Press, 2009.

Wall, Robert W. "The Priority of James." Pp. 153–60 (Chap. 8) in *The Catholic Epistles and Apostolic Tradition*. Edited by Robert W. Wall and Karl-Wilhelm Niebuhr. Waco: Baylor University Press, 2009.

Wall, Robert W. "Third Sunday of Easter: Acts 9:1–6 (7–20): Exegetical Perspective." Pp. 403–7 in *Feasting on the Word: Preaching the Revised Common Lectionary: Year C, Volume 2*. Edited by David L. Bartlett and Barbara Brown Taylor. Louisville: Westminster John Knox, 2009.

Wall, Robert W. "Fourth Sunday of Easter: Acts 9:36–43: Exegetical Perspective." Pp. 451–55 in *Feasting on the Word: Preaching the Revised Common*

Lectionary: Year C, Volume 2. Edited by David L. Bartlett and Barbara Brown Taylor. Louisville: Westminster John Knox, 2009.

Wall, Robert W. "Fifth Sunday of Easter: Acts 11:1–18: Exegetical Perspective." Pp. 427–31 in *Feasting on the Word: Preaching the Revised Common Lectionary: Year C, Volume 2.* Edited by David L. Bartlett and Barbara Brown Taylor. Louisville: Westminster John Knox, 2009.

Wall, Robert W. "The First Letter of Paul to Timothy" (Introduction and Study Notes). Pp. 1461–67 in *The Wesley Study Bible: NRSV.* Edited by Joel B. Green and William H. Willimon. Nashville: Abingdon, 2009.

Wall, Robert W. "The Second Letter of Paul to Timothy" (Introduction and Study Notes). Pp. 1469–74 in *The Wesley Study Bible: NRSV.* Edited by Joel B. Green and William H. Willimon. Nashville: Abingdon, 2009.

Wall, Robert W. "The Letter of Paul to Titus" (Introduction and Study Notes). Pp. 1475–78 in *The Wesley Study Bible: NRSV.* Edited by Joel B. Green and William H. Willimon. Nashville: Abingdon, 2009.

Wall, Robert W. "The Acts of the Apostles" (Introduction and Study Notes). Pp. 1869–1923 in *The Discipleship Study Bible: New Revised Standard Version including Apocrypha.* Edited by Bruce C. Birch, Brian K. Blount, Thomas G. Long, Gail R. O'Day, and W. Sibley Towner. Louisville: Westminster John Knox, 2008.

Wall, Robert W. "The Bible as Canon." Pp. 6–7 in *The Multi-Faceted Bible: Six Ways in Which the Church Views the Bible.* Seattle: Seattle Pacific University, 2008.

Wall, Robert W. "A Theological Morphology of the Bible: A Prescription for 'Spiritually Disabled' Students." Pp. 41–62 in *Immersed in the Life of God: The Healing Resources of the Christian Faith.* Edited by Paul L. Gavrilyuk, Douglas M. Koskela, and Jason E. Vickers. Grand Rapids: Eerdmans, 2008.

Wall, Robert W. "The Jerusalem Council (Acts 15:1–21) in Canonical Context." Pp. 93–101 in *From Biblical Criticism to Biblical Faith: Essays in Honor of Lee Martin McDonald.* Edited by William H. Brackney and Craig A. Evans. Macon: Mercer University Press, 2007.

Wall, Robert W. "Reading Paul with Acts: The Canonical Shaping of a Holy Church." Pp. 129–47 in *Holiness and Ecclesiology in the New Testament.* Edited by Kent E. Brower and Andy Johnson. Grand Rapids: Eerdmans, 2007.

Wall, Robert W. "The Acts of the Apostles." Pp. 113–33 in *The New Interpreter's Bible New Testament Survey*. Nashville: Abingdon, 2005.

Wall, Robert W. "Introduction to Epistolary Literature." Pp. 137–58 in *The New Interpreter's Bible New Testament Survey*. Nashville: Abingdon, 2005.

Wall, Robert W. "Introduction to the Pastoral Epistles." Pp. 635–40 in *The Bible Knowledge Background Commentary: Acts-Philemon*. Edited by Craig A. Evans. Colorado Springs: Victor, 2004.

Wall, Robert W. "Introduction to 1 Timothy." Pp. 641–42 in *The Bible Knowledge Background Commentary: Acts-Philemon*. Edited by Craig A. Evans. Colorado Springs: Victor, 2004.

Wall, Robert W. "1 Timothy." Pp. 643–60 in *The Bible Knowledge Background Commentary: Acts-Philemon*. Edited by Craig A. Evans. Colorado Springs: Victor, 2004.

Wall, Robert W. "Introduction to 2 Timothy." Pp. 661–62 in *The Bible Knowledge Background Commentary: Acts-Philemon*. Edited by Craig A. Evans. Colorado Springs: Victor, 2004.

Wall, Robert W. "2 Timothy." Pp. 663–75 in *The Bible Knowledge Background Commentary: Acts-Philemon*. Edited by Craig A. Evans. Colorado Springs: Victor, 2004.

Wall, Robert W. "Introduction to Titus." Pp. 677–78 in *The Bible Knowledge Background Commentary: Acts-Philemon*. Edited by Craig A. Evans. Colorado Springs: Victor, 2004.

Wall, Robert W. "Titus." Pp. 679–87 in *The Bible Knowledge Background Commentary: Acts-Philemon*. Edited by Craig A. Evans. Colorado Springs: Victor, 2004.

Wall, Robert W. "A Unifying Theology of the Catholic Epistles: A Canonical Approach." Pp. 43–71 in *The Catholic Epistles and the Tradition*. Edited by J. Schlosser. Leuven: Peeters, 2004.

Wall, Robert W. "The Function of the Pastoral Letters within the Pauline Canon of the New Testament: A Canonical Approach." Pp. 27–44 in *The Pauline Canon*. Edited by Stanley E. Porter. Leiden: Brill, 2004.

Wall, Robert W. "Toward a Wesleyan Hermeneutic of Scripture." Pp. 39–55 in *Reading the Bible in Wesleyan Ways: Some Constructive Proposals*. Edited by Barry L. Callen and Richard P. Thompson. Kansas City, MO: Beacon Hill, 2004.

Wall, Robert W. "Facilitating Scripture's Future Role among Wesleyans." Pp. 107–20 in *Reading the Bible in Wesleyan Ways: Some Constructive Proposals.* Edited by Barry L. Callen and Richard P. Thompson. Kansas City, MO: Beacon Hill, 2004.

Wall, Robert W. "Introduction to Epistolary Literature." Pp. 369–91 in *The Acts of the Apostles, Introduction to Epistolary Literature, The Letter to the Romans, The First Letter to the Corinthians,* vol. 10 of *The New Interpreter's Bible: General Articles & Introduction, Commentary, & Reflections For Each Book of the Bible Including the Apocryphal/Deuterocanonical Books in Twelve Volumes.* Edited by Leander E. Keck. Nashville: Abingdon, 2002.

Wall, Robert W. "The Significance of a Canonical Perspective of the Church's Scripture." Pp. 528–40 in *The Canon Debate.* Edited by Lee Martin McDonald and James A. Sanders. Peabody: Hendrickson, 2002.

Wall, Robert W. "The Intertextuality of Scripture: The Example of Rahab (James 2:25)." Pp. 217–36 in *The Bible at Qumran: Text, Shape, and Interpretation.* Edited by Peter W. Flint and T'ae-hun Kim. Grand Rapids: Eerdmans, 2001.

Wall, Robert W. "Seventeenth Sunday after Pentecost, Year C. Second Lesson: 1 Timothy 1:12–17." Pp. 429–33 in *The Lectionary Commentary: Theological Exegesis for Sunday's Texts: The Second Readings, Acts and the Epistles.* The Lectionary Commentary. Edited by Roger E. Van Harn. Grand Rapids: Eerdmans, 2001.

Wall, Robert W. "Eighteenth Sunday after Pentecost, Year C. Second Lesson: 1 Timothy 2:1–7." Pp. 433–37 in *The Lectionary Commentary: Theological Exegesis for Sunday's Texts: The Second Readings, Acts and the Epistles.* The Lectionary Commentary. Edited by Roger E. Van Harn. Grand Rapids: Eerdmans, 2001.

Wall, Robert W. "Nineteenth Sunday after Pentecost, Year C. Second Lesson: 1 Timothy 6:6–19." Pp. 438–40 in *The Lectionary Commentary: Theological Exegesis for Sunday's Texts: The Second Readings, Acts and the Epistles.* The Lectionary Commentary. Edited by Roger E. Van Harn. Grand Rapids: Eerdmans, 2001.

Wall, Robert W. "Twentieth Sunday after Pentecost, Year C. Second Lesson: 2 Timothy 1:1–14." Pp. 441–45 in *The Lectionary Commentary: Theological Exegesis for Sunday's Texts: The Second Readings, Acts and the*

Epistles. The Lectionary Commentary. Edited by Roger E. Van Harn. Grand Rapids: Eerdmans, 2001.

Wall, Robert W. "Twenty-First Sunday after Pentecost, Year C. Second Lesson: 2 Timothy 2:8–15." Pp. 445–49 in *The Lectionary Commentary: Theological Exegesis for Sunday's Texts: The Second Readings, Acts and the Epistles.* The Lectionary Commentary. Edited by Roger E. Van Harn. Grand Rapids: Eerdmans, 2001.

Wall, Robert W. "Nativity of the Lord (Christmas Day), Years A, B, C. Second Lesson: Titus 2:11–14." Pp. 456–60 in *The Lectionary Commentary: Theological Exegesis for Sunday's Texts: The Second Readings, Acts and the Epistles.* The Lectionary Commentary. Edited by Roger E. Van Harn. Grand Rapids: Eerdmans, 2001.

Wall, Robert W. "Nativity of the Lord (Christmas Day), Years A, B, C. Second Lesson: Titus 3:4–7." Pp. 460–63 in *The Lectionary Commentary: Theological Exegesis for Sunday's Texts: The Second Readings, Acts and the Epistles.* The Lectionary Commentary. Edited by Roger E. Van Harn. Grand Rapids: Eerdmans, 2001.

Wall, Robert W. "Reading the Bible from within Our Traditions: The 'Rule of Faith' in Theological Hermeneutics." Pp. 88–107 (Chap. 5) in *Between Two Horizons: Spanning New Testament Studies and Systematic Theology.* Edited by Joel B. Green and Max Turner. Grand Rapids: Eerdmans, 2000.

Wall, Robert W. "Canonical Context and Canonical Conversations." Pp. 165–82 (Chap. 9) in *Between Two Horizons: Spanning New Testament Studies and Systematic Theology.* Edited by Joel B. Green and Max Turner. Grand Rapids: Eerdmans, 2000.

Wall, Robert [W]. "Israel and the Gentile Mission in Acts and Paul: A Canonical Approach." Pp. 437–57 in *Witness to the Gospel: The Theology of Acts.* Edited by I. Howard Marshall and David Peterson. Grand Rapids: Eerdmans, 1998.

Wall, Robert W. "Canonical Criticism." Pp. 291–312 in *A Handbook to Exegesis of the New Testament.* Edited by Stanley E. Porter. Leiden: Brill, 1997.

Wall, Robert W. "'The Perfect Law of Liberty' (James 1:25)." Pp. 475–97 in *The Quest for Context and Meaning: Studies in Biblical Intertextuality in Honor of James A. Sanders.* Edited by Craig A. Evans and Shemaryahu Talmon. Leiden: Brill, 1997.

Wall, Robert W. "Reading the New Testament in Canonical Context." Pp. 370–93 (Chap. 18) in *Hearing the New Testament: Strategies for Interpretation*. Edited by Joel B. Green. Grand Rapids: Eerdmans, 1995.

Wall, Robert W., and William L. Lane. "Polemic in Hebrews and the Catholic Epistles." Pp. 166–98 (Chap. 9) in *Anti-Semitism and Early Christianity: Issues of Polemic and Faith*. Edited by Craig A. Evans and Donald A. Hagner. Minneapolis: Fortress, 1993.

Wall, Robert W. "Introduction." Pp. 15–25 in *The New Testament as Canon: A Reader in Canonical Criticism*. Edited by Robert W. Wall and Eugene E. Lemcio. Sheffield: Sheffield Academic Press, 1992.

Wall, Robert W. "The Acts of the Apostles in Canonical Context." Pp. 111–28 (Chap. 5) in *The New Testament as Canon: A Reader in Canonical Criticism*. Edited by Robert W. Wall and Eugene E. Lemcio. Sheffield: Sheffield Academic Press, 1992.

Wall, Robert W. "Peter, 'Son' of Jonah: The Conversion of Cornelius in the Context of Canon." Pp. 129–40 (Chap. 6) in *The New Testament as Canon: A Reader in Canonical Criticism*. Edited by Robert W. Wall and Eugene E. Lemcio. Sheffield: Sheffield Academic Press, 1992.

Wall, Robert W. "Romans 1.1–15: An Introduction to the Pauline Corpus of the New Testament." Pp. 142–60 in *The New Testament as Canon: A Reader in Canonical Criticism*. Edited by Robert W. Wall and Eugene E. Lemcio. Sheffield: Sheffield Academic Press, 1992.

Wall, Robert W. "The Problem of the Multiple Letter Canon of the New Testament." Pp. 161–83 (Chap. 8) in *The New Testament as Canon: A Reader in Canonical Criticism*. Edited by Robert W. Wall and Eugene E. Lemcio. Sheffield: Sheffield Academic Press, 1992.

Wall, Robert W. "Ecumenicity and Ecclesiology: The Promise of the Multiple Letter Canon of the New Testament." Pp. 184–207 (Chap. 9) in *The New Testament as Canon: A Reader in Canonical Criticism*. Edited by Robert W. Wall and Eugene E. Lemcio. Sheffield: Sheffield Academic Press, 1992.

Wall, Robert W. "Law and Gospel, Church and Canon." Pp. 208–49 (Chap. 10) in *The New Testament as Canon: A Reader in Canonical Criticism*. Edited by Robert W. Wall and Eugene E. Lemcio. Sheffield: Sheffield Academic Press, 1992.

Wall, Robert W. "James and Paul in Pre-Canonical Context." Pp. 250–71 (Chap. 11) in *The New Testament as Canon: A Reader in Canonical*

Criticism. Edited by Robert W. Wall and Eugene E. Lemcio. Sheffield: Sheffield Academic Press, 1992.

Wall, Robert W. "Apocalypse of the New Testament in Canonical Context." Pp. 274–98 (Chap. 12) in *The New Testament as Canon: A Reader in Canonical Criticism.* Edited by Robert W. Wall and Eugene E. Lemcio. Sheffield: Sheffield Academic Press, 1992.

Wall, Robert W. "Introduction: New Testament Ethics." Pp. 300–334 (Chap. 13) in *The New Testament as Canon: A Reader in Canonical Criticism.* Edited by Robert W. Wall and Eugene E. Lemcio. Sheffield: Sheffield Academic Press, 1992.

Wall, Robert W. "Social Justice and Human Liberation." Pp. 109–27 in *The Church in Response to Human Need.* Edited by Vinay Samuel and Christopher Sugden. Grand Rapids: Eerdmans, 1987.

Wall, Robert W. "Biblical Foundations for Social Justice and Human Liberation: Toward a New Proposal." Pp. 343–72 in *The Church in Response to Human Need.* Edited by Tom Sine. Monrovia: Missions Advanced Research and Communication Center, 1983.

Wall, Robert W. "New Testament Ethics." Pp. 31–75 in *Christian Ethics: An Inquiry into Christian Ethics from a Biblical Theological Perspective.* Edited by Leon O. Hynson and Lane A. Scott. Anderson: Warner, 1983.

Wall, Robert W. "Glorification in the Pauline Letters." Pp. 155–67 in *An Inquiry into Soteriology from a Biblical Theological Perspective.* Edited by John E. Hartley and R. Larry Shelton. Anderson: Warner, 1981.

Articles

Wall, Robert W., and David R. Nienhuis. "On Reading Canonical Collections: A Response." *Journal of Theological Interpretation* 9 (2015) 149–58.

Wall, Robert W. "Waiting on the Holy Spirit (Acts 1.4): Extending a Metaphor to Biblical Interpretation." *Journal of Pentecostal Theology* 22 (2013) 37–53.

Wall, Robert W. "Empire, Church, and Missio Dei: On Praying for Our Kings (1 Timothy 2:1–2): The 2011 Presidential Address." *Wesleyan Theological Journal* 47 (2012) 7–24.

Wall, Robert W. "James's Theological Grammar." *Christian Reflection: A Series in Faith and Ethics* (The Center for Christian Ethics, Baylor University) *The Letter of James* (2012) 36–45.

Wall, Robert W. "John's John: A Wesleyan Theological Reading of 1 John." *Wesleyan Theological Journal* 46 (2011) 105–41.

Wall, Robert W., and Daniel Castelo. "Scripture and the Church: A Précis for an Alternative Analogy." *Journal of Theological Interpretation* 5 (2011) 197–210.

Wall, Robert W. "Tribute for the Smyth/Wynkoop Book Award Winner of 2010" (*The Cambridge Companion to John Wesley* [2010], edited by Randy L. Maddox and Jason E. Vickers). *Wesleyan Theological Journal* 45 (2010) 270–72.

Wall, Robert W. "The 'Rule of Faith' and Biblical Hermeneutics." *Catalyst: Contemporary Evangelical Perspectives for United Methodist Seminarians* 36 (2009) 1–3.

Wall, Robert W. "The Wisdom of James." *Christian Reflection: A Series in Faith and Ethics* (The Center for Christian Ethics, Baylor University) *Where Wisdom is Found* (2009) 27–37.

Wall, Robert W. "Christ in/and the Old Testament: Jesus in the Old Testament." *Journal of Theological Interpretation* 2 (2008) 16–19.

Wall, Robert W. "The Bible as Canon." *Response* (Seattle Pacific University) 30 (2007) 20–21.

Wall, Robert W. "1 Timothy 2:9–15 Reconsidered (Again)." *Bulletin for Biblical Research* 14 (2004) 81–103.

Wall, Robert W. "Teaching 1 Peter as Scripture." *Word & World* 24 (2004) 368–77.

Wall, Robert W. "A Response to Thomas/Alexander, 'And the Signs Are Following' (Mark 16.9–20)." *Journal of Pentecostal Theology* 11 (2003) 171–83.

Wall, Robert W. "The Canonical Function of 2 Peter." *Biblical Interpretation* 9 (2001) 64–81.

Wall, Robert W. "The Function of LXX Habakkuk 1:5 in the Book of Acts." *Bulletin for Biblical Research* 10 (2000) 247–58.

Wall, Robert W. "'Purity and Power' according to the Acts of the Apostles." *Pneuma: The Journal of the Society for Pentecostal Studies* 21 (1999) 215–31.

Wall, Robert [W.], and Douglas Geivett. "Introduction to the Theme Issue—Jesus and the Academy." *Christian Scholar's Review* 28 (1999) 520–21.

Wall, Robert [W.], editor. "Faculty, Who Do You Say That I Am?" [Transcription of an Unrehearsed 'Jesus Forum' of Faculty Held on the Campus of

Seattle Pacific University, 12 November 1998], *Christian Scholar's Review* 28 (1999) 522–31.

Wall, Robert W. "'Purity and Power' according to the Acts of the Apostles." *Wesleyan Theological Journal* 34 (1999) 64–82.

Wall, Robert W. "The Future of Wesleyan Biblical Studies." *Wesleyan Theological Journal* 33 (1998) 101–15.

Wall, Robert W. "The Canonical Approach to Biblical Interpretation." *Catalyst: Contemporary Evangelical Resources for United Methodist Seminarians* 24 (1998) 3–5.

Wall, Robert W. "Pauline Authorship and the Pastoral Epistles: A Response to S. E. Porter." *Bulletin for Biblical Research* 5 (1995) 125–28.

Wall, Robert W. "Toward a Wesleyan Hermeneutics [*sic*] of Scripture." *Wesleyan Theological Journal* 30 (1995) 50–67.

Wall, Robert W. "Planting Churches or Sowing Seeds?" *Light & Life* (Indianapolis, IN) 127.12, no. 5119 (1994) 17.

Wall, Robert W. "Successors to 'The Twelve' according to Acts 12:1–17." *Catholic Biblical Quarterly* 53 (1991) 628–43.

Wall, Robert W. "The *Embourgeoisement* of the Free Methodist Ethos." *Wesleyan Theological Journal* 25 (1990) 117–29.

Wall, Robert W. "James as Apocalyptic Paraenesis." *Restoration Quarterly* 32 (1990) 11–22.

Wall, Robert W. "Martha and Mary (Luke 10.38–42) in the Context of a Christian Deuteronomy." *Journal for the Study of the New Testament* 11, no. 35 (1989) 19–35.

Wall, Robert W. "Wifely Submission in the Context of Ephesians." *Christian Scholar's Review* 17 (1988) 272–85.

Wall, Robert W. "The Acts of the Apostles in Canonical Context." *Biblical Theology Bulletin* 18 (1988) 16–24.

Wall, Robert W. "What the Bible Teaches about Prayer." *Light and Life Magazine* (Winona Lake, IN) 121.1, no. 5037 (1988) 9–10.

Wall, Robert W. "Ecumenicity and Ecclesiology: The Promise of the Multiple Letter Canon of the New Testament." *Christian Scholar's Review* 16 (1987) 336–54.

Wall, Robert W. "Law and Gospel, Church and Canon." *Wesleyan Theological Journal* 22 (1987) 38–70.

Wall, Robert W. "Peter, 'Son' of Jonah: The Conversion of Cornelius in the Context of Canon." *Journal for the Study of the New Testament* 29 (1987) 79–90.

Wall, Robert W. "'The Finger of God': Deuteronomy 9:10 and Luke 11:20." *New Testament Studies* 33 (1987) 144–50.

Wall, Robert W. "A Response to James Davison Hunter's *Evangelicalism: The Coming Generation*." *Seattle Pacific University Review* 6 (1987) 44–55.

Wall, Robert W. "The Problem of the Multiple Letter Canon of the New Testament." *Horizons in Biblical Theology* 8 (1986) 1–31.

Wall, Robert W. "The Canon and Christian Preaching: Sermons Should Reflect the Rich Diversity of Scripture." *The Christian Ministry* 17 (1986) 13, 15–17.

Wall, Robert W. "The Eschatologies of the Peace Movement." *Biblical Theology Bulletin* 15 (1985) 3–11.

Wall, Robert W. "The Preacher: Sage and Prophet." *Kardia: A Journal of Wesleyan Thought* (Western Evangelical Seminary) 1 (1985) 25–32.

Wall, Robert W. "Introduction: New Testament Ethics." *Horizons in Biblical Theology* 5 (1983) 49–94.

Wall, Robert W. "The Problem of Observed Pain: A Study of C. S. Lewis on Suffering." *Journal of the Evangelical Theological Society* 26 (1983) 443–51.

Wall, Robert W. "The Liberated Legalist." *The Christian Century* 100.27 (September 28, 1983) 848–49.

Wall, Robert W. "Pondering Today's Issues Biblically," in "What's Up in '83? Six Views on Issues Facing Evangelical Christians in 1983." *Light and Life* (Winona Lake, IN) 116.1, no. 4977 (1983) 9 (9–12).

Wall, Robert W. "His Coming: Strange and Wonderful: Refreshing Thoughts on the Familiar Story of Christmas." *Light and Life* (Winona Lake, IN) 113.13 =whole no. 4952 (1980) 14–15, 30–31.

Entries in Dictionaries and Encyclopedias

Wall, Robert W. "Canon." Pp. 111–21 in vol. 1 of *The Oxford Dictionary of the Bible and Theology*. Edited by Samuel E. Balentine. Oxford: Oxford University Press, 2015.

Wall, Robert W. "Catholic Epistles." Pp. 62–67 in vol. 1 of *The Oxford Encyclopedia of the Bible and Ethics*. Edited by Robert L. Brawley. Oxford Encyclopedias of the Bible. Oxford: Oxford University Press, 2014.

Wall, Robert W. "Intertextuality." Pp. 265–66 in *Global Wesleyan Dictionary of Theology*. Edited by Al Truesdale. Kansas City, MO: Beacon Hill, 2013.

Wall, Robert W. "Law and Gospel." Pp. 295–97 in *Global Wesleyan Dictionary of Theology*. Edited by Al Truesdale. Kansas City, MO: Beacon Hill, 2013.

Wall, Robert W. "Reconciliation." Pp. 448–49 in *Global Wesleyan Dictionary of Theology*. Edited by Al Truesdale. Kansas City, MO: Beacon Hill, 2013.

Wall, Robert W. "Righteousness." Pp. 471–72 in *Global Wesleyan Dictionary of Theology*. Edited by Al Truesdale. Kansas City, MO: Beacon Hill, 2013.

Wall, Robert W. "Canonical Approach. II. New Testament." Pp. 372–73 in vol. 2 (Bia-Chr) of *Religion Past and Present: Encyclopedia of Theology and Religion*. Edited by Hans Dieter Betz, Don S. Browning, Bernd Janowski, and Eberhard Jüngel. Leiden: Brill, 2007.

Wall, Robert W. "Intra-Biblical Interpretation." Pp. 167–69 in *Dictionary of Biblical Criticism and Interpretation*. Edited by Stanley E. Porter. London: Routledge, 2007.

Wall, Robert W. "Canonical Criticism." Pp. 563–64 in vol. 1 (A–C) of *The New Interpreter's Dictionary of the Bible*. Edited by Katharine Doob Sakenfeld. Nashville: Abingdon, 2006.

Wall, Robert W. "Catholic Epistles." Pp. 573–74 in vol. 1 (A–C) of *The New Interpreter's Dictionary of the Bible*. Edited by Katharine Doob Sakenfeld. Nashville: Abingdon, 2006.

Wall, Robert W. "Intertextuality, Biblical." Pp. 541–51 of *Dictionary of New Testament Background*. Edited by Craig A. Evans and Stanley E. Porter. Downers Grove: InterVarsity, 2000.

Wall, Robert W. "Canonical Approach II. Neues Testament." Pp. 54–55 in Bd. 2 (C-E) of *Religion in Geschichte und Gegenwart: Handwörterbuch für Theologie und Religionswissenschaft,* Vierte, völlig neu bearbeitete Auflage. Herausgegeben von Hans Dieter Betz, Don S. Browning, Bernd Janowski, and Eberhard Jüngel. Tübingen: Mohr Siebeck, 1999.

Wall, Robert W. "James, Letter of." Pp. 545–61 of *Dictionary of the Later New Testament and Its Developments*. Edited by Ralph P. Martin and Peter H. Davids. Downers Grove: InterVarsity, 1997.

Wall, Robert W. "Antinomianism." Pp. 263–64 in vol. 1 of *The Anchor Bible Dictionary*. Edited by David Noel Freedman. New York: Doubleday, 1992.

Wall, Robert W. "Community: New Testament *Koinōnia*." Pp. 263–64 in vol. 1 of *The Anchor Bible Dictionary*. Edited by David Noel Freedman. New York: Doubleday, 1992.

Wall, Robert W. "Conscience." Pp. 1128–30 in vol. 1 of *The Anchor Bible Dictionary*. Edited by David Noel Freedman. New York: Doubleday, 1992.

Wall, Robert W. "Divorce." Pp. 217–19 in vol. 2 of *The Anchor Bible Dictionary*. Edited by David Noel Freedman. New York: Doubleday, 1992.

Wall, Robert W. "New Testament Use of the Old Testament." Pp. 614–16 of the *Mercer Dictionary of the Bible*. Edited by Watson E. Mills. Macon: Mercer University Press, 1990.

Wall, Robert W. "Acceptance." P. 26 in *The Beacon Dictionary of Theology*. Edited by Richard S. Taylor. Kansas City, MO: Beacon Hill, 1983.

Wall, Robert W. "Gospel." P. 239 in *The Beacon Dictionary of Theology*. Edited by Richard S. Taylor. Kansas City, MO: Beacon Hill, 1983.

Wall, Robert W. "Hierarchicalism." P. 255 in *The Beacon Dictionary of Theology*. Edited by Richard S. Taylor. Kansas City, MO: Beacon Hill, 1983.

Wall, Robert W. "Mystery, Mysteries." P. 53 in *The Beacon Dictionary of Theology*. Edited by Richard S. Taylor. Kansas City, MO: Beacon Hill, 1983.

Translations

Wall, Robert W., and Team. *1–2 Timothy and Titus*. Common English Bible (CEB). Edited by David L. Petersen, Joel B. Green, David A. de Silva, et al. Nashville: Common English Bible, 2011.

Book Reviews

Wall, Robert W. Review of *The Letter of James* (2011), New International Commentary on the New Testament, by Scot McKnight. *Theology Today* 69 (2013) 522–24.

Wall, Robert W. Review of *Exiles from Eden: Religion and the Academic Vocation in America* (1993), by Mark R. Schwehn. *Christian Scholar's Review* 24 (1995) 316–18.

Wall, Robert W. Review of *The Heavenly Court Judgment of Revelation 4–5* (1992), by R. Dean Davis. *Critical Review of Books in Religion* 6 (1993) 217–19.

Wall, Robert W. Review of *The Anchor Bible Dictionary* (1992), edited by David Noel Freedman. *Christian Scholar's Review* 22 (1992) 418–20.

Wall, Robert W. Review of *People of the Book? The Authority of the Bible in Christianity* (1988), by John Barton. *Christian Scholar's Review* 20 (1990) 188–90.

Wall, Robert W. Review of *The Formation of the Christian Biblical Canon* (1988), by Lee Martin McDonald. *Theology Today* 46 (1989) 248.

Wall, Robert Walter. Review of *New Testament Theology in Dialogue: Christology and Ministry* (1987), by James D. G. Dunn and James P. Mackey. *The Christian Ministry* (Chicago) 20 (1989) 43–44.

Wall, Robert W. Review of *The Canon of the New Testament: Its Origin, Development, and Significance* (1988), by Bruce M. Metzger. *Theology Today* 45 (1989) 496–97.

Wall, Robert W. Review of *The Ethics of the New Testament* (1988), by Wolfgang Schrage. *Critical Review of Books in Religion* 2 (1989) 241–44.

Wall, Robert W. Review of *Christian Morality: Biblical Foundations* (1986), by Raymond F. Collins. *TSF Bulletin* (Theological Students Fellowship) 10 (1987) 32.

Wall, Robert W. Review of *The Wealth of Christians* (1984), by Redmond Mullin. *International Bulletin of Missionary Research* 10 (1986) 90–91.

Wall, Robert W. Review of *Jesus and Social Ethics* (1984), by Stephen Charles Mott. *TSF Bulletin* (Theological Students Fellowship) 9 (1986) 24–25.

Wall, Robert W. Review of *Christian Ethics and Imagination: A Theological Inquiry* (1984), by Philip S. Keane. *Theology Today* 42 (1985) 401–2, 404.

Wall, Robert W. Review of *The Great Reversal: Ethics and the New Testament* (1984), by Allen Verhey. *Theology Today* 42 (1985) 125–28.

Wall, Robert W. Review of *The New Testament and Homosexuality* (1983), by Robin Scroggs. *TSF Bulletin* (Theological Students Fellowship) 8 (1984) 24–25.

Wall, Robert W. Review of *Toward a Theology of the Corporation*, by Michael Novak (1981). *Professional and Business Ethics Journal* 1 (1983) 75–78.

Wall, Robert W. Review of *Pauline Studies: Essays Presented to F. F. Bruce on His 70th Birthday* (1980). *Christian Scholar's Review* 11 (1982) 166–67.

Wall, Robert W. Review of *The Golden Cow: Materialism in the Twentieth-Century Church* (1979), by John White. *Journal of the Evangelical Theological Society* 23 (1980) 258–59.

Wall, Robert W. Review of *Paul's Ethic of Freedom* (1979), by Peter Richardson. *Journal of the Evangelical Theological Society* 23 (1980) 175–76.

Wall, Robert W. Review of *The Moral Teaching of Paul: Selected Issues* (1979), by Victor Paul Furnish, *Journal of the Evangelical Theological Society* 23 (1980) 147–48. [This was written by Dr. Wall, though misattributed by the journal to William J. Kinnaman.]

Dissertations and Theses

Wall, Robert W. *The Nature of Obedience in the Ethics of Paul: With Special Application to the Problem of Homosexual Ordination for Christian Ministry.* Th.D. diss., Dallas Theological Seminary, 1979.

Wall, Robert W. *The Militant Church in the Theology of Jürgen Moltmann.* Th.M. thesis, Dallas Theological Seminary, 1973.

PART ONE

Essays on Theology and Methodology

Israel as a Figure for the Church: The Radical Nature of a Canonical Approach to Christian Scripture

FRANK ANTHONY SPINA

For over a generation, the hermeneutical significance of the canonization of Christian Scripture has generated a robust discussion among scholars. Documenting this phenomenon is hardly necessary.[1] Once viewed as a secondary or even a tertiary matter in introductory textbooks, canonization has come to be regarded as vital if not essential to a growing number of people for reading the biblical text *as Scripture*. Over the years, canonical approaches have yielded numerous studies with substantial exegetical, theological, and hermeneutical implications. The honoree for this Festschrift, Robert W. Wall, is widely known for his impressive contributions to this body of scholarship. I am deeply grateful to contribute this essay in honor of my colleague and friend.

Introduction

In this essay, I contend that a canonical reading of Christian Scripture requires seeing Israel—*canonical* Israel—as a figure for the church. The church should

---

1. The major impetus for reconsidering canonization for hermeneutical and theological reasons is Brevard S. Childs, *Introduction to the Old Testament as Scripture* (Philadelphia: Fortress, 1979). Childs had adumbrated his position initially with *Biblical Theology in Crisis* (Philadelphia: Westminster, 1970) and his commentary on *Exodus* (OT Library; Philadelphia: Westminster, 1974). Subsequently, Childs wrote a companion volume to his *Introduction*, entitled *The New Testament as Canon: An Introduction* (Philadelphia: Fortress, 1984). James Sanders also was a major voice in this discussion, though his understanding of canon and the canonical process differed substantially from that of Childs. See his *Torah and Canon* (Philadelphia: Westminster, 1972). On the difference between Childs and Sanders, see Frank Anthony Spina, "Canonical Criticism: Childs Versus Sanders," in *Hermeneutics: Interpreting God's Word for Today* (ed. Wayne McCown and James E. Massey; Anderson: Warner, 1982) 165–94; and "Canon" in *Handbook of Christian Theology* (ed. Donald W. Musser and Joseph L. Price; Nashville: Abingdon, 2003) 81–84.

see herself as a figure of Israel just as the synagogue does.[2] This is because both the church and the synagogue achieved their essential and most durable structure after the Second Temple period, a time marked by varied Jewish religious expressions. These expressions more or less dissipated largely as a consequence of Rome's destruction of the Jerusalem Temple in 70 C.E. To be sure, both Judaism and Christianity (as they were eventually to be designated) had antecedents among these prior expressions.[3] But it would be anachronistic to consider either the synagogue or the church before the Temple's destruction as separate religious institutions. Indeed, there is some evidence that Rabbinic Pharisaic Judaism and catholic Christianity defined themselves, to some degree at least, over against each other.[4] In spite of these acrimonious exchanges, both communities believed profoundly that they were not only the heirs of Israel but her valid representation in their religious life.

In one important way, the development of Rabbinic Judaism and catholic Christianity shared parallel strategies. Both of these groups viewed without reservation the Jewish Scripture—TANAK for Judaism, the Old Testament (primarily the Septuagint) for Christianity—as authoritative and foundational for their formation.[5] But that was not the end of the matter. In the case of Rabbinic Judaism, the Jewish Scripture was read in light of the Oral Torah. Judaism regarded the written and Oral Torah as equally valid. In the case of Christianity, the New Testament functioned relative to the Old Testament the way the Oral Torah functioned relative to TANAK for Judaism. Neither religious community read Jewish Scripture exclusively

---

2. I use the terms *synagogue* and *church* as a short-hand way of referring to Judaism—meaning Rabbinic Pharisaic Judaism—and Christianity—meaning the one holy, catholic, and apostolic church—respectively.

3. James Dunn has cited four pillars of Second Temple Judaism: (1) God is One; (2) The election of Israel as God's people, including the people's perpetuity and the land that God promised them; (3) covenant focused on Torah as expressive of God's will; and (4) the Temple. See Dunn, *The Partings of the Ways* (2nd edition; London: SCM, 2006) 26–42. Of course, there were Jewish groups that in one way or another did not conform precisely to these markers. For example, the Essene community did not participate in the cultus of the Jerusalem Temple, nor did the Samaritan community.

4. Both groups in this formative period did not see themselves any longer as engaging in what earlier amounted to an intramural debate. Instead, both saw the other as illegitimate, apostate, or heretical. See Dunn, *Partings*, xxiii. See also Judith Lieu, *Neither Jew Nor Greek: Constructing Early Christianity* (2nd edition; London: Bloomsbury T & T Clark, 2016).

5. For the purposes of this essay, it is immaterial whether the Jewish Scriptures refer to Hebrew or Greek traditions.

according to its plain sense. Jews saw Torah as foundational and pervasive throughout TANAK—even before the Torah was given!—just as Christians read the entirety of the Old Testament in light of Jesus, their risen and exalted Lord.[6] In this sense, Judaism *qua* Oral Torah and Christianity *qua* New Testament are both in effect *novi testamenti*.[7]

Early Developments

However, this parallelism between the two communities flies in the face of how the popular imagination came to perceive Judaism and Christianity. Most saw Judaism as a logical extension of *historical* Israel—Jews *are* Israel in historical and ethnic terms. Equally, most viewed Christianity as a novel revelation and fundamentally a brand new religion—Christians *are* Gentiles. The synagogue welcomes only Jews whereas the church welcomes anyone who confesses that Jesus is the Christ.

Despite this popular perception, however, in point of fact Judaism had to develop its identity, liturgy, ethics, and communal lifestyle *away* from the Promised Land, *without* a monarchy, having *no* political standing, and *no longer* participating in the temple *cultus*. Thus, Judaism cannot be explained merely as an instantiation of the religion found in TANAK.[8] As well, Christianity cannot be seen as an instantiation of the New Testament, if for no other reason than that Jesus was a Torah observant Jew and worshipped in

6. Richard B. Hays makes a compelling a case that the New Testament cannot be dismissed simply as a tendentious reading of the Jewish Bible, as modern criticism largely asserts. At the same time, Hays acknowledges that the Jesus event triggered these figural readings. This means that one had to first believe that Jesus was the Christ and that God had raised him from the dead before one could "see" the Christological figures in the text. Apart from that initial comprehension and commitment, there was no nonarbitrary way to read the text in such a manner. Event preceded interpretation. See Hays, *Reading Backwards: Figural Christology and the Fourfold Gospel Witness* (Waco: Baylor University Press, 2014).

7. The expression is from David Novak, "From Supersessionism to Parallelism in Jewish-Christian Dialogue," in *Jews and Christians: People of God* (ed. Carl E. Braaten and Robert W. Jenson; Grand Rapids: Eerdmans, 2003) 108–10. See also George Lindbeck, "The Church as Israel: Ecclesiology and Ecumenism," in *Jews and Christians,* 87. Jon Levenson is much more specific about the Oral Torah. He notes that the TANAK (*Miqra*) is properly "placed alongside" the Talmud, Midrash, and medieval rabbinic commentaries. See his *The Hebrew Bible, the Old Testament, and Historical Criticism* (Louisville: Westminster John Knox, 1993) 1.

8. Jon Levenson has remarked that the "religion *in* the book" is not the same as the "religion *of* the book." See *Hebrew Bible,* 107.

synagogues (on the Sabbath!). This is why the synagogue and the church had to read their Scriptures—whether TANAK or the Old Testament—in terms laid out by the Oral Torah and the New Testament respectively. Both communities had roots in Israel, but neither were Israel without remainder. Only canonical Israel may serve as a figure for either the synagogue or the church.

When it comes to the church, positing Israel as her figural representation is hardly idiosyncratic. This is the straightforward teaching of the New Testament generally, in spite of the negative sentiments expressed in so many places against Jewish beliefs or religious practices. Even the Apostle Paul thought in such terms. In 1 Corinthians, for example, he admonished the church to evaluate her life in the light of "our fathers," that is, the people of Israel (10:1–11). In effect, this is a way of saying that for Christians to practice being the church they are to apply to their own community what they read about Israel in the Jewish Scripture.[9] Paul also leaves no doubt about Israel's strategic role in God's economy of salvation when he famously asserts that she is the olive tree into which the church has been grafted (Rom 11:17–24). Finally, he says in no uncertain terms that the gifts of God to Israel as well as God's call of Israel, were irrevocable (Rom 11:29). Even the Epistle to the Hebrews is not supersessionist. Though it asserts that the old covenant is obsolete (Heb 8:13), God's elected people certainly are not.[10] After all, it was Jeremiah who made the original claim that God would in the future make a new covenant for God's people Israel (Jer 31:31–34).

In addition, Jesus' own ministry as recounted in the Gospels was geared to prompting Jews—all of whom in one way or another thought of themselves as Israelites—to repent and prepare for the newly proclaimed arrival of the Kingdom of God/Heaven (Matt 3:17; Mark 1:14–15; Luke 4:42–44). According to the Gospels, this kingdom was tantamount to the dawning messianic age about which the prophets had so prominently and regularly spoken. Though Gentiles would also be eventually included in the eschatological

---

9. Lindbeck, "The Church as Israel" 81. Of course, my use here of "Christians" is an anachronism. Considerable time had to pass before those who believed that Jesus was the Messiah/Christ called themselves *Christians*. See Lieu, *Neither Jew Nor Greek*, 204.

10. See the treatment on God's election of Israel in Joel S. Kaminsky, *Yet I Loved Jacob: Reclaiming the Biblical Conception of Election* (Nashville: Abingdon, 2007). See also Frank Anthony Spina, *The Faith of the Outsider: Exclusion and Inclusion in the Biblical Story* (Grand Rapids: Eerdmans, 2005) 1–11.

messianic age (Isa 19:16–25), Jesus' own mission involved principally Israel (Matt 15:24). At the same time, Jesus' work was at least implicitly favorable to including Gentiles.[11] To the extent that Jesus is depicted as fulfilling biblical prophecy, precisely this Gentile inclusion should be expected. In other words, the Gentile mission in and of itself did not preclude the church from seeing itself as a figure of Israel.[12]

The Church's Supersessionism

Unfortunately, while the church initially saw herself as a figure of Israel as depicted in the New Testament, before long she transformed this identification in a manner that not only excluded the synagogue but vilified it.[13] The concept of God's unconditional election, which guaranteed the existence of Israel in perpetuity (Jer 31:35–37), was soon replaced by a church who saw herself as superseding Jews as God's people. The thinking was that because Israel had been persistently unfaithful to the God who had elected her, as the prophets were never tired of pointing out, and because this unfaithfulness was never more pronounced than when she rejected Jesus as the Israelite messiah, those who believed in and followed Jesus as the Christ became *ipso facto* God's exclusive people. God's unconditional election of Israel was jettisoned in favor of lauding the faithfulness of the church, which was more and more Gentile in make-up.[14]

In the course of time, in spite of her obvious Jewish origins, Jesus' inarguable identity as a Jew, the utterly Jewish flavor of the New Testament, including perhaps even the concept of Incarnation itself as compatible with some strains of Jewish thought, and the retention of the Jewish Scriptures,

11. See the discussion of references to Jesus and Gentile outsiders in Spina, *The Faith of the Outsider*, 137–44.

12. In fact, Gentiles were also attracted to the synagogue, Jewish life, and the Jewish Scriptures in this formative period. Some of these were referred to as *God-Fearers*. In this sense at least, Judaism's seeing herself as a figure of Israel did not by any means preclude Gentile participation in that community. See Lieu, *Neither Jew Nor Greek*, 23.

13. The synagogue reciprocated these acrimonious sentiments, but soon found itself as having minority status after Constantine. The repercussions of this social and political situation were increasingly tragic.

14. George Lindbeck, "The Church," in *Keeping the Faith: Essays to Mark the Centenary of Lux Mundi* (ed. Geoffrey Wainwright; Philadelphia: Fortress, 1988) 186.

the church became the antithesis of the synagogue.[15] Granted, for the first few centuries of the church's existence, she and the synagogue were not hermetically sealed from each other, at least as far as ordinary people were concerned. As late as the fourth century, for instance, Christian leaders rebuked congregations—or at least sub-sections of them—for attending synagogue and observing Jewish feasts and customs.[16] Nevertheless, Christianity did not abandon the conviction that Judaism had been superseded. Even the denunciation of Marcion (2nd century) for his wholesale rejection of Jewish religion, not to mention his repudiation of the Jewish Bible and the Jewish deity, did not ultimately mitigate the church's embrace of supersessionism.[17]

Throughout history, then, Christianity has persisted in this belief that she had replaced Judaism as God's people. On occasion, the church's seeing herself as Israel involved counter claims among Christians themselves, most especially Protestants and Roman Catholics. In this particular confrontation, both groups argued vociferously and vehemently that they were the *true* Israel, meaning by that the southern kingdom Judah as opposed to the northern kingdom Israel, which was seen as schismatic and heretical. Somehow, both groups paid little attention to either the fact that Solomon and his son Rehoboam *of Judah* were primarily at fault in precipitating the schism or that both kingdoms were egregiously sinful and consequently exiled at God's hand.[18]

However, these internecine battles were not the norm. Instead, the church persisted in seeing herself as a *new Israel* who was theologically, morally, and spiritually superior to the synagogue. In fact, the church went

15. The work of Daniel Boyarin has recently fostered rethinking the Jewish flavor of New Testament claims about Jesus as Messiah and Son of God. See his *Border Lines: The Partition of Judaeo-Christianity* (Philadelphia: University of Pennsylvania Press, 2004) and *The Jewish Gospels: The Story of the Jewish Christ* (New York: The New Press, 2012).

16. Dunn, *The Partings*, xx. The presence of the Epistle of James in the New Testament canon as well as Paul's warnings against so-called "Judaizers" (as found, for instance, in Galatians) reflect this situation early on.

17. Jon Levenson, "Did God Forgive Adam? An Exercise in Comparative Midrash," in *Jews and Christians*, 152.

18. See Ephraim Radner, *The End of the Church: A Pneumatology of Christian Division in the West* (Grand Rapids: Eerdmans, 1998) 35–36. See also 1 Kgs 11–12; 2 Kgs 17:1–18; 24–25. Almost immediately, the southern kingdom was just as idolatrous as the northern kingdom (1 Kgs 12:25–33; 14:21–24).

so far as to anathematize the synagogue by protesting that the latter was too deficient to be anything other than a detriment to the human community.[19] Yet in spite of the church's insistence that she had replaced the synagogue as God's special people, in reality this stance soon enough became a "dead metaphor" in that the rich biblical material that was at the church's disposal was all but ignored.[20] For the most part, the Old Testament at a practical level did not fund the spiritual, theological, and ethical dimensions of the church as the New Testament did. The unpalatable fact is that the Old Testament had become in the Christian outlook a *Jewish* document while the New Testament had become a *Christian* one. The church seems not to have noticed that in her creedal affirmations she confessed regularly that what God had done in Jesus the Christ was "according to the Scriptures," something that was first asserted by none other than the Apostle Paul (1 Cor 15:3). Marcion may have been formally repudiated, but informally his legacy lived on in the church that had ostensibly rejected his teaching.

After the Shoah/Holocaust

As might be expected, after the horrors of the Holocaust in World War II the church became increasingly reluctant to see herself as a figure of Israel. This compelled not only a rethinking of the church's presenting herself as a figure of Israel but also of seriously reconsidering the triumphalist claim that she had actually displaced Judaism as the elect people of God. Unfortunately, this rethinking has come at a glacial pace. The belief that the church superseded Judaism has been challenged only relatively recently, and mostly

19. There were efforts—of whatever success may be debatable—in the church to see the relationship between the church and the synagogue in more nuanced and less supersessionistic ways. See Matthew A. Tapie, *Aquinas on Israel and the Church: The Question of Supersessionism in the Theology of Thomas Aquinas* (Eugene: Pickwick, 2014). See also Stephen E. Fowl, "Selections from Thomas Aquinas's Commentary on Romans," in *The Theological Interpretation of Scripture: Classic and Contemporary Readings* (ed. Stephen E. Fowl; Cambridge, MA: Blackwell, 1997) 320–37.

20. This sentiment is expressed by George Lindbeck, who argues that the references to the church as Israel became "dead metaphors devoid of the powerful typological realism they once possessed." See Lindbeck, "What of the Future? A Christian Response," in *Christianity in Jewish Terms* (ed. Tikva Frymer-Kensky et al.; Boulder: Westview, 2000) 360.

by a small number of Christian theologians.[21] Equally, various Christian denominations have also—again, relatively recently—confessed their historic anti-Judaism which had eventuated in terrible mistreatment of the synagogue over the centuries. At best, Christian supersessionism came to be seen as unseemly in the light of the Holocaust. At worst, this stubborn stance served to foster a vicious form of anti-Semitism which fertilized the very soil which, for example, the Nazis were able to cultivate for their depraved purposes.[22] Since the Shoah/Holocaust, it is now increasingly the case that Christians, including not only theologians but growing numbers of clergy and laity as well, have not only become more positive about the religious contributions of Judaism generally but find less and less attractive the idea that the church's claim to be the new Israel at the expense of Judaism's claim is legitimate.

While these more ecumenical developments have been welcomed by some Jews and some Christians, this change in the church's thinking has come at a cost. By rejecting the notion that the church superseded the synagogue—which is to be lauded—the unfortunate consequence of this move has been the virtually complete denial of the church's Jewish roots. Marcionism has once again raised its ugly head. If, however, the church wants effectively to reject Marcionism not only in word but deed it needs to ask whether it is possible for Israel to be a figure of the church (*and* Judaism)

---

21. See, for example, the essays contributed by Christian scholars in Carl E. Braaten and Robert W. Jensen, eds., *Jews and Christians: People of God* (Grand Rapids: Eerdmans, 2003). See also R. Kendall Soulen, *The God of Israel and Christian Theology* (Minneapolis: Fortress, 1996; and Michael J. Vlach, *Has the Church Replaced Israel? A Theological Evaluation* (Nashville: B & H, 2010).

22. Christianity was not the cause of Nazism, but almost surely this monstrous ideology could not have taken hold apart from the long history of the church's anti-Judaism position as well as the church's passive or sometimes active participation in the violence perpetrated against Jews throughout the ages. See "*Dabru Emet*: A Jewish Statement on Christians and Christianity," Braaten and Jensen, *Jews and Christians*, 180. In general, the church's stance is a fundamentally religious and theological one, not an ethnic one. To be sure, that is a distinction that was regularly violated by Christians. But for the most part, Christians did not discriminate against Jews because they were Jews (as the Nazis and others did) but as a function of substantial theological disagreement. At the same time, Christians were all too often complicit in violence against Jews that, for all practical purposes, was indistinguishable from anti-Semitism generally.

in a non-supersessionist guise. In my judgment, that is not only a possibility for the church but a theological necessity. The New Testament teaches that those who put their faith in Jesus—even Gentiles—have an inexorable connection to Israel.[23] If Jesus is the Christ/Messiah, he is *Israel's* Christ/Messiah. One cannot be a Messiah without a messianic community. If Jesus is God incarnate, the God in question is Israel's God, the God of Abraham, Isaac, and Jacob. If this is not true, then Marcion in the final analysis wins. Obviously, these are unabashed Christian claims. But they are claims that do not require—and should not be seen to require—holding tenaciously to the false belief that Christianity replaced Judaism. The church's being figured by Israel does not preclude Judaism's also being figured by Israel. Both groups have equal access to TANAK/Old Testament as they work out their identity.

Israel as a Figure of the Church

Some time ago George Lindbeck made a strong case that canonical Israel should indeed be understood as a figure for the church even, perhaps especially, in this modern post-Holocaust era. As we saw, the earliest Christians (though they did not call themselves at this point *Christians*) were a Jewish sect, one of several in the Second Temple period. They understood their community as *ekklesia* or *qahal*; indeed, as the assembly of Israel in a new age.[24] These followers of Jesus as the Christ argued that they were that part of the people of God who lived in the times after the messianic era had begun but before its ultimate completion. Four heuristic guidelines were the basis of this conviction. First, these particular Jews saw themselves identified by a narrative, specifically Israel's narrative. Second, Israel's history was their singular history. The Jewish Scriptures—whether in its Hebrew or Greek form—were the sole ecclesiological textbook. Third, Israel's story

---

23. Patrick D. Miller goes so far in this direction as to argue for altering the first article of the Apostles' and Nicene creeds. He advocates supplying the phrase ". . . who delivered Israel from Egyptian bondage" after the statement, "I believe in God the Father Almighty, Creator of heaven and earth." He argues for this change for theological, liturgical, and pedagogical reasons. See his "Rethinking the First Article of the Creed," *Theology Today* 61 (2005) 499–508.

24. Lindbeck, "The Church" 182.

was wholly appropriated, including not only grace but judgment. Fourth, Israel and these Jews who believed in Jesus were one people. Discontinuity and nonidentity were not problems for this sect per se, but for "unbelieving Jews" and later Gentile Christians, respectively.[25] In the Second Temple period, then, the church (not yet understood as absolutely separate from other Jewish religious expressions) was simply one of a number of Jewish sects that claimed allegiance to and saw themselves as representing elect Israel.

The claim that Israel was a figure for the community that believed in Jesus took on a much different meaning after the destruction of the Temple in 70 C.E. Subsequent to this catastrophe, Rabbinic Pharisaic Judaism and catholic Christianity began to take form now in terms that completely denied their religious enemy's counter claims, since both groups were convinced that these claims were mutually exclusive. Neither community realized in the polemical postures they assumed relative to each other that their Scriptures were a sufficiently capacious instrument of God's spirit and able to bestow their unity-and-community building power on both.[26] Both Judaism and Christianity lived in the world of Israel's story, tried mightily to serve Israel's God, and believed with all their hearts and souls that they were God's chosen. Simultaneously, both insisted that one was absolutely right and the other was absolutely wrong. Is it possible that both communities assessed this situation incorrectly? Neither the synagogue nor the church could claim exclusively that she was *the* figure of Israel. If this is the case, then the church has an equal right, so to speak, to see herself in these terms just as she did initially.

Perhaps the biggest obstacle to overcome in making a cogent argument that the church may legitimately forge her self-identity as a figure for Israel—either initially or in the present—is the idea that the Jews are a pure ethnic group. In reference to the Pauline botanical metaphor, not every type of plant could be grafted into an olive tree (for example, a tomato plant!). This means by definition that Gentile foliage could never be grafted into a Jewish tree, contrary to the Apostle's insistence. How might this formidable obstacle be overcome?

25. Lindbeck, "The Church" 183–84.
26. Lindbeck, "The Church as Israel" 87.

It is doubtless true that most people today—whether Jewish or Gentile—think of Israel in general and Judaism in particular as comprising ethnic Jews. Is this not the plain teaching of the Jewish Scriptures themselves? The answer to this question, as it turns out, depends on to whom the question is addressed. For example, Jon Levenson leaves no doubt about the presentation of Israel in the Jewish Scripture as basically a kin-group.[27] For the most part, Levenson's articulation of the ethnic make-up of canonical Israel and the continuation of that ethnicity in Rabbinic Judaism is the view held popularly not only by Jews but by Christians. In fact, whether seen from either a religious or a secular viewpoint that is the way Jews are generally understood regardless of their particular cultural or geographical location.

But there are counter voices. Jacob Neusner suggests that there is no ethnic Israel that is distinct from religious Israel.[28] For Neusner, though ethnic identity is transmitted genealogically, as far as Torah is concerned a place in Israel is reserved for every Gentile who accepts the unity of God and the yoke of the Torah, which is God's revealed will for humanity. This means that Israel is, for Neusner, a "supernatural entity," not simply an ethnic one. To be sure, Israel consists of those born in Israel. But Neusner excepts those who deny the principles of the faith.[29] Neusner even goes so far as to criticize the Apostle Paul for presenting Israel in ethnic terms, which he opines is incompatible with later Rabbinic Judaism.[30]

Of course, Judaism has every right to define itself in any terms it pleases. But because we are concentrating on *canonical Israel*, the issue of ethnicity turns on what the Jewish Scriptures themselves say (whether TANAK or Old Testament). I would agree that Israel as it is pictured in Scripture has an ethnic *element*, but I do not think the text itself may be reduced to that element. When God called Abraham, soon it became clear that only one of the patriarch's children—the one born to Sarah—would be the child of

---

27. Levenson, *The Hebrew Bible*, 153. See also Levenson, "The Perils of Engaged Scholarship: A Rejoinder to Jorge Pixley," in *Jews, Christians, and the Theology of the Hebrew Scriptures* (ed. Alice O. Bellis and Joel Kaminsky; SBL Symposium Series 8; Atlanta: Society of Biblical Literature, 2000) 239–46.

28. Jacob Neusner, "Was Rabbinic Judaism Really 'Ethnic'?," *Catholic Biblical Quarterly* 57 (1995) 283.

29. Ibid., 284–85.

30. Ibid., 303.

promise (Gen 17:15–21). Other children, although related to Abraham by blood, did not inherit God's promise (Gen 21:12; 25:1–6). Isaac famously fathered twin sons, only one of whom would be heir of the promise (Gen 25:23; 28:4). Obviously, Esau—the eponymous ancestor of Edom—was just as much related to his father and mother as Jacob, but he was excluded from the promised future.

Even if one wants to trace Israelite ethnicity to Jacob/Israel, the issue remains problematic. Judah fathered the line of the great David, but he did this by being tricked by his Canaanite daughter-in-law, Tamar (Genesis 38). Joseph, too, married outside his kin-group (Gen 41:45). This meant that the tribes of Judah, Ephraim, and Manasseh had women forebears who were outside the extended family.[31] Moses also had a foreign wife, Zipporah (Exod 2:16–22). Of course, Solomon shattered the record for marrying foreign wives (1 Kgs 11:1–2)!

Perhaps it is fair to mention in this survey of non-ethnic examples of Israelites the inclusion of the Gibeonites in Joshua. These people used a ruse to avoid the total destruction to which the rest of the Canaanite population was subjected (Josh 9:1–15). Though the leaders and Joshua himself were upset over this blatant deception, they honored the agreement with this outsider group who remained "to this day" with Israel (9:27). Even the punishment inflicted on the Gibeonites had an ironic twist. These foreigners were relegated to be hewers of wood and drawers of water. But they were to do these seemingly menial tasks "for all the congregation," at the "altar of the Lord," and, according to Joshua himself, in the "house of my God" (9:21, 23, 27). Not only were these meaningful sacerdotal activities but the phrase "the house of my God" occurs only one other place in the Old Testament, Psalm 84:11 (Eng. v. 10). There the sentiment is expressed that even being a doorkeeper in the "house of my God" is preferable to dwelling in the tents of the wicked. The Gibeonites ended up doing meaningful religious work in the Israelite community.

In this same book, the quintessential Canaanite Rahab and her family become part of Israel whereas the quintessential Israelite Achan and his

---

31. One could make a case that Ruth—a Moabite—is part of this pattern, though technically she is related in that Moab came about due to the incestuous relationship that Lot, Abraham's nephew, had with his daughters (Gen 19:30–38).

family are condemned.[32] Finally, it is fair to bring up the case when Samson casts his eye on a Philistine woman, an action that bothered his parents. They did not know, however, that Samson's predilection for a foreign woman was "from the Lord" (Judg 14:1–4). These examples—and there are more— seem to indicate that ethnicity may be a factor in Israel's identity according to TANAK/Old Testament, but certainly not in any absolute manner.

Ezra-Nehemiah, however, is of a different order entirely. In this material, the *golah*-group (that is, those who had been exiled) emphasized ethnic purity as indispensable for Israelite identity. Those who returned from the Babylonian exile apparently applied a strict construction of Deuteronomy 7:1–6. For this reason, the returnees demanded divorces from those who had intermarried (Ezra 9). To the extent that Rabbinic Judaism thought of itself exclusively in ethnic terms, Ezra-Nehemiah certainly played a decisive role.[33] At the same time, this is only part of the whole TANAK. Plus, once pure ethnicity is *contaminated* by those outside the group, as it were, it cannot be recovered. The point remains that at best only parts of TANAK/Old Testament unambiguously presents Israel as an ethnic entity. It also needs to be kept in mind that even though Judaism has not been a proselyting religion, it has always welcomed converts who are, by definition, Gentiles.

In this light, there is no reason why the church cannot be grafted into the Israelite tree. A return to seeing Israel as a figure for the church is, therefore, in order, even in these post-Holocaust times, just as Lindbeck argued. This theological move on the part of the church need not, and must not be, in supersessionist terms.[34] Plus, the church dare not forget the terrible cost of divorcing itself from Israel's election or Israel's God. This changes the very essence of Christian thought.[35]

---

32. Spina, *The Faith of the Outsider*, 52–71.

33. See Joseph Blenkinsopp, *Judaism: The First Phase: The Place of Ezra and Nehemiah in the Origins of Judaism* (Grand Rapids: Eerdmans, 2009).

34. Robert Wall rejects supersessionism in his book *Why the Church?* (Nashville: Abingdon, 2015) 21. At the same time, he avers that the Incarnation is a "qualitatively superior" self-presentation to that of God's sojourn with Israel. Most Jews would see such a statement, I would think, as inherently supersessionist. That is, most Jews operate on the assumption that God's sojourn with Israel was in no way deficient.

35. See Christoph Schwöbel, "Das Christusbekenntnis im Kontext des jüdisch-christlichen Dialogs," in his *Gott in Beziehung: Studien zur Dogmatik* (Tübingen: Mohr Siebeck, 2002) 308.

Israel as a Figure for the Church: Implications

To conclude this essay, I will sketch out a few implications for taking seriously that canonical Israel is indeed a figure for the church. As will be obvious, each of these items would require several essays, or even a book-length treatment, to do them justice. That goes beyond the bounds of a single programmatic essay. For now, I will be content to bring up discussion points.

First, if Israel is a figure for the church then she needs to see herself as *elected*. Just as Israel was chosen by God's amazing grace, the church should see herself in similar terms. If the church is grafted into a tree, which itself came into existence because of God's inscrutable will and utter graciousness, then being grafted is itself an equal manifestation of God's electing grace.

At one level, this seems unremarkable. The church might respond by reminding herself, as well as outsiders, that she has always regarded divine grace as central. But at another level, the church has often succumbed to a posture of *works* precisely in her supersessionist attitudes and claims. The church has typically seen herself as obedient to God and has accused the synagogue of being disobedient to that same God. That is, Israel lost her election status by bad behavior and apostasy. The logic is that the church gained her election by her faith in Christ and subsequent good behavior. But this comes very close to the church trumpeting works, not primarily as a response to God's grace but as a way of inducing it. This is the very opposite of grace in the biblical pattern. In point of fact, this posture trades on justification by works, a charge that the church most (in-)famously has leveled against the synagogue. When the church contends that God rejected Israel for her disbelief and sinful behaviors, the church also condemns herself for her corresponding disbelief and sinful behaviors. Just as God remained committed to God's chosen people regardless of sin, then a church that is also elected may thankfully count on God's commitments regardless of her sin. If the synagogue can lose its election status by in effect bad works, how does the church exempt herself from losing election status for the same reasons? The question is rhetorical.

Second, if Israel is a figure for the church, then the church is as liable to divine judgment as Israel was in the biblical story. The church has little difficulty in confessing sins at an individual level. Christians sin, confess, repent, and experience God's forgiveness through Christ. That is all to the good. But the church as a collective, as a community, as the very Body of Christ, seldom repents for her corporate sins. Why is this? Does the church, precisely because she is the Body of Christ, take the position that she is incapable of sin? Perhaps such thinking has in part given rise to the church as *invisible*, and therefore known only to God. But Israel was not *invisible*. She was all too visible, and as such she was not able to avoid God's judgment. An *invisible* church is a gnostic church. The actual church consists of flesh and blood people living in a myriad of cultures and subject to sin, not only as individuals but also as a community. This *visible* church, a figure of canonical Israel, cannot reduce sin to an individual matter and believe that she is somehow collectively not liable to God's wrath or judgment.

There are numerous stories in the Old Testament about the sins of individuals. Sin is a problem even for the most famous characters. At this level, the church sees no problem in identifying with Israelites. As a matter of fact, both the synagogue and the church have been in tandem in interpreting a great deal of the biblical material moralistically. We teach our children not to be unbrotherly or deceive (like Cain or Jacob), not to disregard the future (like Judah), or not to commit adultery and murder (like David). These are all heinous sins that require repentance and amendment of life.

However, there are sins of which Israel as a whole is guilty that elicit God's disfavor and often judgment. Many narratives emphasize divine judgment on Israel as a community (for example, Judg 4–16; 1 Sam 4–6). The ultimate divine judgment in the Old Testament is the Exile (2 Kgs 22–25). Yet, not even this most dire of punishments means that God abandons the elect community. Why should not the same obtain for the church? Should it not expect a holy and righteous deity to exact punishment on the whole community when it does not live up to her covenant commitment? Again, the question is rhetorical.

Since we are neither prophets nor apostles, it is all but impossible to cite any particular divine judgments that have been visited on the church. But we need not be prophets or apostles to name the church's sins that seem to demand punishment. The church may deny committing such sins, but outsiders will not refrain from pointing out the church's most egregious sins.

There are at least two sins committed persistently, pervasively, and even arrogantly by the church that surely have provoked God. One of these sins is the consistent mistreatment of the synagogue. Sinning against the synagogue did not involve only harsh and unloving words. Nor were the church's calumnies against the synagogue confined to the earliest formative period, in which both Judaism and Christianity exchanged rancorous salvos that were hardly becoming to either religious community. There are some exceptions to the church's distasteful language that disparaged Judaism, but they were just that: exceptions.

But, as noted, the church did not limit herself only to deprecating Judaism. The church sometimes fostered violence against the synagogue, or at least remained deafening silent when the synagogue was subjected to persecution on the part of people who did not need to fear prosecution from authorities or sometimes on the part of authorities themselves. Again, the long history of anti-Judaism in Europe made all too possible the anti-Semitic horrors of Hitler. If the church had no other sins on her ledger, this one is more than enough to evoke God's terrifying punishment.

There is another corporate sin for which the church bears enormous responsibility: racism. Even though the global church has been racist at times, the American church deserves special consideration on this score. It is all but impossible to deny that racism is America's original sin.[36] Christians were involved in America's system of slavery from top to bottom, from beginning to end. Likewise, Christians fought tooth and nail in the American Civil War for the Confederacy to preserve slavery. Even after slavery was abolished, Christians participated callously and cruelly in the segregationist policies of the Jim Crow South.[37] Northern Christians were no better in breaking racial barriers. Even today, while overt racism is no longer in vogue in the broader culture, the insidious forms of systemic racism continue to plague every feature of American life. Of course, some Christians spoke out against slavery, did what they could to abolish this vile institution, participated in the Underground Railroad, and were prophetic voices against not only slavery but segregation, lynching, and racism in general. These courageous Christians, unfortunately, again were exceptions to the rule.

---

36. See the work of Jim Wallis, *America's Original Sin: Racism, White Privilege and the Bridge to a New America* (Grand Rapids: Brazos, 2016).

37. James Cone devastatingly criticizes the white Christian church for its participation not only in segregation but in the vile, extrajudicial practice of lynching. Even the venerable Christian ethicist, Reinhold Niebuhr, all but ignored racism in general and lynching in particular. See *The Cross and the Lynching Tree* (Maryknoll: Orbis, 2011).

Most white Christians in one way or another have been complicit in racism in all of its pernicious forms.

The Christian Scriptures teach unambiguously that God created humanity in God's very own image and likeness (Gen 1:26–27). In the realm of racism, Christians have failed miserably to act as though they believe this fundamental truth. Would not God grieve about this depressing pattern of sin? More importantly, would racism of this duration and extent on the part of the white church (why is there a "white church" in the first place?) not anger God? What makes the white church think that because it is *under grace*, it need not worry about divine wrath and punishment? Israel was also under grace, and suffered immensely in the Exile for its many sins, at least some of which were no worse than the deplorable sin of racism. Perhaps the white church continues to be in denial about its racist sins. Perhaps it does not see, or cannot see, any evidence of God's judgment against the church. If this is so, the church might want to consider repenting at a corporate level sooner rather than later.

The third implication of viewing canonical Israel as a figure for the church involves the *law*. For the most part, law—referring to the legal material in TANAK/Old Testament—is viewed positively by Jews and negatively by Christians. Jews follow the law as a response to God's grace as demonstrated in the election of Abraham and Sarah generally (Gen 12:1–3) and the rescue from bondage in Egypt particularly (Exod 20:1).[38] Christians reject the law because they believe it subverts the conviction that they are saved by grace alone. But there is confusion on this issue in that almost every Christian rejects antinomianism at the same time that they view law negatively.

Even the Apostle Paul, who is mostly responsible for a negative view of law in the popular Christian imagination, does not dismiss *doing* right out of hand (see Rom 2:10; 12:21; 13:3). Dunn suggests that Paul was not against the law as such, or even *good works*. Instead, the Apostle argued against the law understood and practiced in such a way as to deny the grace of God to Gentiles.[39] Granted, this is a subtle argument (if Dunn is correct). Jews in Paul's day as much as Jews throughout history saw Paul as contradictory in maintaining that God's promises to Israel were irrevocable (Romans 11:29),

---

38. Miller, "Rethinking" 502.
39. Dunn, *Partings*, 181–82.

but at the same time allowing that the law was dispensable for following God.

This is neither the time nor the place to sort out Paul's theology, for which I lack the requisite competence in any case. However, Paul's epistles notwithstanding, if Israel is a figure of the church then something has to be done with the law, since it remains part of the Christian canon.[40] There was a time when the church distinguished between the *moral* law (the Ten Commandments) and the *ceremonial* law (the other commandments scattered throughout the Torah/Pentateuch). But this is not a canonical distinction. All the laws have God as their source.

Now, I readily concede that the law may be appropriated by the church only at a figural level. That is hardly problematic in that the whole Old Testament is available to the church primarily at a figural level. Otherwise, one reads Scripture in terms of a past history that no longer speaks to future generations. Indeed, reading the Old Testament figurally is the main hermeneutical method employed by every writer of the New Testament.[41] The church will always take seriously the New Testament's take on the Old Testament material, but she is not confined to appropriate only those texts that appear explicitly or are alluded to in the documents themselves. The whole text is available to the church, whether New Testament writers made use of them or not.

This usage of the legal material will involve considerably more familiarity with the Old Testament text than is the case today. But that is a good problem. Treasures await a more complete knowledge of the biblical text. Knowing the Old Testament backward and forward will shed light on the New Testament itself as well.[42] This requires steady, hard work, the use of a sanctified imagination, and being open to the Holy Spirit. But such an effort

---

40. Levenson points out that even Christian scholars who took a so-called historical approach to the Bible were not able to hide their Christian and primarily Protestant bias in relegating the legal material in the canon as devoid of spiritual or theological significance. See his "Why Jews are not Interested in Biblical Theology," in *Hebrew Bible*, 33–61.

41. Hays, *Reading Backwards*, 1–15. For a comprehensive theological approach to figural reading, see Ephraim Radner, *Time and the Word: Figural Reading of the Christian Scriptures* (Grand Rapids: Eerdmans, 2016).

42. Richard B. Hays is a master of paying attention to the use of Scripture in the New Testament. In addition to his *Reading Backwards*, see also *The Conversion of the Imagination: Paul as Interpreter of Israel's Scripture* (Grand Rapids: Eerdmans, 2005); *Echoes of Scripture in the Letters of Paul* (New Haven: Yale University Press, 1989); and "Reading Scripture in

will open up a whole new area of the Old Testament that has been forgotten or ignored for far too long. If the church wants to take her canon seriously, and if Israel is a figure of the church, then the church must now attend to this greatly neglected area.[43]

The last implication to be drawn in light of Israel as a figure of the church has to do with polity. Usually, polity is seen as a way of organizing church life with no one form being better than another. Whatever polity a church employs is a matter of convenience and tradition. Polity in this sense is a neutral matter that has no theological heft.

But is this true? Is polity inherently theological, as a matter of fact? Is there no theological difference between a denominational and a non-denominational church? Is a congregational church the same theologically as a church that is managed by an episcopal or presbyterian or synodical system? What even constitutes a church in theological terms? May I plant a church simply because I am a Christian, have a Bible that I think I can alone interpret, and preach with power and conviction? May I celebrate the sacraments simply because I want to celebrate them? May I ordain myself? At the very least, these are ecclesiological questions. And, ecclesiological questions are also theological questions. The question, then, is: Does Israel being a figure of the church affect the polity in any way of the one, holy, catholic, and apostolic church? It seems so. Because the church involves people, it will have an institutional form of some sort, notwithstanding the tired complaints about "the institutional church." As it turns out, as long as people make up the church, that is the only kind of church there is. There is no such thing as a noninstitutional church. Even a so-called noninstitutional church is institutional, whether this is recognized or not. I submit that seeing Israel as a figure for the church requires a rethinking even of ecclesiology.

If Israel is a figure of the church, then just as an Israelite is born into Israel a Christian is also born into the church. This birthright is not unique to Jews who are born into Judaism. The logic of this position is as follows. A child born to Christian parents (or even one Christian parent) will be

---

the Light of the Resurrection," in *The Art of Reading Scripture* (ed. Ellen Davis and Richard Hays; Grand Rapids: Eerdmans, 2003) 216–38.

43. One effort to read the law figurally is Ephraim Radner, *Leviticus* (Grand Rapids: Brazos, 2008).

baptized, a sacrament that seals the child as Christ's child—and part of the church, the Body of Christ—forever. The baptized child's parents (as well as the godparents and congregation) will promise to bring up the child in every aspect of Christian faith. This is why catechism is one of the church's most awesome responsibilities. At an appropriate time, this same child will confirm what his or her parents and godparents and congregation affirmed on his or her behalf. There is no need for conversion. Conversion is reserved for those who are outside the church.

Might a person baptized as an infant decide to abandon the Christian faith at a later time? There is no guarantee that this might not happen. But there is equally no guarantee that a person baptized as an adult—or who undergoes a "born again" experience—will honor his or her Christian commitments in perpetuity. Does such a practice rob a child from the spiritual vitality that is often felt by and expressed by a new convert? Only if the church is neglectful. This is why ongoing spiritual formation is part of the sanctifying process. The church should always foster the revitalization that derives from the practice of prayer, regular worship, a holy liturgy, spirit-led preaching, religious retreat, Christian education, developing discipleship, serious Bible study, engaging in manifold good works, being open to the Holy Spirit, and the like. This means that revival is a constant task of the church. But one can only *revive* if there has been an initial *vive*. Conversion to the one, holy, catholic, and apostolic church is always an evangelical possibility. Conversion is for those outside the church.

Israelites taught their children every feature of Israelite faith. They did not have to *become* Israelites. They *were* Israelites. Jews teach their children every feature of Jewish faith. They did not have to *become* Jews. They *are* Jews. Likewise, if Israel is a figure for the church, then Christians will teach their children every feature of Christian faith. They do not have to *become* Christians. They *are* Christians.

Conclusion

We have explored the possibility of seeing both Judaism and Christianity as figures of canonical Israel. Both figural readings are legitimate appropriations of TANAK and the Old Testament. Born approximately in the same era, these twin communities—joined at the hip[44]—have survived for two millennia and, with God's help and blessing, will continue to survive until the Israelite God recreates finally the new heaven and the new earth, at which time Jews—so they fervently believe—will expect to greet their Messiah for the first time, and Christians—so they fervently believe—will expect to greet their Messiah for the second time.[45]

44. See Boyarin's contention that Judaism was not the mother of Christianity; instead, Judaism and Christianity are twins, joined at the hip. Boyarin, *Border Lines*, 5.

45. See the remarks of Walter Brueggemann, *Theology of the Old Testament: Testimony, Dispute, Advocacy* (Minneapolis: Fortress, 1997) 449.

The Role of Historical Criticism in Wesleyan Biblical Hermeneutics

ANDREW KNAPP

Unlike most contributors to a Festschrift, I was never a graduate student of the honoree, nor a departmental colleague, nor a scholar working on the same material with overlapping research. Instead, Dr. Wall taught me when I was an undergraduate at Seattle Pacific University. After some courses with him, I requested that he guide my senior thesis, a commentary on Titus, and he graciously complied. I shudder to recall what sort of drivel I presented to him (and although I am certain copies exist, I pray they never see the light of day), but it was apparently passable enough for him to encourage me to pursue graduate work in biblical studies, which I did. In the ensuing years, however, my interests turned from the New Testament to the Hebrew Bible and the ancient Near East, far afield of Rob Wall's main wheelhouse. But it is fair to say that without Rob Wall's influence, alongside that of the other Bible faculty at Seattle Pacific, I would not have pursued biblical studies as a career. So I am delighted to contribute to a volume in his honor.

Despite my straying from Rob's primary area of research, when presented with the opportunity to write in this book I immediately knew what topic I wanted to pursue. My own work to date has been steeped in historical criticism, but I have always remained interested in theological interpretation of Scripture and the use of the Bible in the church. Given Rob's immense contributions in this field, this seems an appropriate occasion to visit this issue in light of my education since leaving Seattle Pacific. I want to look at Wesleyan biblical interpretation specifically, given Rob's own ecclesial location and concerns. Additionally, the time seems ripe to explore this topic. After years of only limited engagement with the idea of how Wesleyan scholars should interpret Scripture, the last two decades have seen a flurry of activity on the topic. Yet little attention has been paid to the place of historical criticism within Wesleyan biblical interpretation, despite the serious theological questions raised by such a hermeneutic. For example, one of the first monographs dedicated to constructing a distinctively Wesleyan biblical hermeneutic, Steven Joe Koskie's *Reading the Way to Heaven: A Wesleyan Theological Hermeneutic of Scripture*, barely acknowledges the issue except to state in passing that "a redefined role for historical criticism is legitimate" in Wesleyan biblical interpretation.[1]

My goal here is not a descriptive survey of how Wesleyan biblical scholars have engaged the results of historical criticism in their interpretation; neither do I intend to impose this as a one-size-fits-all prescriptive decree of how Wesleyan interpreters should deal with this issue. Rather, I intend to lay out how I, as one initially formed in a Wesleyan institution and then trained primarily in a nonconfessional institution that espoused historical criticism, synthesize the diverse means of approaching the Bible/Scripture that I have encountered. Thus, the next three sections lay out in broad strokes how I approach the issues, then in the fourth and final section, I provide a worked example, interpreting Psalm 29 with the strategies presented.

The Historical-Critical Method
and the Bible as Scripture

In its narrowest sense, historical criticism simply refers to the historian's attempt to determine "what really happened," assessing the correlation between historical event and the historiographical account of said event in the biblical record.[2] More commonly, though, scholars demonstrate a broader understanding of historical criticism as the umbrella covering an array of critical approaches to the Bible (such as form-, redaction-, source-, and other critical methods), all of which seek to explain the various ways in which the Bible relates to history and is itself a product of historical

---

1. Steven Joe Koskie Jr., *Reading the Way to Heaven: A Wesleyan Theological Hermeneutic of Scripture* (Winona Lake: Eisenbrauns, 2014) 127. I hasten to add that Koskie's book is an excellent step forward on this subject despite this lacuna. Sarah Heaner Lancaster's treatment of Scripture and revelation in Methodism provides an excellent survey of Wesleyan approaches to Scripture from the time of John Wesley until the present, but it also addresses the issue of historical criticism only tangentially ("Scripture and Revelation," in William J. Abraham and James E. Kirby, eds., *The Oxford Handbook of Methodist Studies* [Oxford: Oxford University Press, 2009] 489–504).

2. For one example of this understanding of historical criticism, see Daniel J. Harrington, *Interpreting the Old Testament: A Practical Guide* (Collegeville: Liturgical, 1991) 27–38.

processes. Key here is the diachronic emphasis of historical criticism; original meaning and textual development are privileged over contemporary
application and final form. In investigating the text in such a fashion, the
historical-critical exegete strives for objectivity and autonomy. John Collins
notes that the historian must not worry about results conforming to authorities and should be "opposed not only to ecclesiastical interference but also
to undue deference to received opinion."[3]

The theological interpreter, on the other hand, traditionally begins not
by emancipating the interpretation from all external "interference" but by
subjecting it to the Rule of Faith. The theological interpreter reads the Bible
not as any other book but as Scripture, the revealed word of God, and deliberately keeps theological concerns at the forefront of the reading.[4] Some
would maintain that these different starting points and concerns render
historical criticism inherently inimical to theological interpretation. I do not
have space in this essay to detail my objections to this position, so I must
state here as a premise for the following work that I do not find the two
approaches to be mutually exclusive—or, at the very least, I do not see historical critical work as precluding confessionally driven readings of Scripture.
Historical criticism does not require any sort of methodological atheism
and rejection of the supernatural out of hand. But the method does require
a certain theological agnosticism—to use the common parlance, the (tem-
porary) "bracketing out" of one's faith commitments—when exegeting a text.

I suggest that one might best consider the two approaches not as in
conflict but as nonoverlapping magisteria. How they relate will be addressed
throughout this essay, but before moving on, some remarks on the more
general relationship between the two ways of interpreting the Bible are in
order. For much of the twentieth century, the majority of biblical scholars—
including those who professed to be believers in the Christian (or Jewish)

---

3. John J. Collins, *The Bible after Babel: Historical Criticism in a Postmodern Age* (Grand
Rapids: Eerdmans, 2005) 5.

4. Like "historical criticism," "theological interpretation of Scripture" is notoriously
difficult to define. For example, in his oft-cited introductory article, Kevin J. Vanhoozer
defines theological interpretation negatively, focusing on what it is not rather than what it is
(Vanhoozer, "What Is Theological Interpretation of the Bible?" in Kevin J. Vanhoozer, ed.,
Dictionary for Theological Interpretation of the Bible [Grand Rapids: Baker, 2005] 19–23).
Also like historical criticism, theological interpretation is an umbrella term that covers many
discrete hermeneutical methods.

faith and those who did not hold to any particular creed—espoused historical criticism as the primary lens through which to view the Bible.[5] As the century drew to a close, however, an increasing number of scholars expressed dissatisfaction with this position. Sundry reasons for this were put forward, which I will boil down to two for simplicity.

First, historical criticism by definition is not theological. One may employ historical criticism to investigate historically situated religion but not to plumb the mysteries of the transcendent. Christian theology begins with the Bible as Scripture, an incomprehensible category from a historical-critical perspective. In the words of Frank Spina, "There is no question that the Bible can legitimately be studied from a number of perspectives: as ancient literature, as a potential source for historical reconstruction, as a cultural artifact, as political propaganda, as data for observing the development of language, as expressive of different ideologies, etc. But none of these require[s] a self-conscious acceptance of the Bible as 'Scripture,' which is a *theological* category."[6] This recognition does not divest historical criticism of all worth—in fact, later in the same essay Spina writes that "we need more historical critical investigation, not less"[7]—but it does relegate historical criticism as, at best, an auxiliary approach to the Bible for the theologian.

The second reason for searching for new approaches to the Bible for the purposes of theology is that historical criticism tends to restrict the meaning of the biblical text at the time of its original authorship, thus stripping the text of its polyvalence. The present jubilarian has expressed this issue well: "The methodological interests of historical criticism, which seem preoccupied by those contingencies that shaped particular biblical writings at various points of origin in the ancient world, tend to subvert Scripture's intended use as a means of grace and rule of faith by which believers are initiated into their new life with Christ in the realm of his Spirit. For all their exegetical utility, the tools of historical criticism misplace Scripture's theological reference point with a historical one, freezing its normative meaning in ancient

---

5. Within the Christian tradition, there has always been a significant group (namely fundamentalists) holding to a high view of inerrancy that leads to the dismissal of historical criticism *tout court*. This is an enormous issue in its own right but not one that I will discuss in the present essay.

6. Frank Anthony Spina, "Wesleyan Faith Seeking Biblical Understanding," *Wesleyan Theological Journal* 30 (1995) 36.

7. Ibid., 42.

worlds that do not bear upon today's church."[8] Elsewhere he sharpens this point: "There can be no single, original sense of a multivalent Scripture that can effectively broker the Word of God for every people of God."[9]

Despite these negative appraisals, in recent years an increasing number of Christian traditions have actually been more willing to explicitly acknowledge a place, and even a need, for historical criticism in theology. In the Roman Catholic tradition, for example, historical criticism is now essential. As is well known, Pope Paul VI encouraged Catholic biblical scholars to engage this approach in the landmark statement *Dei verbum* in 1965 at Vatican II. More recently, Joseph Cardinal Ratzinger (now Pope Emeritus Benedict XVI) helped the Pontifical Biblical Commission promulgate "The Interpretation of the Bible in the Church," which reinforces the church's pro-critical position. Early on, this document states: "The historical-critical method is the indispensable method for the scientific study of the meaning of ancient texts. Holy Scripture, inasmuch as it is the 'word of God in human language,' has been composed by human authors in all its various parts and in all the sources that lie behind them. Because of this, its proper understanding not only admits the use of this method but actually requires it." The document goes on to acknowledge that the historical-critical method has certain limitations—including the fact that it is not concerned with "possibilities of meaning which have been revealed at later stages of the biblical revelation and the history of the church," an idea discussed in the previous section—and that it must be carried out "in an objective manner" without "a priori principles."[10] But when this occurs, historical criticism and theology go hand in hand: "This method has contributed to the production of works of exegesis and of biblical theology which are of great value."[11]

8. Robert W. Wall, "Canonical Contexts and Canonical Conversations," in Joel B. Green and Max Turner, eds., *Between Two Horizons: Spanning New Testament Studies & Systematic Theology* (Grand Rapids: Eerdmans, 2000) 166.

9. Robert W. Wall, "Toward a Wesleyan Hermeneutic of Scripture," in Barry L. Callen and Richard P. Thompson, eds., *Reading the Bible in Wesleyan Ways: Some Constructive Proposals* (Kansas City, MO: Beacon Hill, 2004) 53.

10. The mention of "a priori principles" clearly refers to those who assert that historical criticism, especially in light of Troeltsch's principle of analogy, excludes the supernatural.

11. Pontifical Biblical Commission, "The Interpretation of the Bible in the Church," presented March 18, 1994. http://www.ewtn.com/library/curia/pbcinter.htm#8. Accessed January 3, 2016.

The Reformed tradition demonstrates a similar orientation. Although there is no lengthy statement on historical criticism such as that of the Pontifical Biblical Commission, the Confession of 1967, issued by the Presbyterian Church (USA), declares an "obligation" on the part of the church to utilize such an approach: "The Bible is to be interpreted in the light of its witness to God's work of reconciliation in Christ. The Scriptures, given under the guidance of the Holy Spirit, are nevertheless the words of men, conditioned by the language, thought forms, and literary fashions of the places and times at which they were written. They reflect views of life, history, and the cosmos which were then current. The church, therefore, has an obligation to approach the Scriptures with literary and historical understanding."[12] Here, again, faithful interpreters are exhorted to bring what they can to understand Scripture historically in order to understand it theologically.

In North America, the tradition most resistant to historical criticism in recent generations has been evangelicalism. But, while it can be treacherous to paint a group as diverse as contemporary evangelicals with a broad brush, one can detect some movement toward embracing historical criticism here as well. To cite just one example, a cadre of young scholars recently published a volume entitled *Evangelical Faith and the Challenge of Historical Criticism*, in which they exhort their colleagues to espouse historical-critical methods when interpreting Scripture.[13] In a closing essay, the volume editors begin with a section titled "The Possibility and Necessity of Evangelical Historical Criticism," in which they write, "Although certain features of modern historical criticism have rightly been chastened, the discipline will persist. And well it should, for it is in history that God revealed himself; it is in history that God inspired and enscripturated his people's reflections on their encounter with him; and it is in history that we encounter that Scripture. We Christian biblical scholars have to do with Scripture *in history*."[14] This book, of course, does not carry authority

---

12. "The Confession of 1967," http://www.creeds.net/reformed/conf67.htm, accessed January 3, 2016.

13. Christopher M. Hays and Christopher B. Ansberry, eds., *Evangelical Faith and the Challenge of Historical Criticism* (Grand Rapids: Baker, 2013).

14. Christopher B. Ansberry and Christopher M. Hays, "Faithful Criticism and a Critical Faith," in Hays and Ansberry, eds., *Evangelical Faith and the Challenge of Historical Criticism*, 204 (emphasis theirs).

within evangelicalism equivalent to the authority carried by the previously examined statements within Catholicism and Presbyterianism, and indeed it has generated some controversy among its intended audience, receiving high praise from many in the evangelical camp and scathing critique from others. But its very existence and the discussion it has generated bespeak increasing openness toward some kind of historical criticism in evangelical biblical hermeneutics.

In terms of magisterial teaching on biblical interpretation, Wesleyanism is somewhere between evangelicalism and Catholicism. The Articles of Religion display much restraint on what one must believe about the nature of Scripture.[15] The United Methodist *Book of Discipline* goes into further detail about the nature of Scripture, in some ways resembling *Dei Verbum*, but it is less explicit about critical work, noting only in passing that "we draw upon the careful historical, literary, and textual studies of recent years, which have enriched our understanding of the Bible."[16] I will explore how well historical criticism fits in with historical Wesleyan biblical scholarship in the final section, but first I will briefly outline *why* historical criticism has such sanction in so many Christian denominations if, as was discussed in the previous section, it is insufficient for the theological task.

The Role of Historical Criticism in Biblical Interpretation by Wesleyans

There are different ways of approaching the contribution of historical criticism to general Christian biblical hermeneutics, but I contend that it serves the task of biblical theology primarily by providing boundaries to legitimate interpretation. On one side, historical criticism places a boundary against

---

15. "The Holy Scripture containeth all things necessary to salvation; so that whatsoever is not read therein, nor may be proved thereby, is not to be required of any man that it should be believed as an article of faith, or be thought requisite or necessary to salvation. In the name of the Holy Scripture we do understand those canonical books of the Old and New Testament of whose authority was never any doubt in the church." After this the canonical books of both Testaments are listed ("The Articles of Religion of the Methodist Church." http://www.umc.org/what-we-believe/the-articles-of-religion-of-the-methodist-church. Accessed January 3, 2016).

16. *The Book of Discipline of the United Methodist Church* (Nashville: United Methodist Church) 82, §105.

the historicism of fundamentalism, namely the approach to Scripture that favors plain-sense exegesis to the point that it locates the Bible's theological message within its historical reporting. As many have previously noted, such an approach can become a sort of biblical docetism,[17] valuing Scripture's status as the Word of God so highly that it dismisses all indications that this Word was mediated through the (fallible, historically particular) words of humans—the Bible only "seems" to be a human product.[18] Emphasis on such a "high" view of Scripture can have deleterious effects on one's faith when one confronts problems with the model. Ansberry and Hays write in this regard, if somewhat polemically, "Fundamentalist obscurantism can also imperil the faithful. Far too many believers have been taught to understand the Bible in modern terms removed by millennia from the ancient cultures that composed the sacred texts. In this way, Christian doctrine has been pitted against science, archaeology and ancient history. Under such sad conditions, people's faith can be snatched and devoured by evolutionary biology, by the Epic of Gilgamesh, by *vaticinium ex eventu*, by an archaeological record lacking evidence of a million-persons-march from Egypt, or by a Gospel Synopsis that shows divergent details in the Evangelists' depictions of Christ. Sure, atheistic critical scholarship is dangerous, but so is benighted pietism."[19]

The Jewish scholar Jon Levenson expresses this somewhat differently in a fine essay on the interaction of historical criticism and biblical theology. Levenson cites the example of two apparently contradictory laws, one in Exodus and the other in Deuteronomy. He juxtaposes the manner of dealing with this contradiction by historical critics and (rabbinic) traditionalists.

---

17. For this point I am indebted to Brent A. Strawn, "Docetism, Käsemann, and Christology: Can Historical Criticism Help Christological Orthodoxy (and Other Theology) After All?" *Journal of Theological Interpretation* 2 (2008) 161–80.

18. Drawing an analogy between biblical and Christological docetism in some ways presupposes an incarnational view of Scripture, at least if one is to press the analogy. The incarnational view is, in my view, quite helpful, although not without its shortcomings. The incarnational view has a long and illustrious history but was put forth most accessibly by Peter Enns (*Inspiration and Incarnation: Evangelicals and the Problem of the Old Testament* [Grand Rapids: Baker, 2005]). For some of the problems with this approach and an intriguing alternative, see Daniel Castelo and Robert W. Wall, "Scripture and the Church: A Précis for an Alternative Analogy," *Journal of Theological Interpretation* 5 (2011) 197–210.

19. Ansberry and Hays, "Faithful Criticism and a Critical Faith" 205.

The latter construct a convoluted scheme of harmonizing the two texts in blatant violation of the plain-sense meaning in both; to historical critics "this operation is a historically indefensible homogenization of the past" and they prefer to let the contradiction stand, appealing to the discrete historical situations behind the two texts.[20] Levenson is clearly sympathetic to traditional, noncritical approaches to Scripture, and he appreciates the value of rabbinic interpretation, but he also acknowledges that it is sometimes "historically indefensible." Here we see the safeguard provided by historical criticism at work—historical criticism can be used in service of biblical theology not by being used as a weapon to destroy theologically driven attempts to establish a coherent voice within Scripture, but to caution against attributing such a voice to historical reality. In short, historical criticism requires the faithful exegete to "do" theology because it reveals that theological meaning cannot simply be mined from the biblical text. The consummate historian would not necessarily be a perfect theologian.

In addition to guarding against historicism, historical criticism also furnishes a barrier at the opposite end of the interpretive spectrum. It protects Scripture from the excesses of postmodernism, specifically those that allow the reader to impute nearly any meaning on to a given text. By asserting that texts do have inherent meanings, the historical critic declares that not anything goes when interpreting the biblical text. John Collins writes, "What historical criticism does is set limits to the conversation, by saying what a given text could or could not mean in its ancient context. A text may have more than one possible meaning, but it may not mean just anything at all."[21] There are multiple valid reading strategies, but the text does have a "determinate core of meaning" that controls how one may apply such strategies.[22] Collins writes favorably of such postmodern readings as deconstructionism and ideological criticism, adducing especially Derrida and Foucault, respectively. In fact, he writes that such approaches to the text in actuality essentialize historical criticism and push it to its limits.[23] He uses Yvonne

---

20. This discussion comes from the titular essay of Levenson's collection, *The Hebrew Bible, the Old Testament, and Historical Criticism* (Louisville: Westminster John Knox, 1993) 3.

21. Collins, *The Bible after Babel*, 10.

22. Ibid., 14.

23. Ibid., 22, 25.

Sherwood's deconstructive reading of Hosea[24] as an example, remarking that Sherwood successfully problematizes the tendency of avowed historical critics to accept without question the prophet's premise that Yahweh is morally and in other ways superior to Baal, when in fact the text calls into question Yahweh's treatment of his people. Sherwood cuts against the grain in her deconstruction of the text here, but at the same time her reading is constrained, and generated, by the text itself. As such, it is open to acceptance, rejection, or qualification by other readers on critical grounds. What historical criticism would prohibit would be an interpreter ignoring the message of the text to pursue his or her own agenda without allowing for a valid critique of the interpretation.

In providing barriers on either end of the spectrum of exegesis, historical criticism indeed plays a key role in biblical interpretation (theological and otherwise). This role, however, is in no way of a constructive kind. That is, in what we have seen thus far, one does not develop theological doctrine on the basis of historical-critical analysis of Scripture. Some debate exists whether historical criticism *qua* historical criticism should be considered a theological task; I contend that this is a semantic quibble, the answer of which boils down to how broadly one views the theological task. Historical criticism is not inherently theological. One need not be a "faithful tradent" to interpret the text from a historical-critical perspective, but such a requirement is necessary for theological interpretation.[25] Historical criticism does play a crucial role in theology. It may even be valid to think of historical criticism as a preliminary task for doing theology—an act of clearing a foundation and getting permits before one builds a house.

Thus we see warrant for both of the *prima facie* contradictory premises discussed above: the "negative appraisal of the modern historical-critical enterprise"[26] shared by Wall and so many other recent interpreters is merited where one's focus is theology, yet we also see why so many Christian traditions have explicitly embraced historical criticism in recent years.

24. Yvonne Sherwood, *The Prostitute and the Prophet: Hosea's Marriage in Literary-Theoretical Perspective* (Sheffield: Sheffield Academic Press, 1996).

25. See Wall, "Toward a Wesleyan Hermeneutic of Scripture" 43: "Note the importance of theological location as a tacit but critical feature of the interpreter's social context: the talented hermeneut is also a faithful tradent."

26. Wall, "Canonical Context and Canonical Conversations" 166.

On the surface, historical criticism and theological interpretation can seem antithetical. The former is much more adept at demolishing than building; Levenson notes that after taking the text apart "ruthlessly," historical critics "lack a method of putting it back together again."[27] Yet what one requires theologically, and what Levenson advocates, is a means of interpretation that interfaces the historical and canonical[28] contexts of Scripture so that historical-critical efforts would "be dialectically checked by a continual awareness of the need to put the text back together in a way that makes it available in the present and in its entirety—not merely in the past and in the form of historically contextualized fragments."[29] Theological interpretation seeks to create a coherent voice from Scripture—coherent not only with the rest of the canon (often the primary concern of theologians, because detecting a single voice from such a discrete canon is no simple task) but also individually coherent and historically legitimate. We might go so far as to consider historical criticism an *ancilla theologiae*, something outside of theology and fueled by reason but that can be applied to theological ends.

Wesleyan biblical interpretation is, of course, by definition theological.[30] It follows, then, that if historical criticism is indeed important for theological interpretation, even if only in a preliminary or ancillary way, then it must be important for Wesleyan biblical hermeneutics as well. Of course,

27. Levenson, *The Hebrew Bible, the Old Testament, and Historical Criticism*, 2.

28. Note that Levenson does not use the terminology of "theology" and "canon," instead juxtaposing historical and literary contexts. But in light of the rest of this volume (which frequently deals with theology, canon, and similar concepts explicitly), it seems valid to invoke such categories here. At the very least, even if Levenson would object, I would uphold this point when applying this discussion to historical criticism and Christian theological efforts.

29. Levenson, *The Hebrew Bible, the Old Testament, and Historical Criticism*, 79. Interestingly, Wall favorably cites this same passage from Levenson in his discussion of the Wesleyan idea of the simultaneity of Scripture. Wall also appears to see historical and theological/canonical approaches in a sort of dialogue. Although he embraces the idea of Scripture's simultaneity, he remarks that ignoring the "plain sense" of individual passages "undermines the integral nature of Scripture and distorts its full witness to God." Therefore, he contends, ultimately the "critical aim of exegesis" (he does not specify what type of exegesis), after it "successfully exposes the pluriformity of Scripture," is to put the text together again (Wall, "Toward a Wesleyan Hermeneutic of Scripture" 49).

30. Spina, for example, writes, "Whatever else it means to be Wesleyan, or to approach Scripture as a Wesleyan, it cannot mean something besides a theological approach" ("Wesleyan Faith Seeking Biblical Understanding" 36).

in the preceding discussion there is nothing distinctively Wesleyan about utilizing historical criticism in this way. As discussed above, many, perhaps most, nonfundamentalist Christian traditions espouse such an approach. This goes a long way toward explaining why twenty years ago Frank Spina acknowledged that the Wesleyan hermeneutic is often defined more by the scholars doing the interpretation (namely, Wesleyans) than by the specifics of the approach involved.[31] Because not all of Scripture pertains to Wesleyan distinctives, much Wesleyan interpretation may well resemble that of non-Wesleyan faithful interpreters. I will try to illustrate both this last point and the main point of this section, on the general role of historical criticism in theological hermeneutics, with one broad example. When I attended Seattle Pacific University I took a course on Revelation that turned out to be quite formative. Although the course was not taught by Rob Wall, we used his commentary on this book.[32] This commentary does an admirable job of incorporating crucial insights from historical criticism, such as the significance of the book's apocalyptic genre in light of other contemporaneous apocalypses, in a theologically valid way. Wall illuminates how the ancient author likely conceived of the book and how it was interpreted by its ancient audience, and in light of this he calls into question certain ways of interpreting the book as some sort of ecstatic, purely futurist foretelling. But at the same time, he never freezes the meaning of the text in the first century, balancing the moments of origin and composition with the moments of canonization and interpretation.[33] He writes, "the interpreter considers Revelation as a historically conditioned document; its message must be understood in light of its original historical setting, and its messenger as one whose convictions about God shaped what he wrote down."[34] But he clarifies that, contrary to many modern critical commentaries, these concerns are not primary but only serve a greater purpose: "We are primarily interested in the book's (rather than the author's) apostolicity—a more

---

31. "It is difficult to avoid the impression that what is often referred to as a 'Wesleyan hermeneutic' is little more than the adoption of a particular interpretive technique by scholars who consider themselves 'Wesleyan' on grounds having nothing to do with the hermeneutic in question" (Spina, "Wesleyan Faith Seeking Biblical Understanding" 36–37).

32. Robert W. Wall, *Revelation* (Peabody: Hendrickson, 1991).

33. Ibid., 2–40.

34. Ibid., 4.

theological than historical concern. In addition, our interest in the historical crisis which occasioned this composition will finally be more theological than historical."[35] In having the historical situated-ness of Revelation inform his discussion while not allowing it to dictate the end-goal of interpretation, Wall's commentary is exemplary in showing how historical criticism can be used in theological interpretation. He recognizes that the text continues to have meaning for the community of the faithful today and shows how the first-century setting from which Revelation emerged constrains that meaning.

Wall's commentary surely represents Wesleyan interpretation given his affiliation with the tradition and overarching approach, but there is little in the volume that is *distinctively* Wesleyan. That is, his work on Revelation reflects a confessional background, but for the most part, it could reflect a sympathy with any number of ecclesiastical traditions. Can one, indeed, do theological work that is explicitly Wesleyan with regard to the specific way one incorporates historical criticism? This question will serve as the impetus for what follows in this essay.

The Role of Historical Criticism in Wesleyan Biblical Interpretation

Attempting to harness an allegedly objective tool like historical criticism for an overtly agenda-driven project, such as Wesleyan biblical interpretation, is at best a dangerous proposition. "Bracketing out" convictions is tricky business; even with the most pristine intentions, it is easy to let one's theological orientation influence one's historical exegesis. The entire enterprise can resemble political lobbying, allowing a certain agenda to corrupt what should be an analytical process free of external influence. One could point to innumerable examples of the dubious use of historical criticism for theological purposes—namely, instances where the outside observer cannot shake the feeling that the interpreter's theological commitments are driving their allegedly critical investigation. I will point to just one, namely Gerhard von Rad's biblical theology centered around the idea of salvation history (*Heilsgeschichte*). I appeal to von Rad because, although he was a

---

35. Ibid., 6.

Lutheran, his particular brand of biblical theology might on the surface appeal to Wesleyans. One of the distinctives of Wesleyan theology is a focus on the soteriological reading of Scripture (see below), so if one could show that exegesis reveals that God's redemptive activity unifies the overarching, diverse biblical narrative, it would lend tremendous historical imprimatur to this theology. Unfortunately, in order to fit the entire Old Testament into his schema, von Rad in fact takes several passages out of their original contexts, not exegeting them as discrete texts but interpreting them in light of the whole of Scripture. For an evaluation of von Rad's overall theology I will again invoke Levenson: "Within the limited context of theological interpretation informed by historical criticism—the context von Rad intended—his essay must be judged unsuccessful. Within another limited context, however—the confessional elucidation of scripture for purposes of Lutheran reaffirmation—it is an impressive success."[36] As noted above, if the devotion to historical criticism of the twentieth century (including by most Christian biblical scholars) taught us anything, it is that historical criticism is not in itself sufficient for the constructive theological task.

If Wesleyans should not turn to historical criticism to help build a (biblical) theology, then I would recommend attempting to use it in more modest capacities. More to the point, I submit that Wesleyans should examine how they currently interpret Scripture and see if historical-critical examination can enhance any areas of interest. Wesleyan interpretation necessarily begins with John Wesley; but I will echo the present honoree's caveat that "I am not a scholar of Wesley nor the son of one,"[37] so here I rely on the work of others to reconstruct his hermeneutic. A thorough examination of whether historical criticism is consistent with Wesley's own conception

---

36. Levenson, *The Hebrew Bible, the Old Testament, and Historical Criticism*, 61. Levenson is here focusing on one particular essay by von Rad, but one can safely apply this evaluation to von Rad's broader program. Levenson treats von Rad's *Heilsgeschichte* elsewhere in the volume (21–26), at one point offering this incisive critique: "Once again, a historical method—this time, form criticism—has been employed to decompose the received text and to reorder it according to the needs of Christian theology. This use of historical criticism has proven to be the most important in Old Testament theology, for it enables the theologian to find meanings in the book that the *textus receptus* does not suggest. The retrieved past (the Hebrew Bible) can thus be rapidly assimilated to the familiar present (the Old Testament). The man can repress the child within and go about his business as if nothing has changed" (25).

37. Wall, "Toward a Wesleyan Hermeneutic of Scripture" 45 n. 19.

of Scripture is beyond the scope of this study, but the question is worth addressing briefly. It must be remembered that Wesley was active in the early to mid-eighteenth century, at the very dawn of the Enlightenment, rendering him an early modern but essentially precritical reader of Scripture. He did, however, not infrequently remark on the authorship of Scripture and the role of reason in biblical interpretation, which is germane to this discussion.

If we accept that one of the results of historical criticism is that it reveals diverse viewpoints within the Bible, then at first glance Wesley's conception of Scripture would seem to exclude such an approach. For example, responding to a contemporary thinker about his discussion of Scripture, Wesley wrote, "Whether he is a Christian, deist, or atheist, I cannot tell. If he is a Christian, he betrays his own cause by averring that, 'All Scripture is not given by inspiration of God; but the writers of it were sometimes left to themselves and consequently made some mistakes.' Nay, if there be any mistakes in the Bible, there may as well be a thousand. If there be one falsehood in that book, it did not come from the God of truth."[38] Such comments appear to anticipate today's fundamentalist equation of diversity with errors and mistakes, a premise not accepted by many confessional historical critics. Digging deeper, though, reveals that Wesley may not have been entirely satisfied with a black-and-white approach. In one sermon he endorses "a stated rule in interpreting Scripture never to depart from the plain, literal sense, unless it implies an absurdity."[39] Such "absurdities" are items in the Bible that are disproven by reason or science (such as the cosmology evident in the Old Testament) or areas where different biblical passages contradict one another.[40] Scott Jones, one of the main scholars of Wesley's method of biblical interpretation, expounds on this as follows: "Thus, the exceptions to the rule of literal interpretation become critically important. The literal sense

---

38. John R. Tyson, *The Way of the Wesleys* (Grand Rapids: Eerdmans, 2014) 7–8.

39. Scott J. Jones, *John Wesley's Conception and Use of Scripture* (Nashville: Abingdon, 1995) 79. Jones's entire section on "Scripture and Reason" in Wesley's thinking provides helpful background for this discussion (65–80).

40. Jones, *John Wesley's Conception and Use of Scripture*, 79–80. For several examples of Wesley's generally simple solutions to problematic biblical passages, see Stephen Westerholm and Martin Westerholm, *Reading Sacred Scripture: Voices from the History of Biblical Interpretation* (Grand Rapids: Eerdmans, 2016) 296.

cannot be contradictory to other Scriptures, because that would charge God [the author of the entire Bible] with self-contradiction. The literal meaning of a text must be one that coincides with the general tenor of Scripture, which is determined by the analogy of faith." [41] In sum, it appears that while Wesley was certainly no historical critic himself—and probably would not be too interested in such an approach if he were alive today—his conception of Scripture would allow for the methodology. His own manner of interpretation was a precursor to the sort of theological interpretation of Scripture now prevalent among confessional biblical scholars—he did not deny that Scripture contains "absurdities," but when they appear one should appeal to the testimony of the entire biblical text for understanding. [42]

Accepting that Wesley was a precritical (and therefore not anticritical) interpreter of Scripture, [43] and that his conception of Scripture would allow for critical readings, our next step would be to see how Wesley *did* read the Bible so as to see if historical criticism can complement his approach. Today's Wesley scholars tend to identify four characteristics of his approach to the use of Scripture. Wall categorizes these as (1) the sacrament of Scripture; (2) the simultaneity of Scripture; (3) the soteriological use of Scripture; and (4) the sermonic midrash of Scripture. [44] I submit that a Wesleyan, critical scholar could integrate these two discrete approaches to Scripture by adopting the results of independent historical-critical exegesis [45] and then appropriating them for these specifically Wesleyan purposes. In the rest of this essay I will briefly provide an example of such a hybrid approach, using

41. Jones, *John Wesley's Conception and Use of Scripture*, 197. Note, though, that in his conclusion Jones states that "Wesley has a serious problem in his hermeneutics" in that the literal sense does not always line up with the general tenor of Scripture, a tension that is never resolved in Wesley's writings (Ibid., 215).

42. This is consistent with Jones's view of Wesley as well. Jones acknowledges that although Wesley was interested in historical context, there is a "crucial difference between Wesley and historical-critical interpretation. . . . While Wesley is interested in the human side of Scripture, his primary emphasis falls on the divine authorship of the text. For Wesley, the Bible's unity stems from the fact that it has a single ultimate author" (Ibid., 197).

43. Spina, "Wesleyan Faith Seeking Biblical Understanding" 33–34.

44. Wall, "Toward a Wesleyan Hermeneutic of Scripture" 44–54.

45. By "independent" I do not mean to suggest that no single scholar can study a text both critically and in a Wesleyan fashion. I only mean here to reinforce my earlier point that historical-critical work by definition must be performed without an overarching theological agenda—it must be a-Wesleyan, so to speak.

Psalm 29 as a test case. I admit at the outset that Psalm 29 readily lends itself to this sort of reading; not all biblical texts would submit themselves so readily to core Wesleyan emphases.

A Wesleyan Reading of Psalm 29
Informed by Historical Criticism

We should begin this evaluation of Psalm 29 with a summary of the critical consensus regarding the background of this text. The psalm shows several peculiarities that prove vexing for those who wish to interpret it in a traditional way. I will outline three here. First, the introductory verse of the psalm reads, "Ascribe to Yahweh, you gods, ascribe to Yahweh glory and strength." Most translations show some discomfort with this straightforward meaning, so they replace the "gods" with "heavenly beings." But the Hebrew phrase here, *běnê ʾēlîm*, is clear. Most translators take the liberty to transform "gods" into the more generic "heavenly beings" because, of course, one of the main tenets of Christian faith is monotheism, the belief in one god in three persons. But Psalm 29, read literally, seems to accept a whole pantheon of gods, with the main deity Yahweh surrounded by a council of lesser deities.

A second peculiarity of this passage, when read within the Old Testament canon, is that despite being labeled a "psalm of David" at the outset, we read the following in verse 9: "The voice of Yahweh causes the oaks to whirl, and strips the forest bare; and in his temple all say, 'Glory!'" When David became king, of course, Israel had no temple. David longed to build a temple but was informed by the prophet Nathan that not he but his son Solomon would build it. So how is it that in this allegedly Davidic psalm all those in the temple—present tense—declare God's glory?

The third and final peculiarity that has perplexed scholars is this: In early Israel, Yahweh was essentially a tribal god, tied to his people and especially his land. Yahweh was the god of *Israel*. But this psalm seems to care nothing for the territory of Israel. Several geographical markers appear, but they are all north of Israel. In verse 5 Yahweh "breaks the cedars of Lebanon"—Lebanon today is the country immediately north of Israel; in the Bronze and Iron Ages, when this psalm originated, this was the heartland of the region known to readers of the Old Testament as Canaan. In verse 6

Lebanon appears again, and beside it Sirion, a mountain just north of Israel, also in Canaan. In fact, Deuteronomy 3:9 tells us that Sirion was what the Canaanites called Mount Hermon—so in addition to Sirion not being an Israelite location, it is not even an Israelite term. Two verses later we find the "wilderness of Kadesh"—Kadesh was an area in the center of Canaan. Why is the psalmist so concerned with Israel's neighbor, and not at all with Israel itself?

It is fair to say that these three peculiar aspects of Psalm 29 constitute what John Wesley called "absurdities." The apparently polytheistic reference to an assembly of gods seems inconsistent with the overarching theological message of Scripture; the casual mention of the temple that did not yet exist militates against reading with the "plain, literal sense" of this psalm; and the fixation with the land of Canaan without any demonstrable regard for Israel is bewildering with a surface reading of the text. Yet most biblical scholars think that they have the solution to these absurdities. The psalm does not fit naturally in the biblical Psalter, but there is a place where it fits quite well—in the ancient Canaanite cult of Baal.[46] Baal was considered not the only god, but the chief god, with a multitude of subdeities who made up his court. At the time of David, and for several centuries before, there were several temples devoted to his worship. The geographical references make sense as well. What clinches the argument that this psalm originated not with David but with the worshippers of Baal is the imagery used: Baal was the storm god, and one sees allusions to a thunderstorm throughout the psalm. The psalmist focuses on the "voice" or "sound" of the god and explicitly states that "the god of glory thunders." One can also see the powerful storm when the god's voice "breaks the cedars," "flashes forth flames of fire," "shakes the wilderness," "strips the forest bare," and more. As the psalm draws to a close, the deity "sits enthroned over the flood": According to the central Baal myth, Baal became the chief god by emerging victorious after a great battle against the flood deity. Thus, in its original context, it might be more appropriate to say that the god "sits enthroned over Flood," with a capital F.

---

46. For considerations of how early Yahwism may have been influenced by the Baal cult, see the classic essay of Frank Moore Cross, "Yahweh and Ba'l," in his *Canaanite Myth and Hebrew Epic* (Cambridge, MA: Harvard University Press, 1973) 147–94.

With regard to a mechanism for how this psalm came to praise Yahweh and take a prominent place in the psalter, the most common explanation from those in the scholarly guild is simple: somewhere along the way, a pious Israelite encountered the song and appropriated it by simply substituting the name Yahweh for the name Baal throughout.[47]

Such is a historical-critical understanding of Psalm 29, independent (so far as can be achieved) of "ecclesiastical interference," to use John Collins's expression.[48] To interpret this theologically, we must now take an additional step, approaching the text not exegetically as an early Canaanite/Israelite composition but canonically as a small part of Christian Scripture. For this theological interpretation to be specifically Wesleyan, we must pay attention to the previously delineated Wesleyan foci of the sacramental, simultaneous, soteriological, and sermonic aspects of Scripture. I shall do so below.

According to the Wesleyan view, Scripture is sacramental insofar as it serves as a means of grace. As a medium through which God is revealed, Scripture transforms us and enables us to seek God. This transformation, part and parcel of the Wesleyan emphasis on sanctification, does not involve mere intellectual assent to God's message, but passionate response: "God 'authors' Scripture not to warrant some grand system of theological ideas to guide people in orthodox confession, but rather to lead sinful people into thankful worship of a forgiving Lord."[49] This is abundantly clear in Psalm 29, in which the response to Yahweh throughout all creation models the Wesleyan ideal of responding to God. The Wesleyan view of sanctification is not one of quiet, inward response, but of visible transformation and responsiveness to God's call. In the psalm, all the heavenly beings ascribe to Yahweh glory, strength, and splendor in recognition of holiness (29:1–2). Meanwhile, Lebanon leaps like a calf, the cedars break, the desert shakes, and more (29:3–9). The only humans who appear in the psalm, described generically as all those in the temple, proclaim Yahweh's glory (29:9). This vibrant

---

47. Such is the case with Claus Westermann, who writes, "The peculiar thing about Psalm 29 . . . is that a Canaanite psalm could be taken up in Israel's worship with apparently hardly any alteration" (*The Living Psalms* [trans. J. R. Porter; Grand Rapids: Eerdmans, 1989] 236).

48. Collins, *The Bible after Babel*, 5.

49. Wall, "Toward a Wesleyan Hermeneutic of Scripture" 47.

acknowledgment of God's power by divine beings, nature, and humanity draws us into participation in the sort of reaction the gospel should evoke.

Of the four Wesleyan foci under consideration, the emphasis on Scripture's simultaneity is, at least superficially, the most at odds with historical criticism, which exposes the Bible's pluriformity through diachronic investigation.[50] The idea of simultaneity presumes that more important than the sundry human authors who contributed to various parts of Scripture is the single divine author responsible for the entirety. Recognition of this single divine author in turn demands that the diverse passages of Scripture form a coherent whole despite the numerous, often dissonant voices. On this point Jones writes, "Thus, for Wesley, the general tenor of Scripture teaches the analogy of faith: the system of doctrine whose content is the order of salvation and whose function is to serve as a normative guide and limit for theology and as a rule for interpretation."[51] This "general tenor" includes such theological themes as original sin, justification by faith, and sanctification. We will look at this in light of the theme of the faith of the outsider in the discussion of the sermonic use of Scripture below; here I want to call attention to how the principle of simultaneity could help a Wesleyan interpreter address the polytheism that backgrounds Psalm 29. On the one hand, the underlying polytheistic worldview is at odds with the greater biblical message, which unquestionably presents a single God.[52] But the use of the Canaanite divine council image is little different from, for example, Paul's quotations of "pagan" philosophers in his speech on the Areopagus in Acts 17. In both cases the biblical author draws on ideas inconsistent with the gospel message but recontextualizes them to help illustrate the greater point. Just as Paul adopts Aratus's statement that we are the "offspring" of the gods (Acts 17:28) to make a point about the divine nature, so the psalmist appropriates the idea of the subjection of all other deities to Yahweh to praise Yahweh's glory (Ps 29:1). In fact, appeal to the simultaneity of Scripture helps us understand why this text ended up in the canon: Despite its presumed Canaanite origin, when properly situated as a paean to Yahweh it demonstrates the subjection of all things to God.

50. See the discussion of this in the preceding section.

51. Jones, *John Wesley's Conception and Use of Scripture*, 49.

52. Of course, polytheistic imagery similar to that of Psalm 29 lies behind several other OT texts, such as Ps 82, Exod 15, and Deut 32.

The emphasis on the simultaneity of Scripture has another consequence. While not diminishing the historical crux regarding the mention of the temple in a putatively Davidic psalm, this Wesleyan emphasis obviates any potential theological problems caused by more literally focused hermeneutics. Yes, the incongruousness between the psalm's incipit and its contents is an absurdity, but not one that raises theological problems.

Historical-critical analysis of Psalm 29 opens new vistas for reading the text soteriologically. Whereas a surface reading of the psalm reveals little about the humans involved, recognizing its origins outside Israel justifies reading it as a demonstration of God's call to all humanity. James Limburg asserts that the Canaanite background of the psalm allows an ecumenical point to be made, comparing the appropriation of non-Israelite material in the Hebrew Bible to the more recent phenomenon of Christian hymns set to secular tunes.[53] This ecumenical aspect of the psalm does not provide one with a detailed map of "the way to heaven," to invoke a common Wesleyan use of Scripture, but it does encourage us by demonstrating that God has revealed his holiness throughout creation. Westermann notes that when one acknowledges how easily Canaanite divine imagery could be incorporated into Israelite worship, it becomes "perfectly possible to accept what the two religions had in common, awe in the presence of the Creator and His word of power, recognition of God as king and homage paid to Him in worship."[54] Read through a Wesleyan lens, one can see how this coheres with the emphasis on salvation while simultaneously opening up the conversation beyond any potential Wesleyan tribalism.

The emphasis on the "sermonic midrash of Scripture"[55] does not mean only that Scripture should be used homiletically—that much is taken for granted—but that the interpreter is given a certain license to read into Scripture so that it continues to be a living text that addresses contemporary communities of faith.[56] Wesley's sermons were often thematic, mining various biblical passages for material that could address a certain urgent point. I will

---

53. James Limburg, "Psalm 29," in Roger E. Van Harn and Brent A. Strawn, eds., *Psalms for Preaching and Worship* (Grand Rapids: Eerdmans, 2009) 123.

54. Westermann, *The Living Psalms*, 236.

55. Wall, "Toward a Wesleyan Hermeneutic of Scripture" 52.

56. Ibid., 53–54.

fabricate an example here in which Psalm 29 could be helpful, again focusing on the presumed Canaanite background of the psalm. If one were to appeal to Scripture for exhortation to embrace the other, one could turn to several powerful passages: Isaiah 56, in which Yahweh promises to accept the foreigners who come to him, for "[Yahweh's] house shall be called a house of prayer for all peoples" (56:7); 2 Kings 5, in which Naaman the Syrian comes to Elisha and is cured of his leprosy; Matthew 15, in which Jesus heals the Canaanite woman on account of her great faith; and many more. A straightforward, noncritical reading of Scripture reveals ample biblical warrant for the inclusion of the other into the people of God, enough to fill numerous sermons. Yet drawing in the critical understanding of Psalm 29 could help one to reify this point in a different way. The background of the psalm does not just provide a prophetic voice of encouragement for the foreigner, or a parable of inclusion, or even a historical account of an individual coming to know Jesus; we also see here a silent example of God esteeming the Canaanites, Israel's quintessential nemesis, so highly that their liturgy (so to speak) was adopted into the canon, the privileged means of God's self-disclosure. An investigation of Psalm 29 reveals that the Canaanites had great faith, they just did not necessarily grasp the appropriate object of their worship. Elsewhere, Scripture shows that such devotion persisted through the centuries and eventually found proper expression: In Matthew 15, when the Canaanite woman encountered Jesus and begged for help, it was granted on account of her great faith.

Conclusion

Historical criticism has wielded tremendous influence, and yielded tremendous results, in biblical studies over the last two centuries. This approach has raised serious challenges to the traditional reading of Scripture, challenges that cannot be ignored. All those who wish to read Scripture as Scripture, regardless of confession, must factor in the findings of historical-critical exegesis. At the same time, the most recent generations of scholars have demonstrated with increasing clarity that critical examination of the biblical text by itself is insufficient for the theological task. Historical criticism can be used in constructive theology, but only as a complement to more deliberately and self-consciously theological approaches.

I submit that all Wesleyan readings of Scripture should, indeed must, embrace historical criticism for the same reasons as many other confessional traditions: The approach guards against both naïve literalism and anything-goes readings that essentially strip the text of any inherent meaning. There is nothing distinctively Wesleyan about this use of the critical method, though. To employ historical criticism in a distinctively Wesleyan manner, one should highlight where the results of a (non-Wesleyan) critical evaluation of the Bible cohere with traditional Wesleyan emphases in the interpretation of Scripture. Wall writes that "a Wesleyan setting for the reading of Scripture should seek after those particular meanings that occur as the natural and logical yield of participating in a community of believers whose teaching and life are guided by a rule of faith composed in a distinctively Wesleyan heritage context."[57] When examination reveals that not just the world of the biblical text but the world behind the text reveals the gospel message, particularly in light of the divine hope for human sanctification and salvation, one can appeal to such study to interpret the text in a distinctively Wesleyan, thoroughly historical-critical way.

57. Robert W. Wall, "Facilitating Scripture's Future Role among Wesleyans," in Barry L. Callen and Richard P. Thompson, eds., *Reading the Bible in Wesleyan Ways: Some Constructive Proposals* (Kansas City, MO: Beacon Hill, 2004) 119.

Reconsidering Theological Interpretation of Scripture: Barth and Goldingay in Conversation

SHANNON NICOLE SMYTHE

> The church can hardly know anything at all of this incarnate Word except by reading those biblical texts about him, and by living in an abiding relationship with him and his people—a relationship that these same sacred texts both monitor and enrich.
>
> —Robert W. Wall[1]

Among proponents of "theological interpretation of Scripture" there are often intramural disagreements about what assumptions necessarily undergird readings of Scripture that aim to be not merely historical but theological as well. One such recent debate took place within the final pages of John Goldingay's book *Do We Need the New Testament? Letting the Old Testament Speak for Itself*,[2] in a chapter provocatively entitled "Theological Interpretation: Don't Be Christ-Centered, Don't Be Trinitarian, Don't Be Constrained by the Rule of Faith." There, Goldingay, himself a self-identified proponent of theological interpretation, suggests that advocates of theological interpretation have adopted some assumptions about what such interpretation entails, with the result that biblical faith has been rendered "more congenial to Western Christians than one that reflects the Scriptures more broadly."[3]

---

1. As my first New Testament professor, Rob Wall instilled in me the importance of studying Scripture not only critically and contextually but also as an act of worship, formation, and contemplation. I am forever grateful to him for the encouragement and guidance he gave to me as I was discovering my theological vocation as a young woman with a less than supportive family. In particular, I am thankful for the many occasions when we wrestled with New Testament texts about women, fighting to hear the gospel message in, and sometimes even despite, them. It is an honor to dedicate this essay to him.

2. John Goldingay, *Do We Need the New Testament? Letting the Old Testament Speak for Itself* (Downers Grove: InterVarsity, 2015).

3. Ibid., 157.

In order to evaluate Goldingay's critiques, I turn to Karl Barth, whom many consider to be the forerunner of theological interpretation.[4] Within Barth's work, we have some much needed resources for a theological evaluation of Goldingay's argument that "theological interpretation is proper exegesis."[5] Specifically, Barth wrote extensively on both the *nature* of Scripture as well as its *interpretation*. This essay will not attempt a comprehensive representation of Barth's reflections on Holy Scripture but will instead highlight three key aspects of Barth's thinking on the topic, namely: Scripture's Christological basis, the necessity of participatory exegesis, and an account of the relationship of the witness of the prophets and apostles. While a discussion of Barth's approach to these subtopics is instructive in and of itself, the goal of these accounts is to create a constructive dialogue between Barth and Goldingay in order to be able to respond to Goldingay's critiques of Christ-centered and Rule of Faith readings of Scripture.[6]

---

4. Daniel J. Treier, *Introducing Theological Interpretation of Scripture: Recovering a Christian Practice* (Grand Rapids: Baker, 2008) 11. Treier's actual point is that Barth is the forerunner of the *rediscovery* of theological interpretation of Scripture.

5. Goldingay, *Do We Need the New Testament?* 160.

6. I do not take up Goldingay's critique of trinitarian interpretations of Scripture because I believe his points are noncontroversial and quite valid. He summarizes his counterposition this way: "Christian theological interpretation will be trinitarian in the sense that it knows that Yahweh the God of Israel is the God who is Trinity. It will not be Trinitarian in the sense that it looks for reference to the Trinity in Isaiah or Genesis" (*Do We Need the New Testament?* 169). It is worth mentioning that Barth's doctrine of the Trinity supports Goldingay's desire to see interpretation "enable the Scriptures to confront us" (ibid., 176). As David W. Congdon explains: "Barth's Trinitarian theology is, in fact, a form of hermeneutical theology.... First 'revelation is the self-interpretation of this God,' according to Barth.... Put in hermeneutical terms, 'if revelation is the self-interpretation of God, then in it there occurs the fact that God interprets Godself *as* the one whom God *is*.' Second, the event of revelation, understood as God's self-interpretation, establishes the creaturely enterprise of interpreting revelation: '*the revelation of God itself is what makes possible the interpretation of revelation*.' The self-interpretation of God not only brings God's being to speech; it also authorizes and empowers human beings to engage in an ongoing inquiry and interpretation of this divine coming-to-speech.... For this reason the event of God's unveiling does not bypass the hermeneutical problem but makes this problem inescapable and essential to responsible God-talk" (*The Mission of Demythologizing: Rudolf Bultmann's Dialectical Theology* [Minneapolis: Fortress, 2015] 18–19).

Barth, Scripture, and Interpretation[7]

Christological Concentration and the Nature of Scripture
Barth's doctrine of Scripture is actualistic.[8] In contrast to a substantialist construal of the Bible that posits Scripture simply *as* the Word of God, Barth understands the biblical text to be Holy Scripture in the event of God's Word addressed to us. In other words, the Bible *becomes* the Word of God for us by an act of God.[9] Barth's actualistic orientation to Scripture stems from a christological concentration, which is characteristic of his dogmatic reflections on any particular doctrine. The incarnation is the event in which God reveals Godself to be the covenantal God who reconciles the world to Godself in the history of Jesus of Nazareth through the power of the Spirit.[10] One of Barth's pivotal insights into the doctrine of the incarnation is that its theme "is not a phenomenon, or a complex of phenomena, but a history. It is the history of God in his mode of existence as Son, in whom He humbles Himself and becomes also the Son of Man Jesus of Nazareth."[11] Thus, the

---

7. The reading of Barth that I will provide is one that takes for granted his heritage as a dialectical theologian, which was largely a "theology of crisis" that was responding to the liberal theology of the day even as it was setting forth a new approach to theology. This means that I do not understand Barth as either neo-orthodox or postliberal.

8. Barth's actualism "alludes primarily to the way in which Barth, following the witness of Scripture, conceives of God and Jesus Christ, and (derivatively) of human beings, as beings-in-action, existing in a covenant relationship" (Paul T. Nimmo, "Actualism" in *The Westminster Handbook to Karl Barth* [ed. Richard E. Burnett; Louisville: Westminster John Knox, 2013] 1).

9. "For me the Word of God is a *happening*, not a thing. Therefore the Bible must *become* the Word of God, and it does this through the work of the Spirit" (Karl Barth, *Karl Barth's Table Talk* [ed. John D. Godsey; Richmond: John Knox, 1963] 26).

10. Bruce L. McCormack notes that "Barth's understanding of the being-in-becoming of Holy Scripture was a function of his commitment to the being-in-becoming of the God-human, his actualizing of the doctrine of the incarnation, which brought in its wake the necessity of affirming the being-in-becoming of the Trinity, of human beings and, ultimately, of everything that is" ("The Being of Holy Scripture is in Becoming: Karl Barth in Conversation with American Evangelical Criticism," in *Evangelicals & Scripture: Tradition, Authority and Hermeneutics* [ed. Vincent Bacote, Laura C. Miguelez, and Dennis L. Okholm; Downers Grove: InterVarsity, 2009] 63–64).

11. Karl Barth, *Church Dogmatics* IV/2 (ed. Thomas F. Torrance; trans. Geoffrey W. Bromiley; Edinburgh: T & T Clark, 1958) 196. Hereafter cited as *CD* with volume and page number.

center of divine revelation is the sovereign event of God's action in history to reveal Godself to human beings in Jesus Christ.

For Barth, revelation is the history of Jesus Christ, the Word of God incarnate, yet this one Word of God has three forms. Each form of the one Word of God is interrelated in its existence to the other forms. The first and normative form of the one Word of God is Jesus Christ, the Word incarnate. The second form is Scripture, the written Word, and the third form is preaching, the Word proclaimed. Barth arranges these three forms into a concentric circle with Jesus Christ as the center, Scripture as the inner circle, and preaching in the final outer circle. The arrangement of the forms illustrates the unity-in-differentiation of the one Word of God. This allows Barth to distinguish between the definitive event of God's self-revelation in Jesus Christ and the biblical text itself, which bears witness to this event of divine revelation.

The relationship between the Word incarnate and the written Word is one of indirect identity. Jesus Christ alone is the Word of God proper. Holy Scripture and preaching are each constituted as the Word of God only insofar as they bear witness to Jesus Christ in the event of their becoming the Word of God. As Barth remarks,

> The Bible is God's Word to the extent that God causes it to be His Word, to the extent that He speaks through it. . . . The statement that the Bible is God's Word is a confession of faith. . . . We do not accept it as a description of our experience of the Bible. We accept it as a description of God's action in the Bible . . . namely. . . . that God's action on man has become an event, and not therefore that man has grasped at the Bible but that the Bible has grasped at man. The Bible, then, becomes God's Word in this event, and in the statement that the Bible is God's Word the little word 'is' refers to its being in this becoming. [12]

Priority rests in the freedom of God in the event of revelation. Only in the event of God's revelatory speaking is the Bible God's Word. That the "human prophetic and apostolic word" becomes "God's own address" to us "is God's affair and not ours." In divine freedom, God comes and takes hold of us in

12. Barth, *CD* I/1, 109–10.

the revelatory event in which the Bible and preaching become God's Word. "If this takes place . . . all this is grace and not our work."[13]

Denoting Scripture's role as a witness to revelation means that to affirm that the biblical text is God's Word to us is done *sola fide*. The Bible is not the same as revelation so there remains a tension between the human words of the prophets and apostles and the reconciling activity of God by Word and Spirit, which is the event of revelation witnessed to in Scripture. The relationship between the written Word and the Word incarnate is explained by use of the analogy of the relationship between the humanity and divinity of Christ. "It is impossible," Barth writes of both the human and divine natures of Christ and of Scripture, "that there should have been a transmutation of the one into the other or an admixture of the one with the other."[14] To this extent, the human element in Scripture, that Scripture consists of the human words of the prophets and apostles, does not cease to be human nor does it become divine, even as God does not cease to be God.

An important difference in the relationship between God and the humanity of the prophets and apostles is that, unlike the person of Jesus Christ, there is no unity of person. The

> humanity of the prophets and apostles is not taken up into the glory of God. It cannot independently reveal, but only attest, the revelation which did and does take place in the humanity of Jesus Christ. . . . But in its own way and degree it is very God and very man, i.e., a witness of revelation which itself belongs to revelation, and historically a very human literary document.[15]

The human nature of Scripture is not a minor point for Barth. He speaks quite openly about those "whom we hear as witnesses speak[ing] as fallible, erring" people like ourselves such that "[o]nly the miracle of faith and the Word can genuinely and seriously prevent us from taking offence at the Bible."[16] But as the Spirit works in and through the written Word, "in the act

13. Ibid., 109.
14. Barth, *CD* I/2, 499.
15. Ibid., 500–501.
16. Ibid., 507. Elsewhere Barth writes: "the spiritual horizon [of the prophets and apostles] was as limited as—and in an important respect much more limited than—our

of revelation in which the prophets and apostles in their humanity became what they were, and in which alone in their humanity they can become to us what they are,"[17] there the Bible becomes the Word of God. The distinguishing mark of Scripture, the reason we call it Holy Scripture, is derived from its content, that subject matter to which it witnesses, which is none other than the good news of God with us sinners.

Theological Interpretation of Scripture as Participatory Exegesis
Before Barth was well-known as a dogmatic theologian, his commentary on the book of Romans earned him a reputation as an innovative interpreter of the Bible.[18] Yet appreciation for his work as an exegete is a complicated affair and is often overshadowed by a more critical appraisal of his work. Regardless, "throughout his career Barth claimed that biblical exegesis remained the presupposition and goal of all his work."[19] He insisted that "scientific

---

own," and that "their natural science, their world-picture, and to a great extent even their morality cannot be authoritative for us. . . . They were with few exceptions not remarkable theologians. They have only their election and calling to commend them" ("Die Autorität und Bedeutung den Bibel" in *Die Schrift und die Kirche* [Zollikon-Zürich: Evangelischen Verlag A. G., 1947] 6, as quoted in David W. Congdon, *The God Who Saves: A Dogmatic Sketch* [Eugene: Cascade, 2016] 16 n. 22.

17. Barth, *CD* I/2, 508.

18. The first edition of the commentary earned him an honorary professorship at the University of Göttingen, and the second edition made him one of the most influential theologians of his day. As Ernst Käsemann observed, "Barth's *Epistle to the Romans* brought 'thoroughgoing eschatology' back out of its existence among the shades and made it into the keynote of New Testament interpretation in Germany" ("On the Subject of Primitive Christian Apocalyptic," in *New Testament Questions of Today* [trans. W. J. Montague; London: SCM, 1969] 109 n. 2). Similarly, Rudolf Bultmann commented that "Barth has grasped Paul's view . . . in its depths . . . through his exegesis many details have become more alive" ("Karl Barth's *Epistle to the Romans* in Its Second Edition," in *The Beginnings of Dialectic Theology*, vol. 1 [ed. James M. Robinson, trans. Keith R. Crim; Richmond: John Knox, 1962] 119).

19. Richard E. Burnett, *Karl Barth's Theological Exegesis: The Hermeneutical Principles of the* Römerbrief *Period* (Grand Rapids: Eerdmans, 2004) 23. Eduard Thurneysen further adds, "[Barth] does not project theological speculations out of his own mind; he is not concerned about a system; he is and he remains a student and teacher of Holy Scriptures. Whoever tries to understand him as other than this will not understand him at all" ("Die Anfänge," in *Antwort: Karl Barth zum siebzigsten Geburtstag* [ed. Rudolf Frey, et al.; Zürich: Evangelischer Verlag, 1956] 832; ET *Revolutionary Theology in the Making* [trans. James D. Smart; Richmond: John Knox, 1964] 12, as quoted in Burnett, *Karl Barth's Theological Exegesis*, 23). Hence Barth's insistence "that no single item of Christian doctrine is legitimately grounded,

exegesis" of the biblical text ought to be theological exegesis. The first element of theological exegesis is determining what a text meant, while the second is focused on the present meaning of the text. Roughly speaking, the first element is the historical-critical descriptive task while the second task centers on translation and application. Krister Stendahl famously proposed not only a sharp separation between these two tasks of biblical theology but also placed the emphasis on the priority of the first over and above the second.[20] In opposition to such a sharp separation of the two elements of biblical theology, Barth saw both steps as needed in theological exegesis because the tasks designed to attain to both the past meaning and present significance of Scripture were mutually determined.[21] The reason for this mutual determination stems from his belief that the goal of exegesis is "the measuring of all the words and word groups found in a historical document by means of the *Sache* (the "object," the "subject-matter") of which they speak."[22] Barth's *Sachkritik* approach affirms that "we only access what is meant through what is said, which means that interpretation is an ongoing

---

or rightly developed or expounded, unless it can of itself be understood and explained as a part of the responsibility laid upon the hearing and teaching Church towards the self-revelation of God attested in Holy Scripture" (*CD* II/2, 35). George Hunsinger highlights that "in fact, it has been estimated that the Index volume to Barth's great dogmatics includes roughly 15,000 biblical references and more than 2,000 instances of exegetical discussion" ("Postcritical Scriptural Interpretation: Rudolf Smend on Karl Barth," in *Thy Word is Truth: Barth on Scripture* [ed. George Hunsinger; Grand Rapids: Eerdmans, 2012] 30). See also James A. Wharton, "Karl Barth and His Influence on Biblical Interpretation," *Union Seminary Quarterly Review* 28 (1972) 6.

20. See Stendahl's 1962 methodological definition of biblical theology in "Biblical Theology, Contemporary," in *The Interpreter's Dictionary of the Bible*, 5 vols. (ed. George A. Buttrick; Nashville: Abingdon, 1962) 1:418–32.

21. Hence Barth writes in the Preface to the second edition of the Romans commentary that "true apprehension can be achieved only by a strict determination to face, as far as possible without rigidity of mind, the tension displayed more or less clearly in the ideas written in the text" (*The Epistle to the Romans* [trans. Edwyn C. Hoskyns; Oxford: Oxford University Press, 1933] 8).

22. Bruce L. McCormack, "The Significance of Karl Barth's Theological Exegesis of Philippians," in *Orthodox and Modern: Studies in the Theology of Karl Barth* (Grand Rapids: Baker, 2008) 98. Barth strongly insists: "When an investigation is rightly conducted, boulders composed of fortuitous or incidental or merely historical conceptions ought to disappear almost entirely. The Word ought to be exposed in the words. Intelligent comment means that I am driven on till I stand with nothing before me but the enigma of the matter; till I have almost forgotten that I am not its author; till I know the author so well that I allow

process as we continually discern the word that is being spoken to us today in this text. . . . The unity of the hermeneutical process lies in the 'single arch that stretches from the biblical texts to the contemporary preaching of the church.'"[23] For this reason Barth describes the historical-critical work of theological exegesis as "the *preliminary* work" that must lead to and never get in the way of "joining with" the biblical author "in the subject matter, by working with him, by taking each word of his in earnest, so long as it is not proven that he does not deserve such trust."[24] Barth insisted on a critical interrogation of the biblical text "in light of its twofold historicity as both a past artifact and a present event."[25]

In a rather interesting move, Barth lifts up the helpfulness of the doctrine of verbal inspiration for the way it brings the biblical text forward for the reader

> as a living link in a movement which should move us as well. . . . Only through this living context of the past and present will historical understanding be at all possible. I take historical understanding to be a continuous, ever more honest and penetrating dialogue between the truth which *was*, which *comes*, and which is one and the same.[26]

In other words, Barth's theological exegesis aims to create a dialogue between the one and the same truth as it was in the past and is now in the present. The hermeneutical task is a dangerous and risky one both in terms of what one might find in the text (that is, the real possibility that the words of the author

---

him to speak in my name and am even able to speak in his name myself" (*The Epistle to the Romans*, 8).

23. Congdon, *The God Who Saves*, 39.

24. Richard Burnett has provided English translations of Barth's many drafts of his Preface to the first edition of his Romans commentary. See Burnett, *Karl Barth's Theological Exegesis*, Appendix 2, Preface Draft III, 288.

25. Congdon, *The God Who Saves*, 38.

26. Burnett, *Karl Barth's Theological Exegesis*, Appendix 2, Preface Draft III, 288. Barth also suggests that "whoever does not continually 'read in' because he participates in the subject matter cannot 'read out' either" (ibid.). It is in this vein that he admits in his Romans commentary that he "had to write entire chapters and sections directly against myself" (ibid., 289). See Barth, *CD* I/1, where he insists that exegesis "is always a combination of taking and giving, of reading out and reading in" (106).

might prove not to be trustworthy) as well as what the interpreter might import into the text (that is, that we would only read out what we first read in). Nevertheless, it is a hazard of the work that simply cannot be avoided.

It is the risen Jesus who confronts us by his Spirit, addresses us in the biblical text, and calls for a participatory response on our part. Indeed, the risen Jesus is, for Barth, the *Sache* of Scripture. "The heart of the matter, quite soberly, is that the biblical witness in the name of the risen . . . Jesus Christ . . . issues in fact as a summons to men and in fact finds a human hearing and produces a human response of obedience."[27] Therefore, Barth urges that theological exegesis is "not about 'reading something into' the Bible, it is about understanding it. One can only *understand* that for which one *stands*."[28] We have to participate in the subject matter of the text if we are to be grasped by it.[29] In other words, just as Scripture becomes the Word of God in the event of God's speaking through it, so Scripture becomes the Word of God as the Spirit empowers our interpretation of Scripture, which is our participatory response to the living subject matter Jesus Christ. To hear the Scriptures as the Word of God is to hear the living and active God addressing us in the biblical texts.

The Relationship of the Witness of the Prophets and Apostles
Not surprisingly, Barth's understanding of the role of the prophets and apostles in revelation also flows from the Christological concentration that gives shape to his doctrine of Scripture. The witness of the prophets and apostles is indispensable in this time between Christ's resurrection and return in that it is "the visible form of the otherwise hidden presence and Lordship of Jesus Christ."[30] Thus Christ is visibly present to the church, and therefore also to the world, through the old and new witness of Christ

27. Barth, "The Authority and Significance of the Bible: Twelve Theses," in *God Here and Now* (trans. Paul M. van Buren; New York: Routledge Classics, 2003) 62.

28. Burnett, *Karl Barth's Theological Exegesis*, Appendix 2, Preface Draft III, 288.

29. Again, in the preface drafts to the first edition of his *Epistle to the Romans*, Barth writes: "I have consciously raised again the method which has long since been repudiated in theology of 'reading in' our own problems into the thought world of the Bible. . . . But it could not be otherwise . . . because, from the beginning, I felt I was participating in it [the subject matter] much too strongly, because I had heard Paul speaking directly *to us* so clearly" (as quoted in Burnett, *Karl Barth's Theological Exegesis*, Appendix 2, Preface Draft III, 288).

30. Barth, "The Authority and Significance of the Bible: Twelve Theses" 57.

in the second form of the Word of God. The "risen and ascended Jesus speaks to and acts upon women and men in his Word. . . . Jesus' prophecy is Scripture."[31] Not only that, but the Holy Spirit "is the presence and Lordship of Jesus Christ Himself in the visible form of this witness."[32] Christ is "active as a Prophet among them [all persons] in His Word and by His Spirit."[33] The Spirit is "Christ's own interpreter, the One who presses on Christ's followers Christ's own mind as expressed in the prophetic and apostolic testimony."[34] Because Barth understands revelation to be the history of Jesus Christ, it is his own prophetic *self*-witness in and through the attestation of the prophets and apostles that the Spirit reveals. Jesus becomes present to us here and now in his Word and by His Spirit.[35]

Barth's reference to both prophets and apostles makes clear that *all* Scripture, by the sovereign action of God, can become the event of the proclamation of Jesus Christ himself. As "Jesus Christ belongs to Israel, so the prophets of the Old Testament belong to the apostles of the New."[36] Both prophets and the apostles testify to

> one and the same center, subject, and content: *Jesus* of Nazareth. . . . The Old Testament witness (to Yahweh and His Israel) and the New Testament witness (to the one Jesus Christ and His people) agree: in this confronta-tion of the gracious God with sinful man, the history, the action which constitutes the center of all created things, which contains the secret of their origin in God's creation and their goal in a new creation, has now taken place. . . . The Bible asserts this by the fact that it speaks of Jesus Christ.[37]

While the event of Jesus' self-witness comes through both Testaments, the singularity of Scripture's witnesses is grounded in the oneness of God.

---

31. Christopher R. J. Holmes, "Revelation in the Present Tense: On Rethinking Theo-logical Interpretation in the Light of the Prophetic Office of Jesus Christ," *Journal of Theologi-cal Interpretation* 6 (2012) 26.

32. Barth, "The Authority and Significance of the Bible: Twelve Theses" 58.

33. Barth, *CD* IV/3, 497.

34. Holmes, "Revelation in the Present Tense" 26.

35. Barth, *CD* IV/3.2, 497.

36. Barth, "The Authority and Significance of the Bible: Twelve Theses" 58.

37. Ibid., 59.

There is one God. True knowledge of this one God comes from "God's self-testimony" given in the one Word of God, the one Jesus Christ. Likewise, the prophetic and apostolic witnesses are the "*one* visible form of the one Word of the one God."[38] The church's establishment of the biblical canon, comprising the witness of the Old and New Testaments, is its "confession of God's election and calling of His witness."[39]

While the prophetic word and action of Jesus Christ is indeed *sui generis*,[40] Barth nevertheless finds that the prophecy of the history of Israel, in its totality, has four things in common with the prophecy of Jesus Christ. First, it is the history of the Word of God revealing, in the flesh, God's will and action in and with humanity. Second, it is also the light of the world bringing light to every person. Third, it, too, speaks from a center in "the present reality of the lordship of God."[41] Finally, it attests "divine-human unity . . . transcendent God and lowly man . . . together."[42] These elements of similarity lead Barth to claim that while the prophecy of the history of Israel is not identical to that of Jesus Christ, in "all its autonomy and singularity, and therefore in all its distinction, it is a true type and adequate pattern . . . it is fore-telling."[43] He sums up the relationship between the history of Israel to that of Jesus Christ by saying that "it is the pre-history in which He Himself acts and the fore-word in which He Himself speaks."[44] Without downplaying or brushing aside "all the difference of time, place and history," he suggests that both testaments mutually confirm and explain each other on the basis of the one covenant. The fact that the covenant between God and humanity is one covenant gives to the attestation of the Old Testament both the quality of "already" as well as that of "not yet." So, the Old Testament already witnesses to "everything that He would say and thus prepar[es] the way for Him . . . as the one coming Prophet."[45] Even so, there was a missing element. Christ was missing. "And the fact that He was missing is the great qualification which the 'not yet' impresses on everything which is to

38. Ibid., 60.
39. Ibid., 60.
40. Barth, *CD* IV/3.1, 49.
41. Ibid., 65.
42. Ibid., 63.
43. Ibid., 65.
44. Ibid., 66.
45. Ibid., 67.

be seen and understood without reservation as the great distinction of what came before, namely, as its substantial likeness with what comes after."[46]

Barth does not end on this "not yet" note in relationship to the Old Testament witness. Instead, he presses back again toward the other side of the dialectic, emphasizing that "the fact that the history of Israel can have no more continuations does not mean that it is outmoded, replaced or dissolved."[47] God's covenant has already been actualized in its first form in Israel's history. Jesus Christ already spoke and acted in the history of Israel as his type, pre-history, and fore-word. All of this means that the new thing that is witnessed to in the New Testament, namely, Christ's

> coming, appearance, birth and existence—does not merely follow upon the old as something new and different; it proceeds out of it as its fulfill-ment and completion, and therefore in unity with it. If what came before was merely with a view to what comes after, the converse is also true that what comes after follows what came before, so that it could not be what it is, nor be seen and understood as such, without it.[48]

Barth can press back and forth between each side of the dialectic because of his firm stance on the place in which they come together. "In Him the history of what came before and what comes after is one history; the word spoken before and that spoken after is one word; its attestation in the Old Testament and the New is one witness."[49] Just as it is one covenant, so there is one Mediator who is the same "yesterday and today." Barth never loses sight of the "one Prophet of the one covenant in its twofold form, first concealed and then revealed, when we say 'Jesus Christ.'"[50]

Barth and Goldingay in Dialogue

With the foundation of Barth's understanding of Scripture and theological interpretation in place, we can now turn our attention to a constructive

46. Ibid., 69.
47. Ibid., 70
48. Ibid., 70.
49. Ibid., 71.
50. Ibid., 71.

dialogue between Barth and Goldingay. While I have drawn broadly from Barth's literary corpus, I make narrow use of Goldingay, drawing only from his final chapter in *Do We Need the New Testament?* Again, my aim is to bring Barth's rather large and complex contribution to the topic to bear on one current discussion regarding theological interpretation. Goldingay's critique of scriptural readings that are Christ-centered and constrained by the Rule of Faith provides the space for such an engagement. We will look at both of Goldingay's critiques in turn, noting his alternative and allowing Barth to weigh in not only on the critique itself but also on Goldingay's alternative.

Theological but not Christocentric?

Goldingay makes clear that he is "enthusiastic about interpretation of Scripture that is theological and not merely historical."[51] He rightly points out that "[h]istorical exegesis will itself be theological, in the sense of reflecting on the theological questions that are inherent in the texts."[52] He upholds theological interpretation of Scripture because it takes account of the nature and interests of the texts themselves, which for the "Hebrew Bible centers on questions about God and Israel and life."[53] Arguing that Childs' insight into the "unremittingly theocentric" focus of the biblical text is actually "the point of Scripture as a whole"[54] allows Goldingay to juxtapose Scripture's theocentric focus with theological interpretation of Scripture that is necessarily christocentric.

Goldingay's use of inherently vague terms such as "Christ-centered" and "christocentric" would seem to imply a critique of any and all interpretations that give Christ some kind of centrality. Yet we begin to see what he means by christocentric when we consider the example he gives. He takes issue with readings of the Old Testament that assume "*the* point about the First Testament is its witness to Jesus."[55] He also remarks that while one could argue "that the entirety of the New Testament's theological interpretation

---

51. Goldingay, *Do We Need the New Testament?* 158.

52. Ibid., 160.

53. Ibid., 159.

54. Ibid., 160.

55. Ibid., 161. Goldingay also calls out approaches that would proclaim that "any theological hermeneutic worth its salt must be Christocentric" (160).

is in some sense christological . . . it is not christocentric."[56] Should Barth's christocentric conception of Scripture be counted among those approaches critiqued by Goldingay? For Barth, God's self-revelation "is not a *given* confined to these ancient writings; it is much rather a divine *giving* here and now."[57] Thus we can affirm with Goldingay that neither testament's vocation is centered on giving an interpretation of Jesus.[58] Rather, the vocation of all of Scripture is one of *bearing witness* to Christ. It is the vocation of the living Christ, the Word of God revealed, to proclaim *himself* in Scripture.[59] This is a subtle yet crucial distinction. In the event of Christ revealing himself in Scripture, Scripture becomes the Word of God. In and of itself, Scripture has no capacity to bear adequate witness to God. While both testaments are the normative witness to the great event of God's self-revelation in the history of Jesus Christ, neither is directly identical with the *Sache*.

Yet the notion of Scripture's witness alerts us to "*who* witnesses to himself through it, namely, the living and ascended Lord. Scripture is his proclamation, his prophecy."[60] Describing Scripture as "Christ's *self*-witness" has the benefit of pointing to "a happening, a going-on," which relies always on the event of God's self-revelation in and through the texts.[61] It also reminds us that interpretation is not so much about bringing a "theory" to the text, whether it be christocentrism or otherwise, since "Scripture's significance cannot be read off the surface of the text."[62] For that reason, the interpreter "must bring to light the perspective and conceptual world of the author of a given text" so as "to translate his meaning and intention."[63] Those who read the biblical text must have "ears to hear the One who speaks and gives himself to be known in and through these texts."[64] This means that

56. Ibid., 161.

57. Congdon, "The Word as Event" 248.

58. Goldingay is willing to consider that "the entirety of the New Testament's theological interpretation is in some sense christological" (*Do We Need the New Testament?* 161).

59. "The statement that the Bible is the Word of God cannot therefore say that the Word of God is tied to the Bible. On the contrary, what it must say is that the Bible is tied to the Word of God" (Barth, *CD* I/2, 513).

60. Holmes, "Revelation in the Present Tense" 24. Christ is "active as a Prophet among them [all persons] in His Word and by His Spirit" (Barth, *CD* IV/3, 497).

61. Holmes, "Revelation in the Present Tense" 24.

62. Congdon, "The Word as Event" 259.

63. Barth, "Authority and Significance of the Bible" 53.

64. Holmes, "Revelation in the Present Tense" 25.

interpretation "is a matter of hearing the text in accordance with what it *is*: speech proper to the risen Christ. The scriptural Word is the Word by which Christ announces himself, speaks himself, proclaims himself as One whose history not only took place 'then and there' but also takes place and is happening 'here and now.'"[65] To be clear: theological interpretation of Scripture that takes seriously the prophetic office of Christ is less about finding reference to Christ in each and every text or verse of either testament and much more about being summoned by the living Christ to hear and respond to the good news Christ is speaking today through the text.[66] Such a summons can only be heard after the first step of theological exegesis, the use of the historical-critical method, has been taken. Barth's emphasis on historical thinking guards against the approach that every pericope, regardless of where it may be found in the Christian canon, is to be understood as talking about Jesus. Thus Barth's approach avoids the error Goldingay rightly critiques.

Goldingay wants to consider "what God was saying to Israel" in a passage like Isaiah 7 without having to determine how it refers to Jesus.[67] As such, he distinguishes between the two testaments by suggesting that the lens of the First Testament is God. The "First Testament restrains christocentric interpretation of either Testament. It draws our attention to the fact that Christ was not christocentric. 'Christ was theocentric.'"[68] The uniqueness of Jesus comes neither from his revealing something new about God nor from his bringing a new meaning to the First Testament. Goldingay remarks, "Before Jesus, Israel had a perfectly good revelation of God."[69] Jesus embodied God and made it possible for people to make a "proper response" to God's revelation.[70] Goldingay resists positing any new element to the revelation of God in Jesus Christ. He wants a First Testament that is

---

65. Ibid., 25.

66. "To be confronted by a Pauline text is to be confronted by a text written by someone who is seeking to bear witness to the very object (the divine Subject) by which (whom!) I also am confronted" (McCormack, "The Significance of Karl Barth's Theological Exegesis of Philippians" 101).

67. Goldingay, *Do We Need the New Testament?* 161.

68. Ibid., 162.

69. Ibid., 163.

70. Ibid., 163.

complete by itself and acts autonomously. Only then, he believes, will we be able to be confronted by insights of the First Testament.

As seen in Part I, Barth affirms, with Goldingay, the "autonomy, singularity, and distinction" of the prophecy of the history of Israel, but he also calls it the pre-history in which Christ acts and the fore-word in which he speaks. God's covenant has already been actualized in Israel's history. The covenant brings together both forms of God's revelation in the Old and New Testaments. In contradistinction from Goldingay is Barth's claim that Jesus is the missing element in the Old Testament that gives it a "not yet" quality. The problem with Goldingay's suggestion of a First Testament that is complete by itself and acts autonomously is its one-sidedness. Goldingay can say this as long as he does not only say this. He is missing the other side of the dialectic by neglecting to maintain that *God* did something definitively new in Jesus, which is, in effect, to deny that there is also a "not yet" quality to the Old Testament. Barth specifies that what is "new" about the coming of Jesus is not to be understood as something new and different but rather as fulfillment and completion.[71] In response to the rhetorical question "Do we need the New Testament?" Barth would say we need the New Testament but never without the Old Testament. And, we need the Old Testament, but never without the New. I believe Goldingay would agree with the first statement, but it is not clear to me whether he would affirm the second clause as written.

From a theological angle, what Goldingay fails to realize is that if we know God only in and through God's actions, then God did indeed reveal something new about Godself in the history of Jesus Christ. If, in the death and resurrection, Jesus reveals himself to be the Messiah, then the history of Jesus reveals something new about God. While Goldingay is correct to guard against the church's subtle Marcionite tendencies, doing so need not come at the expense of losing sight of the Christian kerygma. Indeed, it is the history of Jesus, which is the eschatological event, that gives both testaments its special character. Thus, the history of Jesus is the fulfillment and completion of the one covenant of God. While Goldingay emphasizes Jesus' oneness with Yahweh, he does not preserve the uniqueness of God's saving

71. Goldingay shows signs of agreeing with this by his suggestion that theological interpretation should "operate in a way that recognizes how Jesus is the decisive moment in God's fulfilling his purpose in the world" (175).

work in Christ. In effect, he ends up restricting the saving work of Jesus to that of a possibility, rather than an actuality. He states that by "embodying God's instinct to sacrifice himself for people . . . Jesus made it possible for God's grace and truth to take hold of us."[72] Whereas the problem before was that the people did not give "a proper response to [God's] revelation [in Israel's story]," the coming of Jesus made "such a response possible."[73] It is not at all clear here if Goldingay is saying both that Jesus himself made the proper response to God for us and in our place and that it is now possible, through faith in Jesus, to make a proper response to God. However, both points need to be said if we are to make clear that Christ's saving work is an actuality and not a possibility.[74] If we follow what Goldingay seems to imply, that Christ's work merely opens up possibilities for right responses to God, rather than affirming that Christ accomplishes our salvation *extra nos*, we end up on theological quicksand. While I am not entirely convinced that this was Goldingay's intention, it does seem that for all he is trying to guard against with christocentric interpretation, he has, intentionally or unintentionally, ended up with a severely truncated picture of the saving work of Christ. Barth's christocentric conception of Scripture does not make the same mistake.[75]

Theological but not Constrained by the Rule of Faith?

Against recent trends that set forth the Rule of Faith as a significant aspect of theological interpretation of Scripture, Goldingay argues for Scripture's

72. Ibid., 163.

73. Ibid., 163.

74. George Hunsinger makes this point with precision: "Whatever preparation, reception, or enactment may have been involved (and continues to be involved), our recognition is not to be conceived as in any sense constituting the truth or actuality of salvation. Our recognition is simply our awakening to the fact that, in Jesus Christ, salvation's truth and actuality really pertain and apply to us as well, that we are included in them, that they are real for us, precisely by having been established apart from us" (*How to Read Karl Barth: The Shape of His Theology* [Oxford: Oxford University Press, 1991] 153).

75. "The Old Testament witness (to Yahweh and His Israel) and the New Testament witness (to the one Jesus Christ and His people) agree: in this confrontation of the gracious God with sinful man, the history, the action which constitutes the center of all created things, which contains the secret of their origin in God's creation and their goal in a new creation, *has now taken place*. . . . The Bible asserts this by the fact that it speaks of Jesus Christ" (Barth, "The Authority and Significance of the Bible: Twelve Theses" 59, emphasis mine).

own internal coherence, which allows it to "be read as a unified story"[76] such that it does not need the "Rule of Faith as a general-purpose guide."[77] Goldingay is concerned by the idea that "'theological interpretation empha- sizes the potentially mutual influence of Scripture and doctrine in theo- logical discourse.'"[78] While he affirms that the "Rule of Faith provides a horizon from within which we may come to understand the Scriptures," it does not follow that the Rule of Faith is necessary in order to render the Scriptures "coherent and relevant; they are coherent and relevant."[79] Indeed, theological interpretation of Scripture should not "assume that the same authority attaches to [the] doctrinal tradition as attaches to the Scriptures themselves."[80]

If we recall that Barth's threefold understanding of the Word of God places the Word of God proclaimed on the outer perimeter of the circle, behind both the Word of God written and the Word of God revealed in Jesus, we will see Barth's agreement with the main thrust of Goldingay's concern that the Rule of Faith and doctrinal tradition not be placed on equal footing with the biblical text. Yet while Barth refuses to collapse revelation into either Scripture or tradition, he also affirms the authority of the creeds of the church, which confess belief in the triune God who comes to us as Word and Spirit. For Barth this means we are to read the Bible under the guidance of these creeds—not with the goal of absolutizing the creeds, plac- ing them beyond criticism, or rendering them "irreformable" in principle, but instead reading the Bible under their guidance and then returning and putting hard questions to them in light of a fresh hearing of the Word of God in the present time. In other words, as important as the Rule of Faith and the creeds are to responsible theological reflection and scriptural interpretation,

76. Goldingay, *Do We Need the New Testament?* 171.

77. Ibid., 170. Goldingay disagrees with Wall's remark that the proper use of Scripture "'depends upon interpretation that constrains the theological teaching of a biblical text by the church's 'Rule of Faith.'" See Robert W. Wall, "Reading the Bible from Within Our Traditions," in *Between Two Horizons: Spanning New Testament Studies & Systematic Theology* (ed. Joel B. Green and Max Turner; Grand Rapids: Eerdmans, 2000) 88, as quoted in Goldingay, *Do We Need the New Testament?* 172.

78. Green, "The (Re-)Turn to Theology," *Journal of Theological Interpretation* 1 (2007) 2, as quoted in Goldingay, *Do We Need the New Testament?* 171.

79. Goldingay, *Do We Need the New Testament?* 173.

80. Ibid., 175.

they can never be fixed or irreformable since they themselves belong to a particular culture and time and are thus open to historical and theological scrutiny. Faithful interpreters must engage tradition without fear, with the freedom to continue the development of the rule itself as God's grace may inspire new rules that help the gospel to be heard in new times and places. [81]

Where Barth and Goldingay differ in their understanding of the Rule of Faith is in how they locate the necessary disruption of the biblical texts on our lives. Goldingay posits an internal relevance and coherence to the scriptural texts in and of themselves. [82] He insists that both a Rule of Faith hermeneutic and our current Western culture prevent us from hearing the broader horizon within Scripture. In contrast to Goldingay, Barth's *Sachkritik* approach to biblical interpretation means that he locates the disruptive element in the gospel itself, or the *Sache* of the text. [83] "The true Word of God

81. Barth warns against the problem of "ecclesiastical and doctrinal orthodoxy in every age," stating that "it ceases to be good when it is linked with indifference to or a depreciation of the incidental but necessary question of the existential determination of the Christian by the content of his witness. However carefully the content is investigated and presented, however resolutely and competently it is conserved in one or another form and protected against misunderstandings and errors, it will harden into a possibly impressive but undoubtedly lifeless idol, and the Christian will find neither joy nor power in attesting it, if it tries to ignore the fact that the living God in Jesus Christ, who is indeed the content of Christian witness, necessarily touches and apprehends the man who is called to attest Him, engaging him in his whole being, making disposition concerning him, finding reflection in his life in the form of personal liberation. We cannot ignore nor abstract away this accompanying phenomenon. We cannot overlook nor suppress nor only partially declare this aspect and significance of vocation. Otherwise even the most conscientious, the sincerest and the strictest orthodoxy becomes an idle pursuit. Otherwise it works in a vacuum in which it quickly becomes alien even to its own supporters because no one can live in it, let alone render service as a Christian witness. Even the trinitarian God of Nicene dogma, or the Christ of the Chalcedonian definition, if seen and proclaimed in exclusive objectivity and with no regard for this accompanying phenomenon, necessarily becomes an idol like all others, with whom one cannot live and whom one cannot therefore attest. And there is something menacing and dangerous in an orthodoxy of this kind" (Barth, *CD* IV/3.2, 655).

82. Goldingay disagrees with John J. Collins that "'the internal pluralism of the Bible, both theological and ethical, has been established beyond dispute,' which implies that we cannot read the Bible as such a unified story" (*Do We Need the New Testament?* 171).

83. Describing his approach, Barth remarks that he hears "in the Bible of the Old and especially of the New Testament not only news from a distant time, but a *message*, a *proclamation*. Bultmann, who is a great scholar, likes to use a foreign word and call it: the 'kerygma.' So, in this point we are also in agreement: there is a kerygma in the Bible. And that is really a

is intrinsic to neither text nor reader, but is rather a *verbum externum* that speaks to us again and again from without."[84] While the Rule of Faith may intend to help us hear this good news, which always comes to us anew in the here and now, we can never equate the Rule of Faith with the gospel. The Rule of Faith is a human witness. The gospel is the powerful event of God's self-proclamation. While it seems that Goldingay may be closer to Barth when he insists that more than the biblical texts themselves, his reading of Scripture is ultimately fixed on the "divine Teacher, whom we are seeking to come to know and follow,"[85] we can see that he has something different in mind when he goes on to state that he is "committed to accepting whatever I find in biblical texts."[86] This comment leads us to wonder whether "acceptance" means an uncritical stance toward the historical-cultural limitations present in the biblical texts themselves.

In contrast, Barth's insistence on hearing the living Christ proclaim himself in and through the text means two things. First, it means that the texts themselves must be critically evaluated in light of the gospel. Barth's insistence that "the historical-critics must become *more critical!*"[87] counters Goldingay's commitment to accept whatever he finds in the biblical texts. Barth does not think the biblical texts are above critique since they are texts written by fallible humans from particular sociocultural locations in history. Second, it means that the living Christ, who has not only come yesterday but continues to come today, must be heard speaking a relevant word in our context. Hence the need to seek after and respond to the *message* of the Bible.[88] In that God freely gives Godself to be known, God comes to us to speak a unique and highly particular Word of grace. This Word of grace

---

lot, that the Bible is for us not just another book, but one in which a voice resounds and calls us" (*Gespräche* 1959–1962, Gesamtausgabe IV [ed. Eberhard Busch; Zürich: Theologischer Verlag] 362, as quoted in Congdon "Theology as Theanthropology: Barth's Theology of Existence in Its Existentialist Context" in *Karl Barth and the Making of Evangelical Theology: A Fifty-Year Perspective* [ed. Clifford B. Anderson and Bruce L. McCormack; Grand Rapids: Eerdmans, 2015] 34).

84. Congdon, "The Word as Event: Barth and Bultmann on Scripture" 263.

85. Goldingay, *Do We Need the New Testament?* 175.

86. Ibid., 175.

87. Barth, *The Epistle to the Romans*, 8.

88. "The object of which Paul speaks is not one we can lay hands on; it is a living Subject who must lay hold of us in the knowing process. But if this be so, then every attempt to

has the dangerous force of an offence which strikes man from without and from a superior height, and in virtue of which he must only try to understand himself, and can only understand himself, as he is understood. Revealing to him this understanding, it sets him at the summit of the pass between what he was and what he will be, leaving him no possibility of retreat but only of advance.[89]

The implication here is that there is no theological interpretation that has "timeless validity as a purely objective truth. To speak of God is simultaneously to speak of oneself in the active service of God."[90]

More than simply fearing that our modern or postmodern context prevents us from hearing Scripture or seeing the aim of interpretation as that of rescuing us "from our narrowness,"[91] we need to recognize that true theological interpretation involves the work of translating the gospel anew into the current context. That is why Barth understood "the whole of his exegetical work in *Romans* as an exercise in what he called 'critical theology.'"[92] Barth would agree with Goldingay's conclusion that proper theological interpretation will allow the biblical text to "nuance our understanding of Jesus' significance" and will "not assume that the same authority attaches to . . . doctrinal tradition as attaches to the Scriptures themselves."[93] He would, however, disagree with Goldingay's suggestion that theological interpretation can operate without faith as a requirement. Goldingay wants the help

describe the true subject matter of the Bible must depend, for its success, on the willingness of God to give [Godself] to the would-be human knower, to allow [Godself] to be brought to expression in human speech" (McCormack, "The Significance of Karl Barth's Theological Exegesis of Philippians" 99).

89. Barth, *CD* IV/3.1, 257.

90. Congdon, "*Apokatastasis* and Apostolicity: A Response to Oliver Crisp on the Question of Barth's Universalism," *Scottish Journal of Theology* 67 (2014) 474.

91. Goldingay, *Do We Need the New Testament?* 176.

92. McCormack, "The Significance of Karl Barth's Theological Exegesis of Philippians," 98 n. 32. As Congdon points out, "Contrary to both historicist liberals and conservative evangelicals, there is no straight line of authority that moves from 'objective' exegesis through biblical and historical theology to its 'subjective' appropriation in systematic and practical theology. Barth . . . point[s] toward a 'third way' which is able to engage in historical research without sacrificing a deeply evangelical emphasis on Scripture's authoritative witness" ("The Word as Event: Barth and Bultmann on Scripture" 262–63).

93. Goldingay, *Do We Need the New Testament?* 175.

of "people who read texts without being personally interested in knowing God" so that they may enable him to see things he does not want to see.[94] Yet what he can gain from such exegetes is only some help in what is but the first step of true theological interpretation. Goldingay not only assumes Stendahl's "two tenses" of meaning in a biblical text, but he neglects to consider the role of divine agency in the being and interpretation of Scripture, which means that only in the event of God's self-revelation in the witness of Scripture and the concurrent responsive hearing and believing of the exegete can Scripture help us to see that which we do not want to see.

Goldingay wants theological interpretation that encourages the process of allowing the Scriptures to confront and rescue us from our narrow ways of thinking and living as these are "decisively shaped by our being modern or postmodern, Western or non-Western people."[95] Yet the truth is that wherever our location in history and whatever our cultural constraints, these same restraints reside in the Scriptures themselves, although they are restraints of a different time and other cultures. Our only hope is to be confronted by the self-proclamation of the *Sache* of Scripture, which comes in and through the texts but is not identical with the texts. The only right response to proclamation is to do the hard work of translating the meaning and intention of the text by listening for what the risen Jesus, who confronts us by his Spirit, is calling us to be and do today.

94. Ibid., 176.
95. Ibid., 176.

Inspiration as Providence

DANIEL CASTELO

Rob Wall and I have cultivated a friendship for just over a decade, and during this time we have had many conversations on a variety of topics, including those related to the kinds of students we see in our classrooms. Part of the responsibilities of teaching in the School of the Theology at Seattle Pacific University involves general education requirements, which are called "University Foundations" courses. We have all kinds of students in these classes, partly because of the nature of the Pacific Northwest, partly because of the kind of institutional culture we foster at SPU (in which a person does not have to be a professing Christian to attend), and other factors. But no doubt some of the things we see in our classrooms from time to time that hit especially home to us are approaches to Scripture that stem from evangelical, sometimes fundamentalist, backgrounds. In my case, I was raised in a Pentecostal denomination that on occasion has aspired to be the Pentecostal version of the Southern Baptist Convention. In Rob's case, in addition to certain family dynamics playing a role in all of this, he is a graduate of Dallas Theological Seminary, a school for which he has deep affection and yet also one from which he must stray on a variety of theological topics, including a doctrine of Scripture. Therefore, we have seen a variety of approaches to Scripture—including evangelical-fundamentalist ones—throughout our lives, and we have gone on to think seriously about how to respond in both a critical and pastoral manner.

One of the questions regarding Scripture often put to us from our students, and one that we constantly have to face with our disciplinary colleagues across the evangelical spectrum, has to do with Scripture's inspiration. Especially given Rob's continued emphasis on canonical criticism, the question often comes up regarding this particular point associated with Scripture's nature, both in terms of how to define inspiration and what role it plays in funding Scripture's authority in believers' lives. In this chapter,

I hope to show features of what I believe Rob's take on biblical inspiration is. This take is informed by many conversations I have had with Rob in addition to running arguments found in some of his works. Given how his views are significantly on the margins of evangelical conversations on Scripture, I believe this chapter will help synthesize and focus Rob's view, which represents in my opinion a vital alternative within a discussion that for far too long seems unable to imagine different possibilities for itself.

Why the Focus on the Historical?

Rob has often found himself in the middle of competing alternatives regarding Scripture's role and authority. On the one hand, Rob has come to see some of the tendencies in fundamentalist-evangelical culture as wrong-headed about Scripture given Scripture's very own claims and characteristics. The matter, as I see it, is not that Rob is trying to be a contrarian (although some might narrate him this way) but that Rob is simply being honest with what he sees in the text and what he believes to be the role the text should play within the community of the faithful, the church, which Rob is fond of calling "Scripture's legal address." But on this last point, Rob is sometimes pushed to the edges by another constituency, the guild of biblical scholarship that for centuries has given methodological privilege to what is generally known as historical-critical studies. This orientation has repeatedly stressed the need to cultivate a kind of critical objectivity within the academy so as to purify the reading of Scripture from the biases and blind spots that allegedly come with churchly and spiritual uses. The way to do this work in this academic guild has typically been the pursuit of a kind of historical contextualization: in other words, these texts must be taken on their own terms, including their embeddedness within wider cultural arrangements. These terms in turn determine what the text "means" since what the author meant and how this was heard in its originating contexts crucially matter for the hermeneutical task. As a result of these commitments, deep and intricate studies in biblical scholarship have been devoted to questions of authorship, date and location of composition, archaeological verification, manuscript integrity, word studies, religious comparative analyses, and so on. In all of this, biblical scholars are oftentimes called to be historians of antiquity, knowing the contexts of the ancient Near East, Second Temple Judaism, or the first century Mediterranean world so as to situate biblical texts culturally, linguistically, and so historically. Of course, there is a certain value to all this endeavoring, but Rob has distinguished himself within the field known as "the theological interpretation of Scripture" precisely because he has felt that the believing biblical scholar, the Christian Bible teacher, cannot simply be a historian; rather, he or she is primarily called to be a doctor of the church as a preacher and teacher of the Word of God for the people of God. In this sense, Rob is mindful of Scripture's contemporary appropriation. The work of historical scrutiny and reconstruction is certainly important to Rob, but such work is in service to Scripture's use and function within the life of the worshiping faithful.

What is ironic about these two constituencies—the evangelical fold and the guild of biblical historical-critical studies—is that for all their professed differences, they have at times demonstrated an ideological connection. Part of the reason why Rob is at the margins of both groups is that these constituencies have occasionally shared certain understandings and convictions. And one such matter has to do with the privileging of history. I have already mentioned this privileging in terms of the biblical studies guild. But from the perspective of the evangelical-fundamentalist fold, the commitment to history is oftentimes registered in terms related to Scripture's inspiration. Expressed directly, evangelicals and fundamentalists tend to think of inspiration as largely a historical phenomenon. The impact of Scripture on the contemporary scene might be registered in terms of "illumination," but "inspiration"—which is associated with the text's coming to be, its identity, and so its constitutional integrity and ongoing relevance—is understood largely in historical terms, typically, in the way the individual authors were "inspired" to write down the text in what are sometimes called "the original autographs." Therefore, when evangelicals and fundamentalists read 2 Timothy 3:16, they see Scripture being "God-breathed" as a characteristic that has been registered in a past process in which human instruments wrote down what God revealed at that time. Now of course, that understanding might be useful to some degree in understanding how prophets or those around them recorded the oracles of God, but in matters related to the inspiration of Scripture, such a process is generalized to the whole of the

Bible's identity. Within this paradigm, it is understood that this process, one lodged within history, is what makes this particular book the authoritative Word of God. This view operates with the assumption that all of Scripture's authors are functionally prophets, and all the words of Scripture should be understood as oracular and so, by implication, bestowed directly by God, thereby being the *vox Dei*.

This casting is certainly a theological one, but biblical scholars in these faith traditions oftentimes devote themselves to historical considerations as a way of keeping it— the theological paradigm— intact. I cannot stress enough just how peculiar this move is. Therefore, matters such as Mosaic authorship of the Pentateuch or Pauline authorship of Ephesians play an important role for some scholars in legitimating the veracity of Scripture and so the upholding of this theological construct. Classes and even professorships dedicated to biblical archaeology sometimes mark the culture of conservative Protestant seminaries and colleges. The running assumption is: History can prove the Bible to be God's word.

These measures and assumptions are all simply indicators that evangelical biblical scholars sometimes find themselves in the trenches, trying to maintain a particular theological viewpoint in relation to Scripture within guilds that do not admit such claims. So, for instance, the rise of the idea of the "original autographs" manages to address variance within manuscript copying and transmission while also allowing the theology of Christian conservative culture to stand. Furthermore, conservatives sometimes devote themselves to "out-archaeologize" the secular archaeologists, seeking to prove the existence of a city or event reported in Scripture, and when the proof is found, it is not just taken to be a statement about the entity in question but about the entire Bible's veracity as well. In all of this, the theology is left to stand. The difficulty, of course, is that biblical studies pursued in this vein is more of a variant within the conventions of the biblical studies guild itself than an ecclesial and theological endeavor pursued for the good of the church's formation.

Scripture Is a Thoroughly Theological Category

Rob's tendency in all these matters is to go to the heart of the theological understanding itself. As we have raised in a number of places, some of his fundamental questions are: What is Scripture? And what is it for?[1] These are basic questions, for sure, but ones that are repeatedly passed by in the guild of biblical scholarship as well as in fundamentalist-evangelical constituencies.

Why are these questions repeatedly ignored? One possible reason is that within the condition of disciplinary fragmentation,[2] theological studies lies on one end and biblical studies on the other, and by being separate from theological studies, biblical studies assumes for itself another methodology besides a theological one, hence the preference for the historical. A purity of inquiry has been sought by the biblical studies guild in the period of modernity and the Enlightenment, and reflected with this agenda is a historical-critical methodology. Again, Rob on both scores finds these developments problematic. His formation while at DTS was significantly theological (there he did work on Moltmann), and he has found that the fragmentation especially of the Christian disciplines is on the whole a mistake. Furthermore, Rob is not convinced (nor am I) that there is such a thing as an "unbiased" reading, for each reading has a certain end or goal at work. People always come to the text looking for something, and this can be understood as a kind of bias. Therefore, the purity sought for via historical-critical examination is at some point an illusion; refinement certainly is possible but not complete objectivity.[3]

Rob's commitments lead to the following conclusion: Scripture is thoroughly a *theological* category. It is intentional that our institutional home, Seattle Pacific, has a School *of Theology*, and that within that School one finds the departments/areas of biblical theology, theological studies, and

---

1. Rob and I have and continue to raise these matters. One iteration of our treatment can be found in our "Reading the Bible as Scripture" in Robert W. Wall and David R. Nienhuis, eds., *A Compact Guide to the Whole Bible* (Grand Rapids: Baker Academic, 2015) 11–26.

2. For some of Rob's thoughts on this situation, see "The Future of Wesleyan Biblical Studies," *Wesleyan Theological Journal* 33 (1998) 101–4.

3. Rob remarks: "We *all* have theological bones to pick. What the honest reader recognizes is that even our most scrupulous study of Scripture engages in a kind of circularity: we bring our religious beliefs and personal preferences with us to the biblical text and we find support for those very beliefs and preferences once we get there. For this reason, *self-criticism may be more important than biblical criticism in interpretation*—the sort of humility, honesty and reverence that engages the sacred text, not to problematize and personalize it but rather allow it to problematize us in bringing our beliefs and preferences into agreement with God's" ("John's John: A Wesleyan Theological Reading of 1 John," *Wesleyan Theological Journal* 46 [2011] 108–9 [italics original]).

practical theology. I have no doubt that Rob played a role in these institutional developments many years ago. Some within the biblical studies guild may find this move on the whole problematic since on the surface it appears to give too much ground to theology. I can imagine that many biblical scholars would not wish to be called "theologians" or would deny that what they do constitutes "biblical theology," generically understood. I believe Rob's reply to these reservations would be that there is no way around the matter: If Scripture is a theological category through and through, then biblical scholars are called to be a species of theologians.

As a way of getting to the matter of what does it mean to say that Scripture is thoroughly theological, let me stress a particular line of inquiry. Why is it that some conservative Christians, even those of a fundamentalist-evangelical kind, at some level ignore the claim of Scripture's theological character in terms of the questions they pursue and the methodologies they employ? Why is it that historical questions and methodologies are sometimes so prevalent? One possible reason has already been alluded to: Perhaps the guild of biblical studies simply puts too much pressure. Maybe its power to set the terms of discussion and the standards for success is simply too much to resist for those trying to gain a voice within it. But in contrast to this, Rob has shown that an alternative approach is possible. Rob has been a very successful New Testament scholar, but he is quite unassuming, both professionally and personally. Yes, he will argue with a kind of exactitude and passion that some might label hubristic, and he himself will say he is not terribly modest, but really, Rob is all about the arguments. He professes to not really care about the pressures of the guild. He's never sought to be professionally famous even though he has written extensively, been an active member of SNTS, a president of a scholarly society, and so forth. Simply, he does not understand his call and work as defined by the guild. Rob loves the guild, and he is both a product of and contributor to the guild, but Rob's call and vocation are not from the guild. I wish other scholars in the theological disciplines would follow his example.

But there may be another reason why especially conservative biblical scholars may tend toward history and away from theology in their work of engaging biblical texts. The reliance on history sets up a specific kind of buffer—one that leaves opportunity for the miraculous, the mystical, and the pneumatological but does so largely in terms of the past. Notice that in the manner "inspiration" is often understood, it is a process of characterizing the text in what seems to be an other-worldly, supernatural fashion: God reveals Godself by "breathing out" Scripture. What an amazing claim! The claim is so radical in fact that its contemporary reception domesticates it to a considerable degree by the additional claim, "That happened in the past, and now that we have the text, the process no longer applies." The canon is closed and presumably with it the dynamics of inspiration. Cessationist arguments in particular operate this way. And for Protestants who typically downplay the role of the church in all of this, what is left is the text and only the text itself. Therefore, the historical plays a role in connecting the contemporary church to the inaccessible, past dynamic of inspiration.

Rob is not interested in sidestepping the radical nature of the process of inspiration. Quite the contrary, he perhaps wishes to radicalize it even further, for Rob's tendency is not to maintain inspiration strictly as a bygone historical dynamic that led to the text having a particular property. On the contrary, inspiration, rather than simply a past event, is understood by Rob as an ongoing process. God did not simply "breathe out" Scripture at the point of its composition; rather, God has been "breathing out" Scripture at various points along the way, including canonization and reception.

Notice what this move necessitates. First and foremost, it requires a vibrant pneumatology. The Spirit has been at work in all aspects of Scripture's role within the worshiping faithful, including its composition, distribution, canonization, copying, modification, and reception. By saying that Scripture is a thoroughly theological category, he (and I) would say that it is first and foremost a "pneumatological phenomenon." God is at the center of Scripture as well as before and after it. A doctrine of God is at the heart of a doctrine of Scripture, and for Rob, it is especially the case that a doctrine of the Holy Spirit—which depicts the Spirit as working *throughout* history— is necessary. As Rob is fond of saying, Scripture is "the auxiliary of the Holy Spirit." What this understanding does functionally is cast inspiration, the work of God "breathing forth" Scripture, as the outworking of divine providence: God stewards the process of Holy Scripture's coming to be and of it being received among the holy faithful for their own good. God is at work in the writing, the transposing, the memory, the apostolic preaching, the transmission, and the sharing of Holy Writ. What may appear to secular historians as random, lucky, or conspiracy-laden processes can be viewed from this perspective as the Spirit putting together the kind of work the Spirit knows God's people need—and this with its many variants, tradents, voices, reworkings, revisions, and so forth.

Frankly, many Christians would find this kind of pneumatological privileging quite dangerous. They would detect a conflict between charisma and institution since, after all, there has to be some kind of stabilizing factor at work in order that spiritual anarchy would not ensue where anybody and everybody could have a revelation from God. For some, this process may just be too chaotic or too random on the surface. Rob would answer such a charge, not by elevating the primacy of an "inspired" text (notice the past tense) but by saying that the church has played a vital role in a God-determined process. And so comes a second point: For Rob's view of inspiration to work, one would also need a vital ecclesiology. Claiming Scripture as a thoroughly theological category means that God's people—those who read Scripture to encounter God's very self—are involved in Scripture being "breathed out." To bring the first two points together: God's Spirit works through God's people to produce a text for their healing and flourishing, that is, for their sanctification. A properly synergistic process is at work here.

The emphasis on healing and flourishing raises a third point: To claim Scripture as a thoroughly theological category means that it must be put to use for theological ends. And in typical Wesleyan-Methodist fashion, for Rob putting something to use for theological ends means employing it and placing it within God's great plan of salvation, within the *oikonomia* of God's self-manifestation and outworking. On this point, Rob has repeatedly appealed to the logic of John Webster in his monumental "dogmatic sketch," *Holy Scripture*. For Webster, sanctification operates as a helpful notion to assert God's election of these texts but in a way that does not diminish their creatureliness.[4] Rob resonates very much with this point, but he does so as a Bible scholar within the Wesleyan-Methodist tradition. Standing in this tradition, Rob will highlight a number of points so as to depict Scripture not simply as a holy text but as a sanctifying text as well.

For instance, as Rob has repeatedly stressed in his writings, it is the second part of 2 Timothy 3:16 that narrates and substantiates what the first part

---

4. John Webster, *Holy Scripture: A Dogmatic Sketch* (Cambridge: Cambridge University Press, 2003) 27–28.

and its elusive term *theopneustos* can mean. It is *because* Scripture is "useful for teaching, for reproof, for correction, and for training in righteousness" that we can go on to say that it is "God-breathed" or "inspired." And the connection to the next verse (v. 17) is also important: The utility or "usefulness" is tied to the teleological and purposeful: "so that everyone who belongs to God may be proficient, equipped for every good work." One of Rob's repeated emphases related to these points and expressed in his commentary on the Pastoral Epistles is the notion of the "performances of Scripture" in these passages: "The adjectives ["God-breathed"] and ["useful"] are existential marks that evince the performances of every Scripture as divinely inspired—that is, as indispensable for wisdom-making."[5] Note the subtle yet powerful point: Scripture's divine inspiration is tied to its performances among the faithful. One should not talk about Scripture's nature or ontology apart from Scripture's role or teleology; they are of a piece, two sides of the same coin.

Later in an excursus in Rob's Pastoral Epistles commentary, he reflects directly on a theology of Scripture:

> A proper theology of Holy Scripture attaches both its production and performance—that is, its material existence as a literary text—to God's providential care for creation and in particular to God's desire to repair all things broken according to God's redemptive purposes. The Bible's authority is not predicated on the identity and intentions of its divinely inspired authors, on the divine nature of its inerrant propositions, or on the artfulness of the biblical text understood in its original historical setting. Rather, the Bible's authority as God's word for the church is predicated on God's persistent use of the Bible to bring to realization God's purposes for the world. In this sense, the Bible's authority is defended here by a long history of evident usefulness as an auxiliary of God's Spirit in the reordering of its faithful readers according to the Creator's good intentions for them—what Paul calls "wisdom for salvation" and "maturity for good works" in 2 Tim 3:15–17.[6]

---

5. Robert W. Wall, with Richard B. Steele, *1 & 2 Timothy and Titus* (Grand Rapids: Eerdmans, 2012) 274.

6. Wall, *1 & 2 Timothy and Titus*, 310.

Notice here that Rob speaks of a theology of Holy Scripture not by denying issues of production but by including them alongside matters related to performance, and these subsumed under "God's providential care for creation," a point which is fundamental for understanding Scripture's place and role among the faithful. Also fundamental here is the shaping and maturing of the church: its instruction and catechesis. Christians read Scripture to encounter and be shaped and transformed by the presence of God. They can do so because God has chosen Scripture as a means by which this can take place.

This focus on Scripture as a "means" suggests a Wesleyan-Methodist idea: Scripture is a "means of grace" bestowed by God so as to cultivate healing and transformation among humankind. Through this Wesleyan-Methodist categorization, Scripture is put in company with other "means of grace," including the Lord's Supper, prayer, and so on.[7] Practically, this makes Scripture sacramental for Christians: a visible, textual sign of an invisible, life-giving grace, that being God's very presence and life.[8] Scripture must be enacted and embodied in this depiction. In other words, Scripture's role among the saints is not simply (and reductively for that matter) to be understood as an "epistemic criterion" that settles questions related to knowing and certainty in ways that are philosophically abstract and speculative. Quite the contrary, Scripture's role is to be one within a community's shared life. The "reordering of faithful hearers" alluded to above in Rob's quoted passage can be quite personal. It can involve the identification and confession of sin; it can mean the raising up of pain and lament; and it also can mean the rejoicing and celebration accompanying answered prayer and deliverance. Put simply, Scripture's function is lodged squarely within a community's shared rhythms of life—its corporate and individuated spirituality. Apart from that life, Scripture can only be appropriated in an impoverished and unhelpful way.

The Spirit's use of Scripture within a community's shared spirituality is with the aim of that community's transformation—that is, its entire

---

7. See Robert W. Wall, "Reading the Bible from within Our Traditions: The 'Rule of Faith' in Theological Hermeneutics" in *Between Two Horizons* (ed. Joel B. Green and Max Turner; Grand Rapids: Eerdmans, 2000) 92.

8. For more on Rob's take on Scripture as a sacrament, see his "Toward a Wesleyan Hermeneutics of Scripture," *Wesleyan Theological Journal* 30 (1995) 58–60.

sanctification. As a Free Methodist elder, Rob is not shy in employing the language of entire sanctification or Christian perfection. In fact, repeatedly as the Paul T. Walls Professor of Scripture and Wesleyan Studies, Rob has used his chair and its annual lecture at Seattle Pacific to prompt conversations as to what it means to be "free" and "entirely sanctified." Of course, Scripture has a role to play in all of this, one being in giving its faithful readers a hopeful imagination for what life in Christ could look like. One such possibility, as already mentioned above, is a shift in focus from the prevalence of "God-breathed" as a qualifier securing Scripture's authority to the second half of 2 Timothy 3:16 and on into verse 17. Another possibility is a renewed sense for the sheer declarative power of Romans 6 and 8 and how these should gain center stage (more so than Romans 7) for marking what life in the Spirit can look like. A further example would be taking seriously the witness of the Catholic Epistles and noting how their role can be cast as complementing the vision of the Pauline Epistles. As Rob highlights in a chapter for student and lay readers, whereas the Pauline witness tends to emphasize sanctification in terms of an identity achieved by Christ and so being in Christ, the Catholic Epistles in no uncertain terms speak to how Christians are to consecrate, purify, and so yes, sanctify themselves as those seeking to be in faithful covenant partnership with the triune God.[9] Finally, in recognizing the privileging granted by John Wesley to the Johannine literature (especially First John), Rob has highlighted the clear and decisive aspects of "sinning no more" in the Christian life.[10] In short, Rob's identity and call as a Methodist pastor and teacher has led him to see that the end-goal of Scripture is to make us saints—those conformed to the image and character of Christ.[11] Again, this is part and parcel to a theology of Holy Scripture, for its role is to prepare us for every good work: (1) the work that

9. See his "Participatory Holiness: A New Testament Perspective" in *Holiness as a Liberal Art* (ed. Daniel Castelo; Eugene: Pickwick, 2012) 40–49.

10. See "John's John" 111–13 and 133–41, as well as broadly, "Wesley as Biblical Interpreter" in *The Cambridge Companion to John Wesley* (ed. Randy Maddox and Jason Vickers; Cambridge: Cambridge University Press, 2010) 113–28.

11. Speaking personally here, I stand fully convinced that Rob's Methodist identity has helped him see these various hermeneutical possibilities, and I would hope that at some point those who are Methodists and pursuing biblical studies will come to see Rob's witness as a compelling model for the integration of these two identities.

God has done for us and that we are yet to witness and realize and (2) the work that we are to partake of as agents within God's unfolding purposes within the *oikonomia*. This speaks to the plans and order of God, that is, to the providence of God. God works throughout history, and God does so for sanctifying purposes. The prospect of beholding the latter should draw us back again and again to the riches of the scriptural witness.

The Prospects for the Future

I believe Rob's proposals are very valuable for a number of constituencies, especially those who love Scripture and who wish to engage it thoughtfully and carefully. Sadly, the value of Rob's views can only be registered within certain, rare conditions within Protestant evangelicalism, and some of these were highlighted above. For instance, one needs both a strong pneumatology and ecclesiology for these approaches to make sense, and unfortunately Protestantism typically ignores or diminishes these doctrines. Conservative evangelical Christians tend to privilege Christology and a very particular doctrine of revelation in their place. However, without a mix of pneumatology and ecclesiology, inspiration cannot help but be registered in the past, a point that simply incapacitates the present by reducing Scripture to a kind of "pneumatological artifact" that perhaps is only recognized via a weak reference to "illumination" or through the exercise of a kind of reasoning/ knowing that operates out of a "common sense" approach.

But if this is so, it raises another, even more basic, consideration: Perhaps it is the case that the Protestant evangelical church is at some level theologically anemic. Rob is keen on this problem, for he has remarked: "[M]ore threatening than the church's biblical illiteracy is its theological ignorance. . . . Sharply put, the pervasive theological ignorance within today's church makes right faith and holy living real impossibilities."[12] This is a most serious set of circumstances. As important as memorizing Scripture and hearing its proclamation during Sunday morning services, the church on the whole has not been trained to think theologically, and this kind of ineptitude necessarily influences how it engages Scripture. The handling of Scripture, no matter how much it is loved or seen as authoritative,

---

12. Wall, "Reading the Bible from within Our Traditions" 107.

is what is being highlighted here, for this handling involves interpretation as well as embodiment and praxis, and these qualities themselves only mark a community that is made wise over time by their attentive intellectual and affective devotion to the things of God. But sadly, God's people are often ill-equipped to trade in the holy mysteries. What is needed is a kind of rapprochement between the academy and the church—a kind of "revolving door," as Rob told me once on a long walk. The academy needs to be more concerned with the parish and the parish more so with the academy, and this for the whole of the gospel's ongoing proclamation and relevance.

Were there to be a "revolving door" between church and academy, I believe Rob's proposals would be more widely considered, for in such conditions, people would be willing to rethink long-held commitments for the sake of their maturation and growth. Such is the need regarding the topic before us. The doctrine of inspiration is typically presented as something historically fixed and so distinct from an expansive account of divine providence, but as I take Rob's proposals, the two are intertwined to such an extent that inspiration may require redefinition. Inspiration is not strictly a past phenomenon; it is a feature of God's Word coming to be—its being "breathed out"—among the worshiping faithful. At all stages of its existence, Scripture is a means of God offering the gift of salvation to those who love God. In the many Scripture debates or "battles for the Bible" that have marred evangelical culture, such a point is often lost. And, one imagines, something of God's work and God's aims with Scripture is lost as well.

But As For You: Pastoral Leadership in a Postinstitutional Time

ANTHONY B. ROBINSON

Amid the "Posts"

In the first decades of the twenty-first century, we live in a time between the times, an advent time of sorts. We stand between what was and what is yet to be. The frequent recourse to the prefix "post," meaning "after," is an indication of this between the times positioning. We are "after" or following something identifiable, but we are less sure how to characterize our own times, let alone the future. So we rely on a variety of "post" constructions.

Recently, for example, I worshipped with a church in Seattle whose mission statement declared that they strive "to be an incarnational presence in a post-modern and post-church culture."[1] They name contemporary culture in the Northwest of the United States as "post-modern" and "post-church." We can say what we are "after," but we are less clear about how to name our new and present time.

In a similar way, I write this essay with an eye toward leadership in a *postinstitutional* time in North America. Of course, institutions, as established patterns and organized forms of human activity and behavior, continue and likely will do so as long as human life continues. Nevertheless, few established institutions today enjoy the taken-for-granted status they once did. From service clubs like Kiwanis and Rotary, to denominational churches named First Presbyterian or First Methodist, to four-year liberal arts colleges such as Seattle Pacific University, to the daily newspaper in most cities, much is in flux. Institutions do not enjoy automatic loyalty or participation from new generations. Competing forms, often spawned by and reliant upon new internet-related technologies, challenge institutions that have been established for decades, even centuries.

---

1. Quest Church in Seattle, Washington, during August 2016.

Religious congregations and denominations are foremost among the institutions that feel the tremor of change and challenge. They no longer enjoy the automatic loyalty or participation of new generations. Many congregations have shrunk to the vanishing point, and some historic denominations are threatened by a similar fate.

Other factors contribute to perceived instability as well. Ours is a time of new religious pluralism in North America with a growing Muslim and Buddhist presence, among others. Another element of this pluralism includes a growing disaffection and disassociation from religious faiths and institutions indicated by the so-called "Nones," who indicate no religious affiliation in census studies. "Nones" are the fastest growing segment of American culture, religiously speaking, in the last decade. And the designation "spiritual-but-not-religious" has also become an accepted descriptor for many in contemporary culture, again indicating a disaffection for established religious groups and institutions.

In such a fluid context, pastoral authority is no longer a given of the office nor is it conferred by a denomination's imprimatur. Most pastors are aware that they and their congregations must compete with a wide variety of options for people's time, loyalty, and support. While some denominations continue to guarantee employment to those they ordain, these are the exceptions rather than the rule. Pastors today do not enjoy the security or authority of a churched culture and era in American life.

Of course, the situation is hardly all negative. There are upsides to these trends as well. There are opportunities to plant new churches, to experiment in the form and focus of a congregation, and to bring the ethos of the entrepreneur to the church. Some suggest that North America is a new and fertile mission field where the fields are, in Jesus' words, "white to harvest." Still, neither congregations nor denominations enjoy (or are held captive by) a taken-for-granted status once enjoyed by many. In this sense, ours is a postinstitutional time. What are the implications of this new time for pastoral leaders?

Paul's Final Charge to Timothy

How are pastoral leaders to negotiate such postinstitutional times? Where do we find guidance for our practice of pastoral ministry and congregational leadership in this time between times? What personal qualities and spiritual habits become essential in such a time? What, really, is ordained ministry and pastoral leadership in these times?

We had such questions in view when Robert Wall and I co-authored our book, *Called to Lead: Paul's Letters to Timothy for a New Day*.[2] Paul's letters to Timothy seek to instruct a young pastor on both the essence and practice of congregational leadership in a time when the church itself is quite new and does not enjoy either a taken-for-granted status or an implicit cultural support or sanction. If ours is a "postchurch culture," Timothy's world was a "pre-church culture." As such, it may provide clues and guidance for pastoral leaders today.

With this intuition to guide us, it is especially fruitful to turn to the closing chapters of the Timothy correspondence, to 2 Timothy 3:10–4:8. This section constitutes, as we note in *Called to Lead*, a "Final Charge" from Paul to his protégé, Timothy. Paul writes as one who has "fought the fight and finished the race," and for whom "death is at hand" (2 Tim 4:6–7). These are his "last words," and as such they are particularly freighted and urgent. They are words and counsel that Paul intends Timothy to hold onto and that are intended to hold Timothy in good stead in the days and work to come.

If "post" is often used today to mean "after," there is of course another sense or meaning of the word. A post is also a beam of wood planted in the ground or foundation as a marker and support to a larger structure. It is worthy of note that Paul earlier in these epistles indicates that Timothy as a pastoral leader is to function in just this way in the life of the congregation. "I write these instructions to you so that if I am delayed you will know how you must behave as the pillar and foundation of the truth within the household of God" (1 Tim 3:14–15).

Within the passage that constitutes Paul's final charge to Timothy (2 Tim 3:10–4:8), there is a particular grammatical construction that also serves as a kind of post upon which Paul builds his charge. Three times here Paul uses a rhetorical formula, *sy de*, which may be translated "you, however." It may also be translated (and it is so in both the NRSV and Jerusalem Bible) as the possibly even more emphatic "but as for you." In his repeated use of

---

2. Anthony B. Robinson and Robert W. Wall, *Called to Lead: Paul's Letters to Timothy for a New Day* (Grand Rapids: Eerdmans, 2012).

sy de, Paul not only provides rhetorical continuity and linkage to his charge to Timothy but also communicates something similar to what is normally meant when someone uses the phrase "stick to your knitting."

It is my observation as a pastor, teacher of pastors, and congregational consultant that effective leaders and effective congregations do "stick to their knitting." That is, they are reasonably clear about their core purpose or business, and they stay focused on that. They do not become easily distracted. They do not try to do everything, but they try to do a vital few things well. They know who they are, whose they are, and why they are. Paul's *sy de*, "but as for you," has the effect of calling his possibly easily distractible young apprentice, Timothy, to stay focused on his own work and core purpose.

For pastoral leaders in our postinstitutional time, this "but as for you" has sobering and calming consequence. Paul, in effect, says, "Yes, there are evil-doers about, but as for you, pay attention to your work and your teaching; yes, there are people in a congregation who are upset or upsetting, but as for you, pay attention to your work and to your teaching; yes, people will have 'itchy ears' and seek teachers who will 'tell them what they want to hear' (2 Tim 4:3), but as for you, stick to your knitting. Don't be pulled off course by the many possible distractions that inevitably come to a pastor." As a contemporary phrase goes, "The main thing is to keep the main thing the main thing."

This emphasis on paying attention to his own vocation finds parallel and confirmation in some of the most compelling literature on leadership in our time. In the 2007 book *Failure of Nerve: Leadership in the Age of the Quick Fix,* Edwin Friedman argues that what counts most for leaders is not—contrary to conventional wisdom—technique, data, or know-how. Having the newest or latest method of market analysis, using social media, or having a mixed media preaching style is not what is really important. "What counts," argues Friedman, "is the leader's presence and being."[3] Friedman, who was both a rabbi and a psychotherapist, describes the effective leader as one who is "self-differentiated." By this he means one who defines himself or herself clearly, who has clarity about his or her own life goals, and is, "[t]herefore, someone who is less likely to become lost in the anxious

---

3. Edwin H. Friedman, *A Failure of Nerve: Leadership in the Age of a Quick Fix* (Church Publishing, 2007) 17.

emotional processes swirling about. I mean someone who can be separate while still remaining connected, and therefore can maintain a modifying, non-anxious, and sometimes challenging presence."[4]

There is a parallel between Friedman's theme of a leader's capacity for clarity and self-differentiation within a complex emotional system and Paul's insistent and recurrent "but as for you" pivot in the closing words to a young pastor. Paul summons Timothy to attend to his own vocation first, not as a way of avoiding other duties or responsibilities but as a way of best fulfilling them. Friedman goes on to argue that leaders who have this capacity, who are clear about their own goals and purposes, and who are able to define themselves clearly "function as the immune systems of their institutions."[5] "It is the integrity of the leader that promotes the integrity or prevents the 'dis-integr-ation' of the system he or she is leading."[6] Paul's charge to Timothy is, in essence, a call to such vocational clarity, integrity, and focus.

Much of the conventional wisdom about leadership emphasizes having the newest technique or skill-set. While both technique and skills can be useful, Friedman's argument is that they are far less significant than the integrity of a leader and his or her capacity for self-differentiation amid a complex and emotionally charged system like a congregation. There is a paradox here. Leaders lead best when they pay attention first to their own functioning and core values. This does not of course mean self-absorption or narcissism. It means clarity about vocation, identity, and convictions, and the capacity to communicate these core values in a nonanxious way.

Friedman's argument is confirmed by my own observations of effective leadership, or its absence, in literally hundreds of congregations with which I have worked. Healthy congregations almost without exception have a healthy leader. Effective congregations tend to have a leader who is clear about his or her core commitments and who is able to communicate those with a certain calm and consistency.

Friedman does, however, include an important qualifier to his discussion: "I want to stress that by a well-differentiated leader I do not mean an autocrat who tells others what to do or orders them around . . . Rather I

4. Ibid., 14.
5. Ibid., 17.
6. Ibid., 19.

mean someone who has clarity about his or her own life goals."[7] Self-differentiation does not translate into coercing, still less bullying, others. In fact, well-defined leaders are able to tolerate dissent and receive feedback because they are clear about their own identity and commitments. Self-knowledge allows one the security to know and be open to others.

One additional caveat regarding the self-differentiated leader: Being such a leader does not mean that a person no longer has need for growth, further learning, or even correction. Paul's warning in 1 Corinthians 10:12 ("So if you think you are standing, watch out that you do not fall") is apt. Effective leaders are committed to their own continuing growth and learning.

There is a remarkable parallel between the ancient wisdom of Paul's charge to Timothy (with its emphasis on his vocational clarity and integrity and paying attention to one's own functioning) and some of the best of contemporary literature on leadership which stresses a leader's capacity for self-differentiation within a complex system. Paul's "but as for you" finds echo and confirmation in the leadership studies and discussions which stress the integrity, self-knowledge, and self-awareness of a leader.[8]

When we analyze Paul's final charge to Timothy, we find that Paul employs the *sy de* formulation three times. As he does so, Paul fleshes out his call to vocational integrity on Timothy's part. After each *sy de*, Paul enlarges on the meaning of Timothy's calling—of what it means to "stick to his knitting."

Following the initial *sy de* in 3:10, Paul turns to the importance of those qualities of personal character demonstrated in his own life as a model for Timothy's practice. He lists "my teaching, way of life, purpose, faith, loyalty, love, patience, physical abuse, and my suffering." Timothy is to pay attention to his mentor, Paul, as a model and guide to evaluating his own character and personal practices, which include suffering in the cause of faith.

When Paul next says "but as for you" (3:14), it is to urge Timothy to keep his ministry rooted in Scripture. "But as for you, stay steady in what you have learned and found convincing, knowing from whom you learned, from

7. Ibid., 14.
8. For an exploration of similar themes, see Ronald Heifetz, *Leadership Without Easy Answers* (Boston: Harvard Business School Press, 2017); Heifetz, *Leadership on the Line* (Cambridge, MA: Belknap, 2003); Peter Steinke, *Congregational Leadership in Anxious Times: Staying Calm and Courageous No Matter What* (Lanham: Rowan & Littlefield, 2014).

infancy you have known the holy writings" (3:14–15). In a time, whether Timothy's or our own, of so many competing truth-claims and when Scripture is often either neglected or distorted to fit a prior agenda, it is easy to stray and lose both focus and confidence. Paul urges Timothy to teach the God-inspired Scripture with confidence.

His final use of *sy de* is part of Paul's stirring exhortation to "do the work of a preacher of the good news" (4:5). Paul notes that the time will come "when people will not tolerate healthy teaching" and will "accumulate teachers who say what they want to hear" (4:3). Every pastor today can look around and see those preachers and teachers who sell a "prosperity gospel" or who trade in conspiracy theories and blame some Other (Muslims, gays, immigrants, the poor, people of color). They often attract large followings as they do. It is difficult, particularly in North America, to argue with success. But Paul urges Timothy to do just that. He is to proclaim the word with courage and urgency, whether "in season or out of season" (4:2 RSV, KJV).

Yes, there will be many seductive voices. There will be other "gospels" proclaimed. There will be false teachers. Nevertheless, Timothy is not to be distracted, to not lose focus. "But as for you," Paul urges, pay attention to the character and holiness of my example and of your own life; pay attention to the holy writings, the Scriptures; and proclaim the gospel message urgently and faithfully. It is always easy, and particularly so in times of flux and uncertainty, to be distracted and to lose a sense of purpose. Paul's *sy de*, "but as for you," sets a steady and steadying beat amid the cacophony.

Another contemporary student of congregational life and leadership, Peter Steinke, has built on the work of Edwin Friedman. In his book, *Congregational Leadership in Anxious Times: Staying Calm and Courageous No Matter What,* Steinke argues that one effect of these postinstitutional times is a heightened congregational anxiety. When the anxiety level grows in a human group, whether a congregation or a body politic, effective leaders help by managing their own anxiety and maintaining disciplined attention on the key challenges facing the group. By insisting that Timothy pay attention to his own spiritual practices, to Scripture, and to the proclamation of the gospel, Paul cues Timothy to provide calm and courageous leadership in his own anxious times—and he cues us to do the same in our own.

Paul's urging to Timothy that he pay attention to himself and his work is not only theologically informed, but it is also psychologically sound. As Paul calls Timothy to attend to his example and to his own spiritual practices, he does acknowledge that there are "wicked people and impostors" who are "deceiving others" (3:13). It is possible to become fixated on, or at least pre-occupied by, such disturbing people and their behaviors and in doing so to neglect oneself or one's own work. Those perceived as "enemies" or as threats to the congregation's life can, in other words, be given too much credit and too much space whether in a congregation's life or in a pastor's mind and heart. While Paul acknowledges the presence of bad actors, his "but as for you" summons Timothy to avoid letting such malcontents grow too large or from becoming a consuming preoccupation. Moreover, if Paul's "but as for you" is a reminder that we cannot control others, it strikes an even more important note: We can take responsibility for ourselves, our actions, our practice. Sure, it is a crazy world and some days people are unfair, irritating, and mean. But the one person you can have some real impact on is you. Focus there. "But as for you" is sound pastoral care for the pastor.

Doing Your Own Work:
What I've Learned from the Recovery Movement

In the third and final portion of this essay, I want to suggest that Paul's *sy de*, the "but as for you" drumbeat of his final charge, has profound implications not only for the focal practice of pastoral leadership but also for the broader life and ministry of the church in our new time. In this instance the "post" to which I attach, or on which I frame, this claim is what has come to be known as "The Recovery Movement."

By "The Recovery Movement," I have in mind 12-Step programs, the first of which was Alcoholics Anonymous. Since the early twentieth century creation of AA, other 12-Step programs have proliferated to help with other forms of addiction and compulsive behavior, including drug addiction, sex addiction, food addiction, co-dependency, and workaholic behaviors. Literally millions of people meet each day in all sorts of venues—often church basements—to "work their program" of recovery.

Over the years as a pastor, I have found myself as a guest at "open" meetings on a number of occasions. Sometimes I was there in support of a new attendee who asked their pastor to accompany them to a first meeting. Other times I was there to hear a parishioner's "First-Step Share" or "testimony" at a Speaker's Meeting. Still other times, I was asked to hear people's "Fourth Step," a person's "searching and fearless" moral self-inventory. On my initial ventures into such 12-Step groups, I brought with me the usual prejudices, imagining the people I would find there would be "a bunch of drunks" or "druggies." Instead, I found people much like myself. Even more to the point, I found people doing hard, honest, and life-saving work.

For some Christians and Christian denominations, the Recovery Movement remains suspect. Such Christians view AA and the other 12-Step programs similarly to the way the disciples viewed the unauthorized exorcist of Mark 9:38–50. There, disciples rushed to Jesus eager to report that they had put a stop, or tried to put a stop, to "someone casting out demons in [Jesus'] name . . . because he was not following [the disciples]." To the disciples' chagrin, Jesus took a more magnanimous view: "Do not stop him; for no one who does a deed of power in my name will be able soon afterward to speak evil of me. Whoever is not against us is for us." The Recovery Movement, while not officially Christian, has been a source of help and healing for many.

Perhaps even more to the point, an argument can be made that the church was the original "Recovery Movement," but it has somehow managed to lose this focus and ethos. Of course, not everyone finds his or her life or well-being threatened by addiction to alcohol or drugs, other substances, or behaviors. But Christian faith asserts something even more basic: We are all in bondage—in bondage to the powers of sin and death.

Contrary to conventional wisdom, sin as understood in Scripture is not a misstep here and there. Nor is it limited to the actions of an individual. Sin is a condition and a ruling power. We are in bondage to our own insatiable egos and their illusion of control. Such hard truth about the human condition has often been set aside in today's church. It has been soft-pedaled or forgotten as churches have opted for the upbeat and positive, or for a faith that says little that is dire or truthful about the human condition.

My hunch is that many people would find it helpful, even transformative, to hear harder truths: that sin and evil are crafty and powerful, that each of us has "stuff"—our own spiritual issues to face—and that all of us need help and saving. And perhaps most importantly, there is the truth that help is available.

A "Third-Step Prayer" evidences the closeness of the Recovery Movement to Christian faith: "God, I offer myself to Thee—to build with me and to do with me as Thou wilt. Relieve me of the bondage of self, that I may better do Thy will. Take away my difficulties, that victory over them may bear witness to those I would help of Thy Power, Thy Love, and Thy Way of Life. May I do Thy will always. Amen."[9] Such a prayer is both honest about the human condition under the power of sin and hopeful about the power of God to liberate human beings from bondage.

In my experience of 12-Step programs, there is a crucial learning and central practice that is strikingly similar to Paul's "but as for you" admonition to Timothy. It is this that links this text, pastoral leadership, and the church of today and tomorrow. In recovery groups and programs, job one, so to speak, is a person's own work, his or her own recovery from the distortions and bondage of addiction. Each one is there to do his or her own work. Encouragement, support, and accountability are found in the group. But a person is not there to work on anyone but him or herself. All are invited to talk about the challenges and temptations they face and the hope, healing, and strength they have found.

While this focus on one's own work could devolve into a kind of self-centered preoccupation, this has not been my observation or experience. Rather, what I have observed, and been blessed by, is the way that people in such groups take responsibility for their own lives and their own work. They may offer and give support to one another, but their clear and primary focus is to do their own work, to be about their own recovery and their own transformation, with the help of God.

This is not how I have generally experienced the church. At least often in my experience of the church, we avoid honest self-examination, confession, repentance, and amendment of life. While all these words may be used, the church in my experience is all too often a place where a certain level of pretense is the norm. Roberta Bondi, the church historian and author of several books on prayer made this point in her remark, "The church tends to call our noble selves. God wants our real selves."[10]

That is, people often act in church as if all is well in their lives and families and as if they have no inner or spiritual work of their own to do.

---

9. Bill Pittman, *Prayers for the Twelve Steps: A Spiritual Journey* (San Diego: RPI, 1993) 2.

10. Bondi made this comment in the context of the Turner Lectures of the Disciples of Christ at Yakima, Washington, in 2000.

The focus often seems to fall upon others. Sometimes this focus upon other people is benign. We seek to help others in need, whether members of the congregation or the larger society. But this other focus has a shadow side as well. Too often we in the church understand ourselves as the healthy or the saved whose task it is to bring health or salvation to others while missing our own need for these realities in our own lives.

The results of such a misplaced focus, of a neglect of doing our own work ("but as for you"), are two-fold. On the one hand, churches become places where we avoid rather than face the truth about ourselves. There is a lack of honesty and accountability that can make church not only artificial but boring. On the other hand, as a result of this failure in churches to do and prioritize our own spiritual work, those who come to church seeking to do just such work may find themselves shuttled off to a project or committee that has little to do with spiritual growth or authenticity.

It is not my intention to be unfairly hard on the church or harsh in my judgment of it. I share in all these failures. And even more importantly, I also know the church often can be a people of spiritual authenticity and transformation we are called to be.[11] It is just not the case as often as one might hope. But just as Paul keeps calling Timothy to pay attention to his own work, to stick to his knitting, so the Recovery Movement has something similar to teach the church today. Instead of "but as for them," we do well to heed Paul's "but as for you" so as to be about the work of human transformation, beginning with the brokenness in our own lives.

There is one particular practice that is standard in 12-Step meetings which both illustrates the focus on one's own work and supports such a focus. This is the practice of "no crosstalk." What that means is that after a person "shares" in a 12-Step meeting—that is, speaks of current challenges and hopes, struggles, and healing—no one responds directly to the speaker. This means that no one rushes to comfort or fix in the event that someone has shared great pain or experienced the advent of tears. Neither does anyone provide advice, saying, "Oh that same thing happened to me; here's how I handled it." No one judges another with comments such as, "What

---

11. An account of one congregation's work and experience of this kind is found in Molly Phinney Baskette, *Standing Naked before God: The Art of Public Confession* (Cleveland: Pilgrim, 2015).

you really need is to get right with the Lord" or "What you need is to stop thinking so much about yourself and help someone else out." People may wish to say such things, but no one does. There is, instead, listening and acceptance and support for people doing their own work.

I have found this no crosstalk practice so compelling and useful that I have adopted it in my work as a consultant to congregations. For example, I may invite people in a congregation that is experiencing conflict to talk about the issues. I invite them, however, to "speak for yourself," not for unnamed-but-concerned others. And I ask the other people present to not respond to the speaker. They are not to agree or disagree with the speaker nor to challenge or confirm what they say; they are simply to listen. This tends to create a safe setting, one in which people take responsibility for themselves.

I have also used this no crosstalk practice in both Bible study and in church planning or visioning exercises. In Bible study, the prompting question may be, "How do you hear God speaking to you in this passage?" Each person is invited to speak for him or herself without someone else offering the authoritative "this is what the text means." There may be a time, elsewhere in study, for information and background on the passage. But at this point, I want each person to feel free and safe to say what each hears God saying to him or her.

As to another example, in a planning exercise the question I offer may be, "Where do you think the Holy Spirit is calling our church to go in the future?" Again, each person is invited to speak for him- or herself without crosstalk. This has the effect of both broadening and leveling the metaphorical table. Without such a norm, some voices will speak more loudly and frequently, while some others will not speak at all or will simply assent to what others have said. But often, at least in my experience, the Holy Spirit speaks through people whom we did not expect to be such instruments. No crosstalk and speaking for yourself are adaptations of the Recovery Movement practice. Moreover, they are ways of taking Paul's "but as for you" seriously in the church. Pay attention to your own work. What is God saying to you?

While these illustrations from my consulting practice may be (I hope) suggestive, the real point is a shift of focus in the church. Instead of pretending we all have our act together and can direct our attention to other people and their issues, let's get real. What are the issues and challenges in my own life? Where is sin powerful? Where do I experience bondage? Where and how am I finding hope and healing?

My hunch is that the churches that permit and encourage this kind of openness and honesty, amid the larger context and embrace of God's saving grace for all people, will thrive and be alive even in our postmodern, postinstitutional, and postchurch culture.

PART TWO

Essays on Biblical Texts and Themes

"Son of Man" in Psalm 8, Psalm 79, and Daniel 7: An Exercise in a Contrapuntal Biblical Theology of the Septuagint[1]

Eugene E. Lemcio

Introduction

Because the honoree uses biblical texts as Scripture (that is, as authoritative for faith and life), I shall attempt to explicate the role of these passages in a version of what has been known as canonical hermeneutics—about which we have both written, starting in the early 1980s.[2] In the process, we have learned much from each other and have shared many of the same views and followed a similar method. However, I am not so sanguine as to believe that Rob will bestow his imprimatur upon what follows, either in approach or conclusions. Nevertheless, I offer it with great respect and affection.

But first a word is in order about the nature and challenges of the task. These days, under the best of circumstances and using original languages, attempting to write a biblical theology (BT) of any kind is looked upon with suspicion and skepticism about motive, method, or competence. James Barr has contended that doing so is neither possible nor legitimate.[3] Consequently, what are the chances of succeeding in murkier waters, where the

---

1. With many, I have used "Septuagint" (LXX) and "Old Greek" (OG) interchangeably. My source for English translation is the NETS, except where noted.

2. The selections found in Robert W. Wall and Eugene E. Lemcio, *The New Testament as Canon: Readings in Canonical Criticism* (Sheffield: Sheffield Academic Press, 1992) 28–77, reproduce essays of mine published elsewhere covering the period of 1981–86. A fresh contribution follows (78–108). Since then, see my "Images of the Church in 1 Corinthians and 1 Timothy: An Exercise in Canonical Hermeneutics," *Asbury Journal* 56 (2001) 45–59, and "The Synoptics and John: The Two So Long Divided. Hearing Canonical Voices for Ecclesial Conversations," *Horizons in Biblical Theology* 26 (2004) 50–96. Because publication of this journal transferred hands, and because sufficient care was not taken to ensure electronic correspondence with the Greek program used originally, the text omits footnote 3 and contains a jumble of accents and breathings, for which the editor apologized in the next number.

3. James Barr, *The Concept of Biblical Theology: An Old Testament Perspective* (Minneapolis: Fortress, 1999).

subject matter (son of man) is so contested,[4] where the uncharted coasts of doing BT of a translation are so unmapped[5] (and rocky!), and where the nature and authority of the LXX have only recently begun to get the kind of attention from academics, within both guild and church, that they deserve? A recent author puts the matter starkly:

> What would modern Christian theology look like if its theologians returned the Septuagint to the place it occupied at the foundation of the church, or at least began to read it alongside the Hebrew Bible, as a witness to the story of the Bible and in acknowledgement of its role in shaping Christianity? The Septuagint has already affected some of Christian theology, but mostly only where the New Testament writers mediate its readings. We saw earlier that the Septuagint, almost exclusively, molds Paul's theology in Romans, and the same can be said for the author of Hebrews. There may be further ideas still, but because the Septuagint has not attracted significant attention from theologians its value for modern Christian thought is still unknown. A full-scale exploration awaits an energetic thinker, but for now it is interesting that even while interest in the theological interpretation of the Bible is increasing the Septuagint has not been given the part it deserves in the drama of the church's reception and use of Scripture.[6]

Since this challenge is so enormous, and the space so limited, I can be only suggestive and illustrative, relying both on the consensus of others and upon

---

4. I preserve the gender-specific designation "son of man" only because it has become a technical term. Otherwise, my aim is to employ gender-neutral categories: "frail, vulnerable human" or "child of dust," for which I argue separately. For examples of this contestation, see Delbert Burkett, *The Son of Man Debate: A History and Evaluation* (Cambridge: Cambridge University Press, 1999); Mogens Müller, *The Expression "Son of Man" and the Development of Christology: A History of Interpretation* (New York: Routledge, 2008).

5. For a reliable guide, consult Martin Rösel, "Towards a 'Theology of the Septuagint,'" in *Septuagint Research: Issues and Challenges in the Study of the Greek Jewish Scriptures* (ed. Wolfgang Kraus and R. Glenn Wooden; Atlanta: Society of Biblical Literature, 2006) 239–52.

6. Timothy Michael Law, *When God Spoke Greek: The Septuagint and the Making of the Christian Bible* (Oxford: Oxford University Press, 2013) 171. See also Mogens Müller, *The First Bible of the Church: A Plea for the Septuagint* (Sheffield: Sheffield Academic Press, 1996).

the soundness of my own presentation of evidence and argument.[7] My primary text is the GOT in its "final" form, understood both as critically reconstructed and as the Scripture inherited by both synagogue and the early church.[8] It presupposes readers who heard or read their Bibles in Greek rather than Hebrew and Aramaic. In viewing the LXX as an independent, free-standing entity (though subject to an ongoing process of interpretation), these observations follow.[9]

The three texts to be studied according to genre are two psalms and a semi-apocalypse. I put it this way in order to give sufficient weight to the narratives of chapters 1–6 of the latter and to the so-called Additions: Susanna and Bel et Draco.[10] So as to reduce (if not eliminate) personal, confessional, and professional bias, I shall avoid exercising preferential treatment, harmonizing, and reducing my chosen texts to an essence. Each of these procedures ignores or denies the radical diversity of the biblical text, made even more so by the longer canon. Positively, I shall conduct a contrapuntal conversation among these three witnesses to son of man, Scripture *per se* being unable to accomplish it. Neither biblical nor secular literature can interpret or teach itself, although uncritical readers and careless scholars personify it as doing just that. An agent is always required.

7. For obvious reasons, the bibliography must be limited to representative scholars engaging issues directly related to the focus of this article: a contrapuntal or dialogical theology of the LXX.

8. Alfred Rahlfs, ed., *Septuaginta* (7th edition; Stuttgart: Württembergische Bibelanstalt, 1962). The great uncials of the full Greek Bible (Codexes Sinaiticus, Vaticanus, and Alexandrinus) remain the foundations of critical reconstruction, for both the LXX and GNT. The *Orthodox Study Bible* (Nashville: Thomas Nelson, 2008) bases its English translation of the OT on the Greek text, regarded as inspired, and its order of books (which include the so-called "deuterocanonical" writings). Noteworthy in the Western, Roman Catholic tradition is *Biblia Sacra. Iuxta Vulgatam Versionem* (ed. Robert Weber; 5th edition; Stuttgart: Deutsche Bibelgesellschaft, 2007), which provides parallel Latin translations of the Psalms from both the HB and the LXX.

9. For a succinct account of scholarly opinion as to how the LXX was intended to function, see Karen H. Jobes and Moisés Silva, *Invitation to the Septuagint* (2nd edition; Grand Rapids: Baker, 2015) 84–90.

10. See my "Daniel: an 'Historical' Sign of the Eschatological Ancient of Days/God Most High? Reading Bel et Draco in Eschatological Contexts: Apocalyptic (Daniel 2 and 7), Prophetic (Esaias 27:1), and Sapiential (Wisdom of Salomon 14:11–14)," in *Orthodoxy and Orthopraxis: Essays in Tribute to Paul Livermore* (ed. Doug Cullum and J. Richard Middleton; Toronto: Clements, forthcoming).

Table 1. Similarities & Differences

	Psalm 8	Psalm 79 (=80 MT)	Daniel 7
1. God	Our Lord	Enthroned Shepherd	Ancient of Days
2. Son of Man	diminished a little from angels	[weakened: 2x]	[without endowments]
3. Endowed	crowned with glory & honor, made lord of creation	made strong (2x)	given kingdom, authority, nations, service, glory
4. Antagonist	enemy & avenger	passersby, boar, wild beast	4 beasts
5. Time[a]	remote past	"present" exile	future
6. Genre	narrative poetry	narrative poetry	apocalyptic myth

[a]Although a canonical approach to the Bible in general and these texts in particular suggests a level of timelessness and placelessness such that one is encouraged to read them synchronically (that is, with immediacy), the heavy presence of narratives, both extensive and brief—as in these psalms and Daniel 7—also encourages a diachronic reading as well. In other words, giving indications of temporality and locality their due has interpretive significance, as I demonstrate throughout.

At first, I will elicit the views of the Greek translator, with an eye to the Hebrew and Aramaic authors.[11] Next comes the challenge of establishing a bridge between those who read these ancient texts and contemporary experience. In the process, perhaps a paradigm will emerge for doing BT with other subjects, on a larger scale (including the NT), and along a broad, ecumenical spectrum.[12]

I begin with a display of commonalities and distinctions among the three passages engaged (Table 1). Central to all is a pattern recounting God's elevation of a lower or subordinate or weakened figure in the context of opposition. This is in keeping with (but is not dependent upon) my view that "son of man" is a biblical idiom for the downside of human experience: its weakness and vulnerability, especially when contrasted with God's majesty and strength.[13] It can be rendered more generically as "child of dust." The reproduction of six consistent categories, whose sequence can vary,

11. W. Rudolph and H. P. Rüger, eds., *Biblia Hebraica Stuttgartensia* (2nd edition; Stuttgart: Deutsche Bibelgesellschaft, 1984).

12. Such an effort, at least in theory, was made by George B. Caird when he attempted to gather and moderate an "Apostolic Conference" of NT authors. However, he was faulted for not allowing contrary voices to be heard. See *New Testament Theology* (ed. and completed by L. D. Hurst; Oxford: Clarendon, 1995) 1–26.

13. Burkett, *Son of Man Debate*, 14–15, shows that this rendering goes back at least five centuries. Forty years ago, John Bowker marshaled a substantial amount of data in support: see his "The Son of Man," *Journal of Theological Studies* n.s. 28 (1977) 19–48.

in each of the three texts suggests a template of sorts—a form, albeit an informal one. The advantage of this minidrama lies in its ability to embrace several themes instead of a single one and to integrate them instead of having to choose the central or unifying motif, which involves a greater level of subjectivity. Such an approach also enables one to valorize both unity and diversity.

Son of Man in LXX Psalm 8

The Psalmist acknowledges the Lord's admirable name throughout the earth, whose magnificence has been raised beyond the heavens (v. 2). A touch of irony follows: praise has poured forth from the most vulnerable and without power, infants and nurslings (v. 3), those who ordinarily cannot speak nor have a voice. In some unknown way, their utterances are involved in putting down both enemy and avenger. The same reversal of conventional wisdom occurs again. In contrast to the majesty of the sky and its heavenly bodies (v. 4), what is man that God pays him any mind, and attends to a frail or subordinate human at that—a condition that both the Hebrew and Greek idiom conveys by the expression "son of man" (v. 5)? Nevertheless, such a one has been invested with vast authority over birds, fish, and land animals (vv. 7–9).

The Psalmist celebrates the awesome privilege and responsibility given to the vulnerable human creation: managing the world that God has created. This is the ideal, the way intended by God at the beginning, what some term "Protology." The author's mode of expression is realistic; his scope is universal; and the time stretches from the beginning of the world into the indefinite future. Nevertheless, all is not well. There is that talk of enemies and vengeance—who are nevertheless to be overcome, the means of victory being unconventional. At base is the issue of power: power manifested in weakness, both apparent and real.

On this point, original and translation largely concur. However, as is often noted, the Septuagint changes the text in a manner that signals a theological slant. More distance is put between the divine and human. Whereas the Hebrew says, "You have made him a little less than God," the Greek renders it thus: "You have diminished him a little in comparison with angels" (v. 6). At first glance, this gives the impression of a further reduction in status. However, seen from another angle, such distancing between the celestial and terrestrial could also suggest an element of trust via non-interference: handing over control of the earth to a "mere human" in a more fundamental way. It would amount to altering the pronoun in the African-American spiritual: "*We've* Got the Whole World in *Our* Hands." So far as the Psalm itself is concerned, there is no future envisioned, no eschatology (unless it be of a very subtle and complex kind), no warrant for expecting things to get better "by and by," either on their own or with outside help.

Son of Man in LXX Psalm 79 (=MT 80)

Such a complication is addressed later in the Psalter by another author and translator, whose structure and content have a good deal in common with the earlier text. It concerns what might be called "estinology": reflection on the way things are. Rather than referring to humankind in general, son of man—thanks to the LXX's syntactical arrangement—is now partly a collective term: a way of referring to Israel, otherwise described as a vine. In the MT, it is בֵּן ("son") who is set in close relation to the vine (vv. 15–16). However, the LXX, by adding ἀνθρώπου, rather than simply translating the Hebrew with υἱόν, makes "son of man" the recipient of this collective association. Such proximity led NT scholar C. H. Dodd to regard it as a complete identification of son of man with the vine. In his judgment, son of man in this instance became a collective symbol for Israel, equivalent to the vine.[14]

However, in my view, Dodd overstated his case. One reason for thinking in terms of association rather than identification is that son of man is spoken of twice as having been strengthened (vv. 16 and 18), something that had not yet occurred to God's people, who repeatedly cry out for salvation (vv. 3, 4, 8, 20). Moreover, the Israel in the Psalm is particular (national, ethnic, and tribal), and therefore, so is the son of man. The names mentioned— Ioseph, Ephraim, Manasses, and Beniamin (vv. 2–3)—are all descended from Rachel, Iakob's greater love.[15] Their Shepherd, close by and protective, is also the One Sitting upon the Cheroubin (v. 2): higher than the angels— near, yet far; immanent, yet removed from their recent experience, about which they lament.

---

14. C. H. Dodd, *According to the Scriptures: The Substructure of New Testament Theology* (New York: Scribners, 1953) 101–2.

15. John Goldingay, *Psalms 42–89* (Grand Rapids: Baker, 2007) 535.

God is also the Vintner, whose right hand—having cleared the ground and prepared it—transplanted a vine from Egypt to a land where its branches could spread from the river (Euphrates) to the sea (Mediterranean). Nevertheless, after such prodigious effort and success, the fence was torn down (v. 13). The fauna that are real in Psalm 8 have become metaphorical in Psalm 79, depicting their assault with particular savagery—a detail enhanced by the LXX. Animals, both clean and unclean (a boar), under no one's control, certainly not a frail human's, have attacked from the forest (v. 14).[16] Were that not enough, fire consumed everything (v. 17).

Lament is followed by appeal: that the Vintner pay attention to the vine, planted by God's own right hand (vv. 15–16); [the] man of God's right hand (v. 18); a son of man. That empowerment of the latter was needed is underscored in the LXX with a double mention (vv. 16 as well as 18). The corollary, that the previous condition was powerlessness, is likewise twice implied by the LXX (once in the MT). If there is a messianic hint here, a contested view, that is all there is.[17] Although strengthened thus, this son of man is given no assignment. Saving the vine is not in his portfolio, rather like the "lord" and Melchizedekian priest in Psalm 109:1 (MT 110:1). He is not the savior, God is (vv. 3–4, 8, 20).

Such is the current state of things. Divine salvation is still in the future, preferably sooner rather than later. In the meantime, God's people, according to the LXX's superscription, are given a directive to voice this Psalm εἰς τὸ τέλος: to the end [of the age] or for fulfillment on behalf of those who will be changed ὑπὲρ τῶν ἀλλοιωθησομένων (v. 1), who are yet to return from

---

16. Mireille Hadas-Lebel, "Rome 'Quatrième Empire' et le symbole du porc," in *Hellenica et Judaica: Hommage à Valentin Nikiprowetzky* (ed. A. Caquot, M. Hadas-Lebel, and J. Riaud; Leuven: Peeters, 1986) 297–312. I owe this reference to John J. Collins, *A Commentary on the Book of Daniel* (Minneapolis: Fortress, 1993) 299 n. 193.

17. Psalm 79 is not mentioned at all either in J. Lust, *Messianism and the Septuagint* (Leuven: Peeters, 2004) or in *The Septuagint and Messianism* (ed. M. A. Knibb; Leuven: Peeters, 2006). Interpreting a messianic tendency here is Joachim Schaper, *Eschatology in the Greek Psalter* (Tübingen: Mohr-Siebeck, 1995) 97 n. 354. See also Heinz-Josef Fabry, "Messianism in the Septuagint," in *Septuagint Research: Issues and Challenges in the Study of the Greek Jewish Scriptures* (ed. W. G. Kraus and R. G. Wooden; Atlanta: Society of Biblical Literature, 2006) 192–205. I am presupposing readers and their listeners who would be familiar with the Psalter and Daniel. In Ps 109 (=MT 110):1–3, God's right hand [man] is the Lord's begotten [son], ἐξεγέννησά σε, there being no equivalent to this clause in v. 3 of MT 110. As such, he is at least a proto-messianic figure. So, it would be in Ps 79, under the influence of the latter text.

captivity or who feel exiled in their native land because someone else is in control (as in the case of Neh 9:36–37).[18] This heightens the particularity of the son of man reference, which C. Vaticanus—the reading chosen by Rahlfs and the NETS—expands further by concluding the superscription with ὑπὲρ τοῦ Ἀσσυρίου ('over the Assyrian').[19] Furthermore, the unique use of μαρτύριον by the translator at this point—of the six instances in the Psalter, only here in the superscription—suggests that he meant for readers to identify Asaph as a witness to these events and composer of the psalm itself.[20]

Son of Man in Daniel 7

Because the past (Ps 8) is not recoverable and the present intolerable (Ps 79), there is only the future (Dan 7) upon which to pin one's hopes: eschatology or, more generally, fulfillment.[21] With Daniel 7, the genre changes from psalm to apocalypse; the medium from rational composition to ecstatic experience; the setting from objective, communal worship to private individual subjectivity.[22] During the dream-vision, natural animal metaphors

18. Albert Pietersma, "Exegesis and Liturgy in the Superscriptions of the Greek Psalter," in *X Congress of the International Organization for Septuagint and Cognate Studies, Oslo 1998* (ed. B. A. Taylor; Atlanta: Society of Biblical Literature, 2001) 122.

19. Alfred Rahlfs, ed., *Psalmi cum Odis* (2nd edition; Göttingen: Vandenhoeck & Ruprecht, 1967); Albert Pietersma and Benjamin G. Wright, eds., *A New English Translation of the Septuagint* [NETS] (Oxford: Oxford University Press, 2007).

20. See the canonical backstory of the Assyrian assault during Hezekiah's reign as recorded in 2 Kgs [4 Kgdms] 19–20, 2 Chr 29–32, and Isa 36–38.

21. I owe this phrasing about time, though not about these texts, to Prof. James A. Sanders [or perhaps Fr. Andrew Greeley] but cannot recall the publication.

22. Although not considering the two Psalms among his examples, the study by Jordan Scheetz is instructive: *The Concept of Canonical Textuality and the Book of Daniel* (Eugene: Wipf and Stock, 2011). I tender my thanks to our honoree for this reference. Unfortunately, it is marred by the total absence of any reference to the Greek translations of Daniel. Scheetz does not discuss whose (or which?) canon. A similar flaw occurs in James M. Hamilton, Jr.'s *With the Clouds of Heaven: The Book of Daniel in Biblical Theology* (Downers Grove: InterVarsity, 2014). The author neglects LXX Daniel throughout, even in his Chapter 7: "Interpretations of Daniel in Early Jewish Literature," although he includes Tobit and 1 Maccabees. Furthermore, Hamilton frequently announces in his "Preliminaries" that the study is conducted with evangelical assumptions, one of them being the "doctrine" (whose? by what authority?) of inerrancy, which then determines his understanding of canon: its contents and its limits. This is a particularly egregious example of how much (even non-evangelical/fundamentalist) biblical study is influenced by confessional assumptions. One has only to look at the index

become the unnatural miscreants of myth. The waters, through which fish swim (Ps 8:9) and by which boundaries are designated (Ps 79:12), become the great [primeval] sea (v. 2) out of which four monsters arise (vv. 3–8). Though possessing some human features, they are for a while subject to no one, certainly not to the mere son of man of Psalm 8.

For the most part, they combine in themselves the most ferocious aspects of the nonhuman, inanimate world: the raw power of empire, according to thrice-repeated interpretations of the vision in vv. 15–27. The monster-kings manifest overwhelming force aimed at the holy ones of the Most High (God's people or the heavenly hosts who are their patrons) and utter blasphemous words against the Most High God.[23] Nevertheless, the kings are mentioned four times as being defeated (once in the original vision, thrice in its interpretation) by a majestic divine figure (vv. 9–12 and throughout vv. 15–27). They stand no chance in the face of power blazing forth from the throne (vv. 9–10).

Afterward, "one as it were a son of man was coming upon the clouds of heaven" to an ancient of days, who invests him with everlasting royal authority, all nations of the earth, honor, service, and an imperishable kingship (7:13–14).[24] Can this be the messianic pretender—even if not technically the Messiah himself? Although not called Χριστός, one would think that—by receiving a kingdom—he would become king and, by implication, God's "anointed." But this remains at the level of inference.[25]

As in the case of the two psalms, the status of an unlikely candidate, a vulnerable human—or fragile community or an angel with human features

---

of passages that fall under the category "Apocrypha" and "Pseudepigrapha." The Roman and Eastern traditions are neglected entirely with such designations.

23. Either interpretation is possible for the Hebrew, the latter being argued for by Collins, *A Commentary on the Book of Daniel*, 10 and 317–18, and Christopher Rowland, *The Open Heaven: A Study of Jewish Apocalyptic in Judaism and Christianity* (New York: Crossroad, 1982) 180–83. However, the OG supports the former, as I argue subsequently.

24. The Greek of v. 14, which contains more diverse vocabulary than NETS, reads: καὶ ἐδόθη αὐτῶι ἐξουσία, καὶ πάντα τὰ ἔθνη τῆς γῆς κατὰ γένη καὶ πᾶσα δόξα αὐτῶι λατρεύουσα· καὶ ἡ ἐξουσία αὐτοῦ ἐξουσία αἰώνιος, ἥτις οὐ μὴ ἀρθῆι, καὶ ἡ βασιλεία αὐτοῦ, ἥτις οὐ μὴ φθαρῆι.

25. Benjamin Reynolds, "The 'One Like a Son of Man' According to the Old Greek of Daniel 7:13–14," *Biblica* (2008) 78. In the MT, the term never appears in the absolute (articular) form, "the Messiah." The situation is different in LXX Daniel, where the appearance and demise of "ὁ χριστός" (anarthrous) occurs at 9:25–26.

from the lower orders—is upgraded. Though appearing on the scene without might, he is given it in abundance. Not previously reigning, he is granted a royal domain. Originally without honor, he nevertheless receives it. The ancient of days figure bestows authority upon him who had lacked it, heretofore. Having been the one to serve, he is now rendered service.[26] This son of man had no more to do with his elevation than the personage to whom the Lord said, "Sit on my right until I make your enemies a footstool for your feet" (Ps 109 [MT 110]:1). And, either because he collectively symbolized them or functioned as an individual (their earthly or heavenly/angelic representative), the same happened to the holy ones and saints.[27]

These dynamics hold true even for the enhancement given to son of man by p967, the earliest (2nd–3rd century C.E.?) pre-Hexaplaric manuscript of the OG.[28] Here he is accompanied by the myriads surrounding the fiery throne (v. 13). Although the great Greek codices follow the Aramaic original in reporting that one like a son of man was brought on the clouds of heaven to [ἕως] the Ancient of Days, this textual tradition (antedating both Origen and the major codices by perhaps a century) reads that a frail human was coming on the clouds and was being present *as* [ὡς] an ancient of days.[29]

26. Such points are ignored or minimized when focusing too narrowly in the results of this minidrama and on the question of the figure's identity rather than on the nature of his prior status. See Eugene E. Lemcio, "'Son of Man,' 'Pitiable Man,' 'Rejected Man'": Equivalent Expressions in the Old Greek of Daniel," *Tyndale Bulletin* 56 (2005) 43–60.

27. See also the bestowal of a kingdom at vv. 18, 22, 27. For scholars taking this view, see Burkett, *Son of Man Debate*, 36–37 and 48–49.

28. Frederic G. Kenyon, ed., *The Chester Beatty Biblical Papyri: Descriptions and Texts of the Twelve Manuscripts on Papyrus of the Greek Bible* (Fasc. VII: *Ezekiel, Daniel, Esther*; London: Emery Walker, 1937) and A. Geissen, ed., *Der Septuaginta-Text des Buches Daniel* (Bonn: Rudolf Habelt Verlag, 1968). Online photos of the document can be accessed at http://www.uni-koeln.de/phil-fak/ifa/NRWakademie/papyrologie/PTheol2.html. Until its discovery, the earliest witnesses to the OG were one eleventh century C.E. hexaplaric cursive (88) and the seventh century C.E. Syro-Hexaplar. See Reynolds, "'The One Like a Son of Man'" for a thorough discussion of the textual tradition and interpretive matters.

29. One need not accept without further ado the widespread claim that cloud travel is necessarily a sign of god-likeness. For example, the LXX at Ps 88:7 reads (without parallel in MT 89): τίς ἐν νεφέλαις ἰσωθήσεται τῶι κυρίωι, καὶ τίς ὁμοιωθήσεται τῶι κυρίωι ἐν υἱοῖς θεοῦ; "[W]ho in the clouds shall be deemed equal to the Lord? And who among divine sons shall be compared with the Lord?" Although Rahlfs did not have access to this manuscript, he nevertheless chose this reading from the later witnesses to the OG. Ziegler-Munnich, though having it, relegated the variant to the apparatus.

At the same time, according to p967, the exalted one became more closely associated with the saints/holy ones. However, in this manuscript, they cannot be holy, supernatural beings, heavenly patrons of the saints because v. 27 renders them as 'holy people of the Most High.'[30] Furthermore, by adding to v. 8 a statement found in v. 21 ("it made war on the holy ones"), the translator created an *inclusio* around "son of man," thereby connecting (if not identifying) his experience with theirs.[31] Does he suffer with them, if not for them? One can reply in the affirmative if suffering results from himself having been at one point deprived (or stripped) of power, for this is how suffering comes about, whatever the source or manner: natural, accidental, or deliberate. However, as was the case in Psalm 8 and Psalm 79, so it is in this manuscript: the son of man figure plays no redemptive/salvific role—a fact that, without further ado, would not qualify him to be a candidate for messiahship.

A Three-Way Conversation

Language and Genre

How then shall we speak about this son of man? What language shall we borrow? Fortunately, the full canon legitimates different genres and idioms by which the same point can be made: psalm and apocalypse, verse and vision, and by singer and seer. One is not locked into an official dialect or form. Clichés and formulae can be challenged and avoided. When grotesque ideas are clothed in sweet reason, grotesque images are needed to strip them away. Furthermore, striving for clarity can be a virtue in some instances, eschewing the luxury of obscurity. On other occasions, code is the better way to go, employing myth to connect one with foundational realities too deep for conventional language and more linear thought.

Thus, the realism of Psalm 8 has its place in bringing the fantastic images of Daniel 7 down to earth. Yet, sometimes the metaphors of Psalm 79 have

---

30. Forms of αγ- in OG Daniel never explicitly modify heavenly beings. But they do characterize loyal Israel: 3:35, 4:19[22], 8:24, and 12:7.

31. Collins, *A Commentary*, 299 n. 199 asserts that the clause intrudes upon the dynamics of the vision, not even considering the possibility that a literary *theological* motive could be at work here—that is, leading the reader to associate God's holy people/saints and son of man more closely from the outset.

to be employed in telling the truth "slant."[32] The defiled outsider, the "boar," must not be allowed to get the point. And there are moments when "reality," defined solely by what "is," needs to be shaken up by the exaggerated (even unnatural) apocalyptic icons of what should be and one day will be. Only so can a heavenly vision be of some earthly good.

Should one be envious of Daniel's ecstatic experience? Oh, to have a private revelation, to see with the inner eye, not just the physical one! Why cannot that son of man reveal himself to me, personally? Longing for such a direct encounter with heavenly realities so as to remove all doubt and uncertainty is challenged within Daniel 7 itself. The privy counselor to kings, called upon to interpret their dreams, is unable to understand his own ἀποκάλυψις of such a son of man (vv. 15–16). This particular truth is not self-evident, even to the great Seer. An Other (together, with the prophet, a community *in nuce*) has to come alongside him, to explain with increasing detail—three times!—what would otherwise have remained a μυστήριον (vv. 17–27).

Moreover, the Psalms in general and these two in particular are said or sung within the context of the community's ongoing worship: Sabbath after Sabbath, feast upon feast, year after year. Psalm 79 is to be read or performed εἰς τὸ τέλος, "to the end of the age" (or "to the time of fulfillment"), routinely and formally reminding the people in their or others' exile of that son of man figure who, as the one at God's right hand, is a sign and seal of their enablement and return. This manner of encounter is more reliable than the *ad hoc*, individualistic, and solitary experience characteristic of "seeing visions and dreaming dreams," inspiring and important though they may be. On the other hand, at the point where liturgy, whose very routine was designed to free up the spirit, becomes instead stifling (and boring?), the breaking through of divine wisdom to a "loner" in unconventional and startling ways (Dan 7) is to be neither denied, diminished, nor demeaned.

The Sense of Time and Place

For those tempted to read Daniel 7 as a proof-text for setting all of their hopes on the future and in a "galaxy far, far away,"[33] Psalms 8 and 79 "earth"

---

32. Emily Dickinson, "Tell All the Truth, but Tell It Slant" in *The Norton Anthology of Modern Poetry* (ed. Richard Ellmann and Robert O'Clair; New York: W. W. Norton, 1973) 41.

33. George Lucas, "Star Wars," Episode 1, Scene 1.

the question of place once and for all. They counter the unbiblical notion that heaven is one's home, a place where we were neither born nor ever visited. Psalm 79:8 speaks of the people's estrangement from their native land, as "strangers in a strange new place,"[34] not of their exile from the earth. Nevertheless, the hint of a "not yet" to finish what had already been accomplished is suggested if one takes with full seriousness the Greek imperatives for God to notice and let the divine hand be upon not only the Vine but also upon the son of man, now brought into close association with God's people.

Furthermore, the son of man's role in dominating the earth may have been frustrated by those mysterious enemies, but it has never been abrogated, according to Psalm 8. And it must be remembered that, although Daniel's vision takes place in the heavens, that sky-screen on which his images are projected, it depicts struggles occurring on earth—according to the three interpretations of the initial dream in vv. 17–27—rather like what used to take place in a war room. Raised high above its observers, the vertical display conveyed by symbols depicts realities happening on the ground.[35] Psalm 79 reinforces this, enabling one to pray that God's rule will be manifested on earth as it is in apocalyptic heaven: "May that future come soon: in our time, with our people, on our land." And Daniel 7 will serve as an eschatological and universal antiphon to this plea.

The Identity of the Enemy, the Nature of the Struggle—and Victory
Because of the increased "historical" emphasis that the superscription of v. 1 adds to the text of Psalm 79, some readers might be tempted to see their struggle and victory primarily (if not exclusively) in local, earthly, ethnic, and human categories (vv. 2–3, in both original and translation).[36] The extremes of such an orientation could lead to chauvinism, tribalism, and exclusivism. But Daniel 7 can serve to expand this vision by portraying their experiences upon a vast global and cosmic canvass, with ultimate and universal issues at stake. Behind the scenes, superhuman forces are at

34. "Anatevka" [Ukraine] from "Fiddler on the Roof."

35. The image is George B. Caird's, but in a different context: *The Revelation of St. John the Divine* (London: A & C Black, 1980) 154–56.

36. Albert Pietersma, "Exegesis and Liturgy in the Superscriptions of the Greek Psalter," in *X Congress of the International Organization for Septuagint and Cognate Studies, Oslo 1998* (ed. B. A. Taylor; Atlanta: Society of Biblical Literature, 2001) 122–24.

work: their activity primordial in origin, apocalyptic in expression, and eschatological in consequence.

However, for readers of Daniel 7 who may be in danger of losing their moorings in the particulars of place, time, and people—being tempted by world-withdrawal and denial of responsibility—then Psalm 79 can serve to ground them in the here and now. Despite these differences, both speak in political terms, but they belong to politics of a different kind.[37] Each rejects conventional wisdom and notions of power. The great reversal to come is not derivative of human genius or striving. God will bestow the kingdom, authority, and glory upon a frail, vulnerable human and the people whom he symbolizes or represents—identity not being the primary issue, but the condition in which he and they find themselves. Psalm 8 bears witness to the other frail agents of the enemy's defeat: children, from whom praise pours forth. The question that remains is, "How then should God's people live?"[38]

The Son of Man: Identity and Role

Described as coming on the clouds of heaven, the danielic son of man might give the impression that his feet can never make contact with the ground, with the so-called "real world." Is he still flesh of our flesh and bone of our bone? Is there any way that this transcendent one can be touched with our immanent sorrows? P967 exacerbates the problem by appearing to iden-tify his "nature" with that of an ancient of days—thus making him even more remote—or seem that way.[39] However, as we saw, he is not responsible for his own elevation/endowment; and the modifications to vv. 8 and 27 strengthen the connection with God's holy people.

Furthermore, it is not the case that son of man as portrayed in Psalm 79 is without similar complications. He, too, is more closely linked with the vine; but his strengthening twice has been said to be for God's self. The prayer for God's hand to establish and be on this son of man carries with it, by implication, the hope that Israel's Lord will exercise this special status in the direction of his kith and kin: for his people—our people. If the future

---

37. I understand politics to be a strategy for distributing power among humans living in community ("the polis").

38. A separate study of "son of man ethics" is in order, about which I have made sug-gestions in n. 43.

39. One must be alert to the dangers of imposing later systematic/dogmatic categories upon this ancient text.

glorification of that son of man and his saints is too lofty and distant, then Psalm 79 links him and them to the here and near. Or, whenever the son of man figure is idealized in the direction of a universal humanity (as in Psalm 8), Psalm 79 roots him in the particulars of people and place, of race and gene pool.[40] There is no other lens by which to gaze into the future of what will be than through the concavity and convexity experienced in the bumbledom and boredom of the ordinary. Nevertheless, should the frail one be construed as merely our elder brother, then Daniel 7 invites the reader to join the Sage's contemplation, for "brighter visions beam afar."

Moreover, a glimpse of both present and future is also evident in the past of Psalm 8. That son of man's original status and role inform the already and not yet. Of him it is said (according to the LXX) that he was "diminished"—from where? The nature of that original status is not spelled out. But it suggests an earlier "equality," perhaps akin to his "likeness" with that ancient of days, according to p967. Is there something in the divine that inclines toward humanity—and frail humanity, at that?

A Brief Postscript

Might reflection on these three texts by the Evangelists who wrote in Greek, and whose citations largely reflect the LXX, have contributed to the three kinds of the Son of Man sayings in the Gospels: present authority; suffering,

---

40. Some interpreters of MT 80 have proposed that the Psalmist had a certain king in mind who embodied the paradigm of the empowered son of man: Hoshea (Otto Eissfeldt, "Psalm 80," in *Geschichte und Altes Testament* [ed. W. F. Albright et al.; Tübingen: Mohr, 1953] 65–78; and "Psalm 80 und Psalm 89," *Die Welt des Orients* 3 [1965] 27–31), Josiah (Erich Zenger, *A Commentary on Psalms 51–100* [Minneapolis: Fortress, 2005] 316), and Zerubbabel (as "some think," says Adam Clarke, *The Holy Bible Containing the Old and New Testaments with a Commentary and Critical Notes*, volume 3 [New York: Abingdon-Cokesbury, n. d. but 18th and early 19th c.] 476). I suggest that, by doubling references to son of man's experiences (implied weakness, explicit strengthening), the translator might have wanted the reader to recall Hezekiah. My hunch (on which nothing in the argument rides) is based upon ways by which the LXX of 4 Kgdms 19–20, 2 Chr 29–32, and Isa 36–38 portray the king as having twice been weakened and recovered: (1) politically and militarily in connection with the Assyrian attack-rebuttal and (2) by a fatal illness later cured. In a separate connection, Pietersma, "Exegesis and Liturgy," 124 observes that the phrase "you that sit on the Cherubim/n" at Ps 79 [=MT 80]:2 has "a verbatim parallel in Hezekiah's prayer in 2Kgs [4 Kgdms]19:15 and Isa 37:16, and the prayer for deliverance in 79(80):4 is paralleled by 2Kgs [4 Kgdms]19:19 and Isa 37:20."

death, and resurrection; and glorious parousia?[41] (I make these distinctions as a literary-theological frame of reference rather than as results of an historical reconstruction.) As in the passages considered, the Son of Man in the Gospels is the supremely narrative category, covering every aspect of Jesus' career. All other terms, "Christ," "Lord," and "Son of God" are exclusively confessional expressions, which he avoids, suppresses, or reinterprets until the resurrection of the Son of Man (see especially Mark 9:9). They are one-sided, addressing only his status and identity. Only with the Son of Man designation does one get a sense of Jesus' role or assignment: that which he is doing or will do.[42] Could an analogous, triangular conversation provide a means by which to reflect theologically upon those three sets of sayings in a similar manner as well? We could then claim to have woven one thread in the tapestry of a theocentric Christology of the entire Greek Bible.[43]

41. Law, *When God Spoke Greek*, 99–104. My late, beloved doctoral supervisor, the Rev. Professor C. F. D. Moule, never tired of reminding all who would listen that "son of man" becomes articular in the singular for the first time in the Gospels, where it functions as a mild demonstrative pronoun. In effect, Jesus is reported to say, "If you want to know what *this* son of man ['frail human'?] is about, refer to *that* son of man ['frail human'?] in Daniel 7." I would extend the range of the article to include Psalms 8 and 79. For a technical discussion of the grammar, see C. D. Moule, *An Idiom-Book of New Testament Greek* (2nd edition; Cambridge: Cambridge University Press, 1963) 111. His latest, published statement of the position appears in *The Origin* [sic] *of Christology* (Cambridge: Cambridge University Press, 1977) 13.

42. Eugene E. Lemcio, *The Past of Jesus in the Gospels* (Cambridge: Cambridge University Press, 1991) 36–39.

43. I put it this way because in all recitals of the Magnalia Dei of Scripture, God is the beginning and end of the story. For an attempt to argue this formally, see my "*Kerygmatic Centrality and Unity in the First Testament?*" 357–73 in *The Quest for Context and Meaning: Studies in Biblical Intertextuality in Honor of James A. Sanders* (ed. C. Evans and S. Talmon; Leiden: Brill, 1997) and "The Unifying Kerygma of the New Testament" 115–31 and 158–62 in *The Past of Jesus*. Then there is the matter of what might be called "son of man ethics." The exaltation of the lowly and vulnerable fits so much of what one finds in the teaching and experience of Jesus as reflected in accounts of his origins, the Sermon on the Mount/Plain, his associations with the marginalized of society, and with the criteria by which the Son of Man will conduct the Great Assize.

Canonical Complexities of Biblical Balaams

Sara M. Koenig

I am now Rob Wall's colleague, but I first met him as a college student in his "Introduction to the New Testament" class. As his student, I was inaugurated into the joys and intricacies of biblical studies; as his colleague, I have benefited from Rob's generous support and encouragement. One of Rob's many adages is that our teaching ought to fuel our scholarship, so it is fitting that my interest in Balaam came from the classroom. A student was working on a term-long project on Balaam, and for the first part of the project, she wrote a paper on Numbers 22–24. She concluded that Balaam was a faithful servant of God, an example of how God speaks even through foreigners and those outside of Israel. Admittedly, he's violent and angry toward his poor loyal donkey, but God uses Balaam as an agent of blessing, and Balaam himself says that he will only say and do what God tells him. But then, for the second paper—in which students were asked to explore intertextuality of their chosen text as well as Jewish interpretations in the Midrash and Talmud—she changed her conclusion, writing, "Now I know that Balaam was wicked, only agreeing to go because he was greedy, and causing the Israelites to fall into sin and worship of idols." When reading only Numbers 22–24, her overall assessment of Balaam was fairly positive. After reading other biblical texts and interpretations, which bore different witness to Balaam, she changed her description. Instead of trying to hold the various pictures of Balaam together, she assumed that one was right and the other wrong, and she needed to choose which was which.

My twenty-something college student's response is both understandable and illustrative of the challenges that come with reading disparate biblical material. Any reader of confusing, contradictory, troubling or terrorizing[1]

---

1. Texts can terrorize in terms of what they are, as in those texts Phyllis Trible identifies as "texts of terror" in her book with the same name: *Texts of Terror: Literary-Feminist*

texts will seek out answers; my student sought a single right answer about
Balaam and assumed that it could be found. "Either-or" assumptions may
be more common for someone who is young and working at an introductory level with the text, but more sophisticated readers are not immune.
Complexity and contradictions are hard; simplicity, symmetry, and harmony are preferred. What makes Balaam such an interesting test case is that
he is not only presented in varying ways throughout the canon, but even
within the two chapters in Numbers 22–24, diverse sources and traditions
about Balaam are evident.[2] That is, it may be less surprising to find Balaam
portrayed in multifaceted ways in the Hebrew Bible and the Greek New
Testament, but competing portraits of Balaam are seen within the pericope
where he first appears. Balaam is also an interesting case because, as he is a
relatively minor character in the larger biblical metanarrative, there is less at
stake theologically in how he is interpreted. On the other hand, our ability
to allow for variegations in Balaam's character may be symptomatic of our
ability to allow for complexity and nuance when reading the entire biblical
canon. We can tinker around with Balaam without needing to take apart
the entire theological engine, but experimenting with Balaam may help us
be more comfortable working on other biblical texts.

Readings of Biblical Narratives (Minneapolis: Fortress, 1984). They also can terrorize in terms
of what they do, or more precisely, how they have been used, as certain biblical texts are
used to terrorize people. For example, the admonition in 1 Tim 2:12 against women teaching or exercising authority has been used to prohibit women from pursuing leadership in
ministry or churches, and Noah's curse of Canaan in Gen 9:25 was used to justify slavery.
For a conversation on what texts do, and those who do things with them, see Nyasha Junior's
response to Brennan Breed's article, "What Can Texts Do? A Proposal for Biblical Studies"
titled "Re/Use of Texts" in http://www.atthispoint.net/editor-notes/reuse-of-texts/265/. Breed
draws on the theory of French philosopher Gilles Deleuze to argue that biblical studies ought
to focus less on what a text *is* and more on what a text does. Junior, on the other hand, points
out that texts themselves do not *do* anything; rather, it is people who do things with texts.

2. See, for example, Julius Wellhausen, *Die Composition des Hexateuchs und der histo-
rischen Bücher des Alten Testaments* (3rd edition; Berlin: Goschen'sche, 1899) 109–16; 347–52;
Sigmund Mowinckel, "Die Ursprung der Bileamsage," *Zeitschrift für die alttestamentliche
Wissenschaft* 48 (1930) 233–71; Otto Eissfeldt, "Die Komposition der Bileam-Erzahlung,"
Zeitschrift für die alttestamentliche Wissenschaft 57 (1939) 212–44; William F. Albright,
"The Oracles of Balaam," *Journal of Biblical Literature* 63 (1944) 207–33; Walter Gross, *Bileam:
Literar- und Formkritische Untersuchung der Prosa in Numbers 22–24* (München: Kisel Verlag,
1974); Hedwige Roiullard, *La Pericope de Balaam* (Paris: J. Gabalda, 1985).

This paper will review options for reading Balaam and discuss how they are illustrative of hermeneutical strategies for dealing with the complications of canonical readings. The options are in no way exhaustive, but might provide a helpful taxonomy for teaching, whether in the academy or in the church.

Majority Rules

A first option is to read through all the biblical texts and add up which portray Balaam positively and which portray him negatively, deciding that the majority rules. To choose this option would be to conclude that Balaam is bad, for there are more texts about Balaam that are negative than positive. The positive texts about Balaam include Numbers 22, where Balaam is the foreigner who will only do and say what the God of Israel will tell and allow, who refers to that god using the personal language of "the Lord my God" (v. 18). In Numbers 23–24, Balaam's words about Israel are blessings and not curses, much to the frustration of Balak, king of Moab, who hired Balaam to curse Israel. Balaam's words glorify Israel, even prophesying future victories and majesty; any words of condemnation are reserved for those nations who are traditionally enemies of Israel (Num 24:17–24). In Micah 6:5, Balaam is lifted up as an example of the saving acts of the Lord. Thus, Balaam is presented positively in three chapters in Numbers and one reference from the prophets. But Numbers 22 also presents Balaam negatively: one whose journey angers God, who beats his donkey, and who, as a seer, is blind to the angel of the Lord standing before him with an unsheathed sword. In Numbers 31:13–15, Moses explains that it was Balaam who instigated the orgy between the Israelite men and the Moabite and Midianite women at Baal Peor in Numbers 25. In Deuteronomy 23:5, Balaam is implied to have wanted to curse Israel; the verse explains that God would not listen to Balaam and instead turned the curse into a blessing (see also Josh 24:9–10 and Neh 13:2). The bad Balaam gets identified in Joshua 13:22 as "the diviner" (הקוסם), a title Baruch A. Levine describes as "a decidedly negative appellation."[3]

---

3. Baruch Levine explains that the process of Balaam's denigration is reflected in this identification in Josh 13:22; see his *Numbers 21–36* (New York: Doubleday, 2000) 454.

The New Testament witnesses to Balaam are univocally negative. In 2 Peter 2:15 he is one who "loved the wages of doing wrong." In Jude 1:11, Balaam is included with Cain and Korah as examples of woe, and those who "abandon themselves to Balaam's error for the sake of gain" are examples of the ungodly. In Revelation 2:14, the church at Pergamum is warned that "you have some there who hold to the teaching of Balaam, who taught Balak to put a stumbling block before the people of Israel, so that they would eat food sacrificed to idols and practice fornication." Seven references to Balaam, therefore, are negative, so in strictly numerical terms, the interpretation of Balaam as negative would "win."

An obvious problem with this approach is inherent in any "democratic" method where the majority rules: the counterevidence—in this situation, the evidence in favor of a positive Balaam—is ignored or "loses." In Barbara Kingsolver's novel *The Poisonwood Bible*, the Congolese leader in the town points out that when there is an election, those who voted against the majority become disenfranchised, and their opinions and perspectives are discounted. The "undemocratic" method used by the tribe in the past was to seek consensus, which certainly takes longer, but allows for the people in this community to eventually come to a common agreement.[4] Even though there is numerically more biblical evidence that would lead someone to conclude Balaam is negative, the option of majority rules might mean that the counterevidence is ignored or suppressed.

It is important to clarify one's criteria for "negative" and "positive," for those terms can be used to describe Balaam's words, actions, ethics, morals, or religious life. The biblical texts refer to Balaam's vices as his blindness, his greed, his desire to curse Israel, his role in instigating orgies, and his pagan practices. Balaam's virtues include his submission to the God of Israel, his

---

4. The tribal leader says, "Our way was to share a fire until it burned down, *ayi*? To speak to each other until every person was satisfied. . . . Now the *Beelezi* tell us the vote of a young, careless man counts the same as the vote of an elder. . . . White men tell us: *Vote, bantu!* They tell us: You do not all have to agree, *ce n'est past necessaire!* If two men vote yes and one says no, the matter is finished. *Á bu*, even a child can see how that will end. It takes three stones in the fire to hold up the pot. Take one away, leave the other two, and what? The pot will spill into the fire" (Barbara Kingsolver, *The Poisonwood Bible* [New York: Harper-Perennial, 1999] 333). After he explains this to the missionary, the people in the village take a vote about whether or not they want to believe in Jesus, and Jesus loses the popular vote.

apparent personal relationship with that deity, and his many words that bless and even glorify Israel. But certainly, what counts as positive or negative for a given interpreter is not universally agreed upon.

Giving More Weight to Certain Texts than Others

A second option, which is in some ways a variation on the first, is to weigh certain texts as more authoritative than others. One could decide that the texts that come first in the biblical canon are primary and foundational, that the picture of Balaam in Numbers 22–24 (which is admittedly complex but still mostly positive) is the lens for reading other, later texts about Balaam. Or, one could choose to give more weight to latter texts. This choice could come from more ideological reasons, such as those who understand the New Testament to be more authoritative than the Old Testament. As mentioned above, the New Testament portrayal of Balaam is wholly negative, so one who chooses this hermeneutical option would understandably read Balaam negatively. A choice to place more emphasis on latter texts could also be inspired by a narrative approach that understands the literary technique of delayed information. When Balaam is introduced in Numbers 22–24, when he is first hired to curse Israel but blesses them, he is drawn in sparse lines, but his motives are shaded in later in the text, such as when he is described as greedy.[5]

---

5. Robert Alter discusses the intentional and purposeful reticence of the biblical narrator by explaining, "the ancient Hebrew narrator displays his omniscience with a drastic selectivity. . . . We are compelled to get at character and motive . . . through a process of inference from fragmentary data, often with crucial pieces of narrative exposition strategically withheld, and this leads to multiple or sometimes even wavering perspectives on the characters" (*The Art of Biblical Narrative* [New York: Basic Books, 1981] 126). Not only does Alter assume the biblical narrator to be omniscient but also reliable and trustworthy. G. Brooke Lester makes the case that the narrative in the book of Daniel withholds information about the titular character, who is presented in Daniel 1–6 as bold and faithful. In Dan 7, however, the text uses the literary device of *analepsis*—sometimes referred to as "flashback" or "retrospection"—to reveal that during the reign of Belshazzar, prior to the actions in chapters 5–6, Daniel had been frightened and confused by his own visions. See *Daniel Evokes Isaiah: Allusive Characterization of Foreign Rule in the Hebrew-Aramaic Book of Daniel* (London: Bloomsbury T & T Clark, 2015) 11–12. There are countless examples of delayed information

This option of weighting certain texts more than others is not limited to just those texts which come "first" or "last." In fact, many readers of Balaam's story have found the hermeneutical key to unlocking the mystery of his character in Moses' words in Numbers 31 that depict Balaam as the one responsible for the Israelite apostasy at Baal Peor that occurs in Numbers 25 when the Israelite men have sex with the Midianite women and worship their god. For example, Christopher Rowland writes that the reference to Balaam in Revelation 2:14 is drawing not on Numbers 22–24, but on Numbers 31.[6] Second, in some midrashim, Balaam is associated with other stereotypical enemies of Israel because of his connection with Numbers 25. In *Midrash Rabbah Numbers*, Balaam is included with Doeg, Ahithophel, and Gehazi as those who "have no share in the world to come."[7] In the *Midrash Rabbah of Numbers*, R. Abba b. Kahana groups Balaam with two other people, Cain and Hezekiah, as "the three persons whom the Holy One, blessed be He, examined and found to be a vessel full of urine."[8]

Josephus also links the texts of Numbers 25 and 31 in the *Jewish Antiquites* to explain Balaam's role in the apostasy at Baal Peor. Josephus imagines a conversation between Balaam and the Midianites after Balaam was unable to curse the Israelites. As Balaam is being sent away, he tells Balak and the Midianites that they couldn't defeat Israel because God's providence and presence is so great, but the way to defeat them is through tools of seduction and apostasy. Josephus' Balaam admits that even this victory will not

in contemporary literature, including the Harry Potter series, which does not reveal details about Snape's character and motivation until the final book, *The Deathly Hallows*.

6. Rowland makes this comment very briefly, succinctly writing in parentheses that Rev 2:14–17 is "a reference to Num 31:16; 25:1–2; compare with 2 Pet 2:15, Jude 11" (Christopher Rowland, "Revelation" in *The New Interpreters Bible Commentary* [vol. 21; Nashville: Abingdon, 1998] 578). Rowland has no discussion about how others might have seen this text as a reference to the Balaam in Numbers 22–24.

7. *Midrash Rabbah Numbers*, 3rd ed. (trans. Judah Slotki; London: Soncino, 1983) 556–57. As is typical for midrash, another perspective is included, that of "those who expound the Scriptures metaphorically." Yet, even those metaphoric expounders say that everyone has a share in the "World to Come" except Balaam. So, even amidst the diverse perspectives, there is apparent agreement that Balaam will not have a share in the "World to Come."

8. *Midrash Rabbah Numbers*, 791. The footnote explains that this can be understood as "a despicable person."

be ultimate because the Israelites flourish after they are brought low, so his specific counsel is as follows:

> So that if you have a mind to gain a victory over them for a short space of time, you will obtain it by following my directions. Do you therefore set out the comeliness of such of your daughters as are most eminent for beauty, and proper to force and conquer the modesty of those that behold them; and these decked and trimmed to the highest degree you are able. Then do you send them to be near the Israelites' camp; and give them in charge, that when the young men of the Hebrews desire their company, they allow it them. And when they see they are enamoured of them, let them take their leaves; and if they entreat them to stay, let them not give their consent, till they have persuaded them to leave off their obedience to their own laws, and the worship of that God who established them; and to worship the Gods of the Midianites and Moabites: for by this means God will be angry at them.[9]

By giving Balaam this speech, Josephus fills in the gap between Numbers 24—when Balaam concludes his oracles and leaves—and Numbers 25—when the Midianite women seduce the Israelite men. Josephus' conclusion to his section on Balaam explains that Balaam's advice to the Midianite leaders was the reason why Moses waged war against the Midianites in Numbers 31.[10]

Instead of emphasizing Numbers 31, other readers understand Deuteronomy 23 as key when Moses explains that Balaam wanted to curse Israel but God turned the curse into a blessing. David Frankel discusses how the Deuteronomic portrayal of Balaam in Deuteronomy 23:5 has subsequent influence on Joshua 24:9–10. The MT and LXX of Joshua 24:9 are essentially the same, "Balak son of Zippor, king of Moab, arose and he fought against Israel, and he sent and he called for Balaam son of Beor to curse you," but

---

9. Josephus, *Ant.* 4.6. http://penelope.uchicago.edu/josephus/ant-4.html.

10. I will discuss Josephus' conclusion in the section on the fifth hermeneutical option, where two or more interpretations of Balaam are allowed. Josephus is an example of how an interpreter can use more than one of these hermenutical strategies for Balaam, and they are not mutually exclusive.

they diverge in Joshua 24:10. The MT of Joshua 24:10 reads, "[B]ut I was not willing to listen to Balaam; he greatly blessed you, and I saved you from his hand" while the LXX reads, "But the Lord your God did not want to destroy you; and he greatly blessed us and rescued us out of their hands." Frankel argues, "The phrase 'their hands' implies that both Balak and Balaam were equally intent on destroying Israel. . . . God saved Israel from Balaam by blessing them, and thus neutralizing the curse."[11] Frankel therefore asserts that the LXX of Joshua 24:9–10 is Deuteronomic, specifically reflecting the tradition of Deuteronomy 23:5–6 that Balaam actually cursed Israel. This Deuteronomic portrayal of Balaam, Frankel suggests, is indicative that there were two independent traditions, one in which Balaam cursed Israel and the other according to which he blessed Israel. Frankel also suggests that the narrative about Balaam in Numbers may have been written as a polemic against the tradition reflected in Deuteronomy 23:5.[12]

Obviously, Numbers 31:13–15 and Deuteronomy 23:5 are different texts, but what they have in common is Moses. Thus, another hermeneutical choice is to give more weight to certain characters than others. Such a choice would be related to the choice to give more weight to certain texts than others. Specifically, Moses may be seen as more trustworthy than Balaam because Moses is the central human character in the Pentateuch. As such, Moses is the star witness in the case against Balaam, and his words provide testimony against Balaam that is hard to refute.[13]

11. David Frankel, "The Deuteronomic Portrayal of Balaam," *Vetus Testamentum* 46 (1996) 34.

12. Frankel, "The Deuteronomic Portrayal of Balaam" 41–42.

13. A similar move is made by those who prioritize Jesus over other NT characters, such as Paul. The argument would be that Jesus' treatment of women as disciples is more authoritative than the writings about women in 1 Tim 2:12 because Jesus is more significant than Paul. There is considerable debate as to whether or not Paul wrote the Timothy letters, but the point still stands. M. Margoliot argued that the purpose of the narrative about Balaam in Numbers is to emphasize Moses' role as Israel's true prophet by depicting Balaam as a false prophet and an "anti-Moses." See Margoliot, "The Connection of the Balaam Narrative with the Pentateuch," *Proceedings of the Sixth World Congress of Jewish Studies* (ed. A. Shinan; Jerusalem: World Union of Jewish Studies, 1977) 285. In contrast to those who might elevate Moses, Adriane Leveen is critical of Moses, asserting that Moses' prophetic authority is diminished by "the non-Israelite seer Balaam whose poetry could be considered a subtle rebuke of Moses' angry (and tired) words aimed at the children of Israel. . . . Balaam's

Read Counter to the Plain Sense of the Text

A third option for interpreting Balaam is to read against the plain sense of the text in Numbers 22–24. In 1885, R. P. Stebbins provided a salient example of how much complex hermeneutical footwork is required to sustain this way of reading. Stebbins explains that the story of Balaam from Numbers 22–24 "has furnished an abundance of merriment to scoffers and bushels of hard nuts for commentators of the old school."[14] Stebbins asserts that "no passage of equal length so fully illustrates the vagaries in which commentators indulge, as this one," describing those vagaries as resulting in "crude, wild and incredible interpretations which have been given of this story by both learned and ignorant men in all the centuries."[15] Rather than participating in such manner of biblical study, he encourages, "Let us then look at this marvelous story in the light of common sense, which is none other than the light of sound criticism."[16] Similar to those who choose option two described above, Stebbins lifts up Numbers 31:16 and concludes that Balaam was "a thoroughly bad, and supremely cunning man," also asserting, "That Balaam was a wicked man does not admit of question, and that he was as shrewd and cunning as he was wicked is equally clear. He understood his business and how to make it profitable."[17] Stebbins then uses his conclusions about Balaam's treacherous character to argue that because Balaam is so wicked, cunning and untrustworthy, there was no encounter with an angel, nor any conversation with his donkey. In Stebbins' words,

> There is not a shadow of proof that this cunning soothsayer ever had a thought from the very first of cursing Israel. Every observing man knew that these panic stricken nations were doomed to fall before these

---

profoundly positive vision of Israel and its future is so necessary at that juncture in the narrative because of its utter absence in the camp of Israel and in Moses' view of his people" (Adriane Leveen, *Memory and Tradition in the Book of Numbers* [Cambridge: Cambridge University Press, 2008] 54–55).

14. R. P. Stebbins, "The Story of Balaam," *The Old Testament Student* 4 (1885) 385.

15. Ibid.

16. Ibid.

17. Ibid., 386.

122 Sara M. Koenig

triumphant hosts. Whatever else Balaam may have been, he was no fool. He told his own story as he pleased; he had no witnesses. He made out the best case he could to excuse his blessing instead of cursing. That he improved the soothsayer's privilege of unlimited lying when he told the absurd story of talking with his ass, and seeing an angel, and communing with the higher powers in the night, and when he went away alone from the altars, is no doubt true.[18]

Stebbins' "sound criticism" and "common sense" require the reader to conclude that what the text says happened in Numbers 22 with the angel and Balaam's donkey did not happen. Certainly, "common sense" in Stebbins' era would be incredulous about an animal's ability to speak. Stebbins is not forthcoming about such an assumption, but he is forthcoming about two other assumptions. First, he assumes that to include Balaam among the prophets will "degrade prophecy . . . degrade the mission of subsequent prophets,"[19] and second, Stebbins believes that to find any sort of messianic prophecy in Balaam's words is to "bring reproach upon the truth and cause of Christ."[20] These strong assertions do not have any further explanation but are the conclusion of Stebbins' very self-confident work.

If Stebbins is an exemplar of a scholar with confidence in his own interpretations, his choice to read Balaam as untrustworthy is not unique. The Midrash has several similar readings. For example, in *Midrash Rabbah of Numbers* it reads,

When Balak sent to [Balaam], and the Holy One, blessed be He, asked him, "*What men are these with thee?*" he should have replied: "Sovereign of the Universe! Everything is manifest to Thee, and there is nothing hidden from Thee; dost Thou then inquire of me?" Instead, he said to Him: "*Balak the son of Zippor, king of Moab, hath sent unto me.*" Said the Holy One, blessed be He: "Since you speak in this way, *Thou shalt not curse the people* (Num 22:23). Vilest of sinners!" said the Holy One, blessed be He. "It is written of Israel, *Surely, he that toucheth you toucheth the apple of his*

18. Ibid., 394.
19. Ibid., 395.
20. Ibid.

eye (Zech 11:12)! And you are going to injure them and to curse them, are you? Let your eye fall out!" Thus it says [of Balaam], *The man whose eye is closed*[21] (Num 24:3). This serves to confirm the text, "*He that toucheth you toucheth the apple of his eye.*"[22]

A similar filling in the gaps is done with Numbers 22:18, when Balaam tells the courtiers that even if Balak were to give him all his gold and silver, Balaam would not go with Balak. Read straightforwardly, it would seem that Balaam is refusing Balak. The Midrash, however, uses this verse to infer that Balaam possessed an evil eye, a haughty spirit, and a greedy soul. In particular, the greedy soul is explained as follows:

> Because it is written, "*If Balak would give me his house full of silver and gold.*" "If," he told them, "Balak desired to hire for himself armies to fight against them, he would be doubt as to whether they would be victorious or whether they would fall. Is it not worth his while that he should give me all that wealth and be sure of victory?" Thus you learn that he actually asked for this.[23]

Midrashic inferences about the bad Balaam are also found in a comment on Numbers 23:10, which compares Balaam unfavorably to Moses.[24] The comparison hinges on the simile for Israel's greatness, "as the stars of the sky" and "as the dust of the earth." *Midrash Rabbah Numbers* explains that while Moses, who loved Israel, compared them with the stars in Deuteronomy

21. This reading of Num 24:3 rests on reading the letter as a *sin*, "eye is closed," but if it is a *shin*, it would be translated as "eye is opened." Rashi explains the root as *shin-taw-mem* (שתם) "to open, make an opening," which is also attested in Rabbinic Hebrew and Aramaic, referring to opening a hole in a barrel, jug, or other vessel in order to extract wine for tasting or inspection. See Levine, *Numbers*, 192.

22. *Midrash Rabbah Numbers*, 792.

23. Ibid., 796. The "evil eye" is taken from Num 24:2, which explains that Balaam lifted up his eyes and saw Israel dwelling by tribes, but the "haughty spirit" comes from Num 22:13 when Balaam says "the Lord refuses to let me go."

24. Moses does not appear—at all—in the texts of Numbers 22–24, and in fact, Moses and Balaam are never in the same scenes together. The closest they appear to one another is in Numbers 31 when Moses commands the Israelites to kill the Midianites, and they also kill Balaam. As was discussed in footnote 13, Margoliot is an example of a contemporary scholar who, like the Midrash, receives Moses with approval and Balaam disapprovingly.

1:10, Balaam, who hated them, compared them to dust; as it is said, "*Who hath counted the dust of Jacob?*"[25]

Both Stebbins and the rabbis approach the texts of Numbers 22–24 with a hermeneutic of suspicion regarding Balaam's character, but that suspicion gets directed toward different places. Stebbins believes that the encounter between Balaam, his donkey, and the angel in Numbers 22 never happened; he effectively seems to conflate Balaam with the narrator of the text. In the same volume in which Stebbins' article was first published, the editorial notes explain,

> Our readers will be interested in the attempt of Dr. Stebbins to interpret the narrative of Balaam from a naturalistic standpoint. . . . The question arises, however, whether Dr. Stebbins has not gone too far. . . . It is well, we believe, to emphasize the human element in Scripture; this element has been, and is, lost sight of by too many interpreters. And in just so far as it is lost sight of, there is a failure to grasp the true force and meaning of the Sacred narrative. But while giving due consideration to this element, we must not forget the other, the divine element. Not to appreciate this is attended with many serious consequences.[26]

Stebbins' lack of appreciation of a divine element in the story of Balaam is a stark contrast with the rabbis. In James Kugel's words, Midrash assumes that the biblical text is "divinely sanctioned," meaning that it is of divine provenance or is divinely inspired.[27]

Using Extrabiblical Sources to Understand the Bible

A fourth option for interpreting Balaam would be to look outside the biblical text itself for extrabiblical sources to help explain his character. The fragmentary texts found at Deir ʿAlla refer to a divine seer named "Balaam son of Beor" (*blʿm brbʿr*) who receives visions from the gods in the night

---

25. *Midrash Rabbah Numbers*, 55.

26. *The Old Testament Student* 4 (1885) 425.

27. James Kugel, *The Bible As it Was* (Cambridge, MA: Belknap, 1999) 18–22.

and an utterance from El.[28] The identification with the biblical Balaam is not certain, but there are obvious connections with the name, as well as communications with the gods at night.[29] These Deir ʿAlla texts depict an authoritative visionary who sees a divine vision and communicates it to his people and community leaders. He seems to be a compassionate person, weeping at the news of destruction[30] and interceding for the people. The Deir ʿAlla texts do not mention Israel's God YHWH, but refer to the general ANE god El. Balaam uses that divine epithet in Numbers 23:8, 22, 23 and Numbers 24:4, 8, 16 and 23.[31]

If the Deir ʿAlla account answers questions about Balaam's character, it raises other questions: Is this "proof" of the historical veracity of the biblical account? Is the authority of the biblical text eroded if a section,

---

28. Christopher B. Hays notes that the word used for "utterance" or "oracle" is equivalent with the Hebrew term *maśśāʾ* used for oracles against the nations in Isa 13:1, 14:28, 15:1, and elsewhere. See Christopher B. Hays, *Hidden Riches: A Sourcebook for the Comparative Study of the Hebrew Bible and Ancient Near East* (Louisville: Westminster John Knox, 2014) 261. The Deir ʿAlla texts get referred to as inscriptions, but they were texts pieced together from fragments of plaster that had fallen to the floor from inner walls of a building; written in ink on plaster with a nib, displayed on the walls. These were discovered in 1967 during a Dutch-led expedition at Tell Deir ʿAlla, a site east of the Jordan, not far from the northern bank of the Yabbok/Zerqa river. The reassembly process exacerbated the problems with the physical condition of the text. See Levine, "The Deir ʿAlla Plaster Inscriptions (2.27)" in *The Context of Scripture*, volume 2 (ed. William W. Hallo and K. Lawson Younger, Jr.; Leiden: Brill, 2000) 141.

29. Other connections include visions of destruction for the nations and animal imagery in the vision. Line 14 of the Deir ʿAlla texts refer to a long list of birds, many of which are included in the category of forbidden fowl in Leviticus 11 and Deuteronomy 14. See Levine, "The Deir ʿAlla Plaster Inscriptions (2.27)" 143. In Balaam's oracles, he compares God to the "horns of the wild ox" (Num 23:22; 24:8), and Israel to the lion and lioness (Num 23:24; 24:9).

30. Manfred Weippert, however, suggests that weeping is a common motif in Ugaritic and Israelite literature, often leading someone to ask the cause of the weeping. For example, when King Kurit wept, El asked him why (Krt A I 26–42), and the angel of the Lord asks Hagar why she is weeping in Gen 21:16 and following ("The Balaam Text from Deir ʿAllā and the Study of the Old Testament" in *The Balaam Text from Deir ʿAllā Re-evaluated: Proceedings of the International Symposium Held at Leiden 21–24 August 1989* [ed. J. Hoftijzer and G. Van Der Kooij; Leiden: Brill, 1991] 168–69).

31. Num 22–24 also uses the divine epithets YHWH and Elohim. In the Deir ʿAlla texts, the "Shadday gods" are also mentioned in lines 12 and 14, but they are planning punishment and destruction.

or character, is borrowed from literature from the surrounding geographical regions? One who chooses this hermeneutical option enters into the larger questions of reception history of texts with their attending possibilities and problems, especially the hermeneutical cycle that emerges when someone hears/sees/reads a reception, and then reads that back into the text.[32]

Allow for Contradictory Interpretations

A fifth hermeneutical option for Balaam is to allow for two—or more— contradictory or even competing interpretations of him. Midrash is especially amenable to this, as it does not insist on a single voice presenting a systematic, coherent interpretation; instead, it is thoroughly dialogic in nature. This dialogue has been collected and codified in the Talmud and volumes of midrashim, and the juxtaposition of one rabbi's interpretation with another's can often contradict.[33] For example, *Midrash Rabbah Numbers,* which contains the aforementioned interpretation of Numbers 23:10, also includes the following interpretation of that same verse: "The blessing of Jacob that he should be like the dust of the earth was fulfilled in the days of Balaam; for so it is written, *Who hath counted the dust of Jacob?*"[34] Not

---

32. B. F. Simpson's rejoinder to Stebbins in 1885 included the following comment, "It is well always to make the connected history a matter of careful study. But it is necessary, nevertheless, to bear in mind that our knowledge of this environing history is of necessity incomplete, and that in most cases we are almost solely dependent on the statements of Scripture for what we do know of it. It will scarcely be logical, in such cases, to depend on the Scripture statement for our knowledge of the historical surrounding, and then use our knowledge of such surroundings as a test of the veracity of Scripture" (*The Old Testament Student* 5 [1885] 126).

33. Gerald Bruns, however, explains that there is no conflict of authority in a conflict of interpretations, because it is the whole dialogue that is authoritative, not just the isolated interpretations that emerge from it. "Midrashic interpretation is multiform and extravagant but also holistic as a social practice; no one interpretation stands by itself, because no one rabbi speaks as a solitary reader—no one rabbi speaks purely and simply in his own name and on his own private authority. . . . This means that there is neither occasion nor cause to determine the authority or correctness of this or that isolated interpretation. Interpretations are not logical propositions concerning which we have to decide for and against, true or false. They are modes of participation in the dialogue with Torah . . ." ("Midrash and Allegory: The Beginnings of Scriptural Interpretation" in *The Literary Guide to the Bible* [ed. Robert Alter and Frank Kermode; Cambridge, MA: Belknap, 1990] 632).

34. *Midrash Rabbah Numbers,* 44.

only does the Midrash juxtapose different interpretations of the same verse but it does so without saying which interpretation is "right."

A subset of this hermeneutical option is to draw on source criticism, especially with reference to Numbers 22–24.[35] Source criticism has an inherent willingness, if not insistence, to allow for contradictory perspectives. The obvious example of how source criticism has been helpful in explaining Balaam is that Numbers 22:22–35, the tale of Balaam's donkey, derives from a different source than the preceding section of Numbers 22:2–21. God tells Balaam to go in 22:21, but then God is angered at Balaam's going in 22:22, and these various sources have been redacted together to tell a larger story of God and God's messengers. Canonical criticism is related to redaction criticism and is thus an extension of source criticism. Attending to the individual sources may be analogous to separating out distinct instruments in a symphonic piece of music: identifying J is like listening to only the percussion, and E is like the melody played by the strings. In practice, it can take so much time and attention to clarify sources that a source critic may miss out on the fullness of the sound that comes when they get "played" together.

---

35. The dominant consensus for several years was that Numbers 22–24 was composed of two separate sources of J and E, but more recent source criticism finds even more possibilities. Richard Friedman explains, "The Balaam episode is perhaps the hardest section in the Torah in which to delineate sources. Most scholars regard this three-chapter story as a composite: first, because they think of the accounts of repeated sets of ambassadors to Balaam as a doublet; and second, because they think there is a contradiction in the story when God tells Balaam to go with the Moabites but then is angry at him for going. The several embassies to Balaam, each composed of more distinguished ambassadors, may well be the original progression of the story. And the confusion over God's sending Balaam and then being angry at him is surprising but still understandable as a single author's development, and it is not easily resolved by separating the section into two sources in any case. Evidence of language is a stronger marker of sources than these considerations. The vast majority of the terms and phrases here that are identifiable with a particular source are typical of E, while only three are typical of J. And there is a particular cluster of terms and phrases here that are also found in Exodus 10 (E). And the deity is referred to as God (Elohim) in narration here seven times. I therefore have marked the story as wholly E, except that I have marked those three J passages so that one can observe them and make of it what one will. The first verse of the story . . . refers to the defeat of the Amorites, which had occurred only in J, not in E. This verse, therefore, either comes from J or else was added by RJE as a means of connecting the J story of the defeat of the Amorites and the E story of the defeat of the Moabites" (Richard Elliot Friedman, *The Bible with Sources Revealed* [New York: HarperSanFrancisco, 2003] 280).

Two ancient interpreters who held Balaam's complexity were Josephus and Origen. In his conclusion to the section on Balaam, Josephus reiterates both the bad that Balaam did, in giving the advice to the Midianites as to how to corrupt the Israelites, and the good, by writing down the complimentary prophecies about them. Josephus further explains how the writing down of the prophecies could be seen negatively and positively. The potential negative is that Balaam would "claim this glory to himself, and make men believe they were his own predictions, there being no one that could be a witness against him, and accuse him for so doing," but what was positive is that Balaam attested to God and did God honor in the written account.[36] Josephus' final sentence in this section on Balaam is, "But let every one think of these matters as he pleases."[37] Such a concluding sentence is striking, especially given that Josephus' stated purpose in the *Antiquities* was to correct those who had "perverted the truth" of the history of the Jewish people. Perhaps the freedom of interpretation that Josephus suggested regarding Balaam was a rhetorical strategy, or perhaps the seeming lack of definitiveness as to how people *should* think of "these matters" can be explained by Balaam's minor status compared to other Israelite heroes.

Origen wrote a series of homilies about Balaam in his commentary on Numbers, and viewed him as "most famous in the magic arts and foremost in harmful incantations."[38] But this same Balaam was chosen by God to give a true prophecy that included a messianic message. Judith Baskin points out how the reference to the star rising from Jacob in Numbers 24:17 was widely understood as a messianic oracle, and therefore early Christians saw Balaam not only as a villain, but also as a divinely inspired prophet.[39] For Origen, Balaam was not a true prophet: the word of God was placed only in Balaam's

---

36. Josephus, *Ant.* 4.13. http://penelope.uchicago.edu/josephus/ant-4.html.

37. Ibid.

38. Origen, *Homily* 15.4 (PG 12, 671 C).

39. Judith R. Baskin, "Origen on Balaam: The Dilemma of the Unworthy Prophet," *Vigiliae Christianae* 37 (1983) 23. Other church fathers, however, attempt to distance the prophecy in Numbers from Balaam. For example, Baskin writes, "Justin cites Numbers 24:17 in his *Apology* as an Old Testament verification of the Incarnation, but he amalgates Balaam's star prophecy with the root of Jesse prediction of Isaiah, and attributes the whole to that author. . . . A similar effort to separate the man from his words is found in an oration of Athanasius. In the *Incarnation of the Word*, the fourth century Father quotes Balaam's prophecy under the name of Moses" (23).

mouth and not in his heart (see Num 22:38; 23:5, 12, 16). Origen explained, "Since, however, his heart was filled with greed for wealth and money, God's word could be placed only in his mouth."[40] The message—from God and not the messenger—is what is important. Ultimately, Origen believed that Balaam found a measure of salvation based on Origen's reading of the LXX of Numbers 23:10, "May I die the death of the righteous, may my seed be like his."[41] In Origen's words:

> From the fact that Balaam says "Let my seed be as the seed of the righteous," we can discern that these Magi who came from the East to be the first to adore Jesus are seen to be from his seed, whether through the succession of his seed, or through the disciples of his tradition.[42] It is evident from the fact that they recognized the star which Balaam foretold would rise in Israel, and that they came and adored the king who was born in Israel. . . . Nor are we speaking only of these, that their seed would be like the seed of the righteous, but all of those of the nations who believed in Christ are saved.[43]

Thus, Origen finds some redemption in that his seed—gentile believers—are saved. Baskin uses the phrase "inspired miscreant"[44] to describe Origen's view of Balaam; Balaam warranted condemnation because of his incantations, but Balaam was worthy of redemption because he was chosen to prophesy about the messiah and because of the merits of his descendants. She writes that for Origen, "both biblical Balaams are accounted for and a lesson in redemption and gentile salvation imparted."[45]

---

40. Origen, *Homily* 14.3 (PG 12, 621D-682A).

41. The Hebrew is more literally, "may my end be like theirs" (ותהי אהריתי כמהו), but the LXX reads "after" as "seed." See Baskin, "Origen on Balaam" 35 n. 54.

42. Hieronymous Bosch's triptych painting, variously titled *The Adoration of the Magi* or *The Epiphany*, includes a character inside the stable who has been identified as Balaam. See Walter Bosing, *Hieronymus Bosch C. 1450–1516: Between Heaven and Hell* (Koln: Taschen, 1987) 72. If this is the case, Bosch places Balaam in the background of the Magi's adoration of the infant Jesus.

43. Origen, Homily 15.4 (PG 12, 689D-690A).

44. Baskin, "Origen on Balaam" 22.

45. Ibid., 30.

Michael S. Moore and Dennis Olson are two examples of recent interpreters who try to hold at least two Balaams together. With Origen, Moore
notes Balaam's involvement in the realm of magic, referring to him as a
"magico-religious specialist."[46] Moore posits that such a view of Balaam was
preserved in Numbers 22–24, as seen in the various rituals Balaam performs
before his oracles. Moore also argues, "As the biblical tradition gradually
passed through the hands of Israelite tradents, however, any pluralistic view
of Balaam which may have lain at its core began to creak and groan under
the increasing strain."[47] Moore does not want to suggest any rigid evolutionary view of Israel's religious history, especially because there is no hard
and fast evidence of such an occurrence. He does, however, believe that discomfort with Balaam's "magical" roles led to a focus on God and God's role.
Moore explains, "The ultimate rationale behind this final biblical attempt to
solve the 'Balaam problem' seems to be as profound as it was simple: Yahweh
your God loves you (Deut 23:6)."[48]

Olson focuses on the literary characterization of Balaam as well as the
role of Balaam's oracles in the larger literary text of the book of Numbers.
Olson describes Balaam as enigmatic, on the one hand acting obediently as
God's intermediary in Numbers 22–24, but on the other hand, according to
Numbers 31, killed for causing Israel's apostasy in Numbers 25. Olson goes
on to say that the literary portrait of Balaam in Numbers holds these two
sides together in a theologically significant manner. He writes,

---

46. Michael S. Moore, *The Balaam Traditions: Their Character and Development*
(Atlanta: Scholars, 1990) 18. Moore takes a phenomenological approach to Balaam, seeing
his role on a social and cultural continuum between magic and religious.

47. Ibid., 118.

48. Ibid., 122. The quote continues with Moore saying, "This adamant theocentric posture, independently emerging alongside the persistent problem of unresolved role strain
over the Balaam problem ultimately led to a reformulation of the tradition which reset
its parameters along an entirely different spatio-temporal continuum. The advantages of
this 'solution' were simple and several: (1) both role-sets ('diviner/seer' and 'exorcist') could
be recognized and preserved, thus demonstrating a genuine concern for some measure
of sociohistorical accuracy; (2) both 'official' versions of Israel's common history could be
maintained with a minimum of role-conflict, thus demonstrating a reverence for the totality
of Israel's epic tradition; and most importantly, (3) Yahweh could be restored to his 'rightful'
place, demonstrating above all an intense concern for restoring a theocentric perspective to
the telling of Israelite history."

Balaam is a legitimate instrument of God by which God affirms and continues his promises to the people. He is a true servant of God. But Balaam's subsequent actions which incite rebellion and apostasy oppose God's will and purpose which leads to Balaam's death. Balaam is a paradigm for the ways of God in the world, whether Israel or any other people. Obedience to the will of God leads to life; disobedience leads to death. . . . No less than Balaam or the wilderness generation, the new generation will live if they act faithfully, but they will come under judgment if they act rebelliously.[49]

Olson also argues for the theological significance of Balaam's oracles in the literary structure of the book of Numbers, as they come after the first generation has been condemned to die in the wilderness (Num 14) and before the new generation enters into the promised land. Balaam's words are words of promise and hope, "in the new leaders who emerge in both the priestly office (Phinehas) and the Mosaic office (Joshua), and the hope of a successful and obedient entrance into the promised land which is anticipated but not yet consummated at the end of the book."[50]

Symphonies, Symmetries, and Quilts

Hermeneutical options that allow for contradiction may ultimately be seeking harmony.[51] To return to a musical metaphor, reading the biblical canon as a whole allows the reader to bring various separate sources and books together in a rich and beautiful sound. A single textual pericope may be like a single instrument, able to play a lovely tune on its own but lacking the rich and symphonic depth of sound when other texts, books,

---

49. Dennis Olson, *The Death of the Old and the Birth of the New: The Framework of the Book of Numbers and the Pentateuch* (Chico: Scholars, 1985) 160–61.

50. Ibid., 162.

51. Baskin says as much about Origen's view of Balaam, writing, "Origen's Balaam, then, is no longer contradictory. As a miscreant who summoned up demons and harmed others through incantations, he certainly warranted condemnation. Yet in Origen's eyes Balaam becomes worthy of redemption, both because he was chosen, however involuntarily, to deliver a prophecy of Christ which could bring the nations to true worship, and because of the merit of his descendants" ("Origen on Balaam" 30).

and canonical instruments are also heard. The preference, musically and hermeneutically, however, is for a sound that all works together, for notes and chords which complement and are consonant with each other. The second Viennese school of music, with composers like Arnold Schönberg, Anton Webern, and Alban Berg, sought to eliminate traditional harmony and thereby highlight melody, rhythm, and emotional contexts of music. They wrote pieces that were deliberately atonal and unapologetically dissonant. Perhaps it is not surprising that their names—and music—are less familiar than Bach or Beethoven, whose music contains dissonant intervals but ultimately resolves them.[52]

Or, to use another metaphor, we prefer symmetry. Even though no natural human face is completely symmetrical, numerous studies document the human bias toward faces that are more symmetrical than asymmetrical. Too much asymmetry is considered unattractive.[53] Even though Balaam in the Bible is neither completely heroic nor completely villainous, it may be more satisfying to explain him as either one or the other. Olson explains, "The history of interpretation of the figure of Balaam is a fascinating chronicle of later reflections on Balaam as saint or sinner, as the prophet *par excellence* or the personification of evil. One side of his character is typically emphasized to the exclusion of the other."[54]

Adriane Leveen describes the various themes in Numbers using the analogy of an intricately designed quilt, where one can detect the individual panels, but an observation of the whole provides a perspective that creates

52. Thanks to our SPU colleague in the Music Department, Brian Chin, who helped me with some of these musical details. In an e-mail exchange, Chin told me that the most dissonant interval is "an augmented 4th (C–F#), or a Tri-tone" that occurs halfway through the octave. In the Middle Ages, the church referred to it as "the Devil's interval."

53. The makeup trend of "contouring" is touted as a way to "minimize asymmetries." Celebrity makeup artist Tina Turnbow explains, "Sometimes by just emphasizing the positives, you'll distract from the asymmetries," http://www.youbeauty.com/beauty/makeup-tips -for-facial-symmetry/ (accessed 12/8/2016). In the visual world of comic books, symmetry is not only associated with beauty but goodness. Villains are depicted with disproportionate heads or as blatantly asymmetrical, as in the examples of Harvey Dent (Two-Face) or Cruella De Vil.

54. Olson, *The Death of the Old and the Birth of the New*, 160. See also Baskin, who argues that while Balaam "tends to be presented in his two contradictory guises . . . neither image ever wholly superseded the other" ("Origen on Balaam" 31).

the dominant impression of the work.[55] Applying this metaphor to canonical readings of Balaam would suggest an overall image that is composed of different smaller images.[56] One's perspective could shift between the individual texts and the larger picture that includes each of the discrete texts. In other words, one could see the overall picture of Balaam but notice how it is composed of smaller, different images: Numbers 24 when the spirit of God comes on Balaam (Num 24:2) and he speaks about Israel's exaltation, and Numbers 31:16 when Moses explains Balaam's role in leading Israel to sin.

A very honest approach to hermeneutics includes doing a cost-benefit analysis of the options, to account for the gains and losses when choosing to read in a particular way. All three of these hermeneutical analogies—listening for harmony, looking for symmetry, or seeing the intricate overall image composed of many varied parts—will yield a different result than allowing the dissonance or asymmetry to remain. The honoree of this volume discusses the diversity of the texts in the canon, explaining that diversity as

> reason for celebration, not disputation. Not only is it impossible to reduce or absolutize the importance of any one part within the whole canon, but the faithful reader is also obliged to relate the Bible's diverse witnesses together in a way that facilitates mutually informing and self-correcting conversations between them.[57]

Though such a statement does not go so far as to champion dissonance or contradiction, it at least allows for a broader conversation than many of the above approaches. My personal concern about the move to harmonize comes from my worry about oversimplification in biblical interpretation. I understand the need for what Olson calls "provisional monologization,"[58] but in a culture that seems increasingly to prefer the monologue over the

---

55. Leveen, *Memory and Tradition,* 23.

56. Moving from fabric to photography, such an image is known as either a "photographic mosaic" or a "photomosaic," where a photograph is divided into usually equally sized sections, each of which is another photograph.

57. Robert W. Wall, "The Bible as Canon," *Response* 30 (Spring 2007), https://spu.edu/depts/uc/response/spring2k7/features/multifaceted-bible4.asp (accessed 10/19/2016).

58. Dennis Olson, "Biblical Theology as Provisional Monologization: A Dialogue with Childs, Brueggemann and Bakhtin," *Biblical Interpretation* 6 (1998) 162–80.

dialogue, such monologization ought not be the end game. If biblical interpretation—and consequent ethics, discipleship, and faith—needs to be simple, it should be a "simplicity on the other side of complexity."[59] In a talk
given in November 2016, Rabbi Lord Jonathan Sacks said, "I believe that
we are in a culture that expects every question to have one answer. I think
we have lost our capacity for complexity, and I think we have to challenge
that . . . to give people the stamina for complexity is the protest we have to
make against a culture of superficiality and simplification."[60] Studying and
interpreting the minor character Balaam throughout the biblical text could
have much to teach us about the stamina for complexity.

---

59. The full quote, which has been attributed to Oliver Wendell Holmes, is, "For the
simplicity that lies this side of complexity, I would not give a fig, but for the simplicity that
lies on the other side of complexity, I would give my life." The attribution is by no means
certain, but the idea is sound.

60. See http://www.rabbisacks.org/faith-future-promise-perils-religion/ (accessed
12/8/2016).

The Spirit in Israel's Story:
An Antidote to Solipsistic Spirituality

JACK LEVISON

Introduction

The Encounter

I was snug in a small white station wagon in Pretoria, South Africa, on my way to visit a township, Nelson Mandela's home, and a few other sites. My seatmate looked like a football player, with sunglasses dangling around his neck. Turns out, that once-upon-a-time football player and, what I would soon learn, larger-than-life personality, was none other than Rob Wall, the honoree of this *Festschrift*.

We hit it off. We spent hours together at that meeting of the Society of New Testament Studies. We ambled through the zoo late at night—and talked. We hung together at a South African festival—and talked.

And we've talked and emailed and argued and laughed for over a decade-and-a-half since that providential first meeting in that inauspicious station wagon. On one occasion—I cannot recall whether it was on one of our walks along the canal in Seattle (we subsequently became colleagues at Seattle Pacific University) or in a European park while we roomed together in Barcelona or Lund—Rob said to me, "You need to write bigger, dude." That is a recollection of what he said. Usually his phrasing is vintage and memorable, cause for a chuckle, but I cannot remember his exact words because I was so struck by their gist: *write bigger*.

I pushed back, not because I felt I'd written big enough—I hadn't—but because I wasn't sure I could. Recently, while spending hours reading the works of N. T. Wright, on whose writings I am co-leading a seminar at Perkins School of Theology, Rob's declaration about my writing resurfaced. I wonder whether I have been too meek in framing the significance of my exegesis for the contemporary world. Wright has many critics, yet none,

I imagine, would criticize him for writing too small, for straining too much insight from too little exegesis.

The Impetus
I have noticed how Wright, in his popular books, states what people get wrong in one or two sentences then turns to offer his own opinion—the *right* way to see things. For instance, many Christians, Wright contends, believe that the gospel is about how individuals who receive Christ will spend eternity in heaven with him. Wright excoriates such "truncated and self-centered readings which have become endemic in Western thought" and labors to convince Christians that they are "not well served by the inward-looking soteriologies that tangle themselves up in a web of detached texts and secondary sources."[1]

I have noticed this pattern and taken to writing "WRONG" then "WRIGHT" in close sequence in the margins of his books. His indictments are sweeping and bold, but Wright makes them nonetheless. Now Wright is not an expert on the opinions he thinks are wrong. He is not a sociologist of religion or an anthropologist. He does not even live in America, from which he draws so much fodder. Yet, on the whole, he may be right, notwithstanding his lack of specific experience or expertise.

What has kept me from making more sweeping statements about the holy spirit is that I am not a sociologist of religion or an anthropologist or an American historian (though I am married to one). In short, I am not an expert. Nor am I a Pentecostal, a charismatic, or a member of the Vineyard fellowship. Given what I am *not*, I am reluctant to say something sweeping and bold—and critical—about the holy spirit in the contemporary church.

Perhaps that should change, and I should take my cue from Rob Wall. Perhaps at the age of sixty, and with a dear colleague whose long-time excellence in teaching and writing warrants this much-deserved Festschrift, I should throw caution—even a modicum of it—to the wind so that my exegesis has purchase. (That's one of Rob's favorite words.) I intend to do this now.

---

1. N. T. Wright, *Justification: God's Plan and Paul's Vision* (Downers Grove: IVP Academic, 2009) 25.

The Problem

N. T. Wright is not the first to point out a flaw in American Christianity: the tendency toward solipsism.[2] Individualism is in our DNA, and we have developed, with ample precedent, a theology tailored to our DNA. Solipsism pervades popular pneumatology. "The Spirit is sent into my heart to give me meaning and purpose, as I relate, one on one to Jesus, in a foretaste of my eternal salvation in heaven."

The tenacity of the individualistic interpretation of the holy spirit is apparent in *The Holy Spirit and His Gifts*, by influential Pentecostal leader Kenneth Hagin. Without hesitation, Hagin applies the metaphor of the Spirit-filled temple to individuals. "Relatively few Christians," Hagin writes, "are really conscious of God *in* them—dwelling in their hearts and bodies as His temple."[3] Hagin tenaciously holds onto this individualistic interpretation although he quotes from the *Amplified Bible* of 1 Corinthians 3:16, where the temple refers to the whole community: "Do you not know *and* understand that you [the church] are the temple of God, and that the Spirit of God dwells [permanently] in you [collectively and individually]?"

It is difficult to overlook the communal dimension of this verse, but Hagin does. Such is the sway of an individualistic interpretation of the indwelling of the holy spirit.[4] Yet, a reader with even a modest knowledge of Greek will notice that the word *you* in the question, "Don't you know you're a temple of the Holy Spirit?" is plural and could better be translated by the southern expression, "y'all." This is not a question posed to individuals.

The Solution

In order to undermine this misunderstanding—or, at least, myopic understanding—of the holy spirit, I will take my cue again from Wright, who has

2. Robert N. Bellah et al., *Habits of the Heart: Individuals and Commitment in American Life* (Berkeley: University of California Press, 1985) 142–43. George Marsden, *Fundamentalism and American Culture* (2nd ed.; Oxford: Oxford University Press, 2006) 37, 71, 85, 92, 100–101. Additionally, Nathan Hatch highlights the emphasis on the primacy of the individual conscience among some early American Christians in his seminal work, *The Democratization of American Christianity* (New Haven: Yale University Press, 1989) 42–43, 136.

3. Kenneth E. Hagin, *The Holy Spirit and His Gifts* (Broken Arrow: Kenneth Hagin Ministries, 1991) 26.

4. See my *Filled with the Spirit* on 1 Corinthians 6:19 (Grand Rapids: Eerdmans, 2009) 294–97.

argued in a variety of ways that the interpretation of New Testament texts without a keen eye toward the story that led to them is, if not to misinterpret them, to interpret them inadequately. As Wright puts it with respect to Paul,

> God had a single plan all along through which he intended to rescue the world and the human race, and that this single plan was centered upon the call of Israel, a call which Paul saw coming to fruition in Israel's representative, the Messiah.[5]

In a rhetorically more compelling way, Wright notes,

> In Galatians 3:29, after heaping up almost all his great theological themes into a single pile—law, faith, children of God, "in Christ," baptism, "putting on Christ," "neither Jew nor Greek," "all one in Christ"—the conclusion is not "You are therefore children of God" or "You are therefore saved by grace through faith," but *"You are Abraham's offspring."*[6]

For Wright, the spirit, too, occupies the lines of Israel's story. Paul, according to Wright, understands the spirit in relation to three elements of Israel's story: the temple, the *shekinah*, and the messiah.

Paul's temple references,[7] notes Wright, combine to confirm a salient Pauline point of reference. Wright believes that "the gospel constituted the long awaited rebuilding of the Temple, and that *the indwelling of the spirit constituted the long-awaited return of YHWH to Zion.*"[8] Temple and spirit are closely aligned with a third element of Israel's story: the messiah. "If the election of Israel," notes Wright, "was the solemn and unbreakable divine promise to save the world through Abraham's seed, Paul sees that promise as *accomplished* in the Messiah and *applied* through the spirit."[9] Temple, *shekinah*, and messiah are all of a piece in Israel's story because all three are, according to Wright, three great expectations of Second Temple Judaism.

5. Wright, *Justification*, 35 (italics removed from original).
6. Ibid., 35–36.
7. 1 Cor 3:16–17, 1 Cor 6:18–20, and 2 Cor 6:14–7:1, alongside Eph 2:19–22.
8. N. T. Wright, *Paul and the Faithfulness of God* (Minneapolis: Fortress, 2013) 712 (italics original).
9. Wright, *Paul and the Faithfulness of God*, 912; see also 956.

One may quibble over details of Israel's story, as Wright understands it, but that is not the point of this essay.[10] I refer to Wright because he has so forcefully made the case for setting pneumatology into the context of Israel's story, which is precisely where pneumatology belongs.

For the remainder of this essay, therefore, I will do just that: set pneumatology in Israel's story, though I will not, as Wright was compelled to do in a book on Pauline theology, begin with the New Testament. To demonstrate, rather, that the spirit breaks the boundaries of solipsistic spirituality, I will focus exclusively upon the Hebrew Bible by looking at the presence of the spirit in three key episodes of Israel's story: in creation, in exodus, and in restoration. In each of these, the spirit shows up in unconventional ways to challenge a dominant, and certainly popular, Christian view of the spirit as God's presence in individual Christians.

The Spirit in Israel's Story

The Spirit and Creation

The Bible's opening words draw readers into an amorphous mystery. What is the spirit of God? Some interpreters understand the spirit as wind: "a wind from God swept over the face of the waters" (NRSV Gen 1:2). Fair enough, given the cosmology of Genesis. In the topography of creation, the waters' as yet untamed waves ripple and surge in the wind, *God's* wind.

Here, however, we appeal to Rob Wall and the canonical prompts to which he has pointed so many of us. The Hebrew construct phrase 'spirit of God' (רוּחַ אֱלֹהִים) invariably points to a peculiar presence of God, which gives wisdom, prophetic insight, frenzy, and inspired speech.[11] The phrase may shade toward wind, such as when Ezekiel is transported in a vision to Chaldea (Ezek 11:24), or breath, such as when Job claims that he will speak with integrity as long as the spirit of God is in his nostrils and breath in

---

10. I have more than quibbled, I hope, in a critique of Wright's pneumatology; see "The Spirit in Its Second Temple Context. An Exegetical Analysis of the Pneumatology of N. T. Wright," in *God and the Faithfulness of Paul: A Critical Examination of the Pauline Theology of N.T. Wright* (ed. Michael F. Bird, Christoph Heilig, and J. Thomas Hewitt; Tübingen: Mohr Siebeck) 439–62.

11. See Gen 41:38; Exod 31:3; 35:31; Num 24:2; 1 Sam 10:10, 11:6, 16:15, 16:23, 18:10, 19:20, 19:23; Ezek 11:24; 2 Chr 15:21, 24:20.

him (Job 27:3; 33:4). Yet the phrase רוּחַ אֱלֹהִים never in the Hebrew canon signals primarily a wind.

When the curtain rises on creation, then, the first presence of God is as the spirit of God—and not principally wind. Wind-like, yes. Wind? Not quite.

The second verb in the Bible confirms this impression. The verb used to describe the spirit's activity, "to hover" (מְרַחֶפֶת), is not something like blowing: the wind of God does not blow over the face of the deep. The verb occurs next in the Hebrew Bible in Deuteronomy 32:11, of an eagle that "stirs up its nest, and hovers over its young; as it spreads its wings, takes them up, and bears them aloft on its pinions." This is an image of both tender care and powerful pinions grasping Israel's neck to "set him atop the heights of the land" (32:13). The spirit of God, at the outset of creation, hovers over an expectant earth, as an eagle hovers over its young.

This verb, in its canonical context, in two poems from different eras in Israelite's history, one placed importantly at the front of the whole history, the other set at the tail end of Torah—a pair of poetic Torah bookends—flies in still another direction. Connected by the verb "hover," these poems interpret one another.

The historically earlier but canonically later poem continues, "[T]he LORD alone guided him; no foreign god was with him" (Deut 32:12); the hovering of the spirit of God reveals God's hegemony over creation. As in the second poem, so in the first: there is no powerful Marduk, no vulnerable Tiamat, whose womb he slices to create the heavens above. No foreign gods come to blow over the topography of creation. The spirit of God *alone* hovers, extending its powerful wings over a fledgling creation.

By the same token, the canonical connection allows the first poem to interpret the second. In the second poem, God rescues Israel, over whom God hovers in liberative presence. Yet this is not merely liberative. It is also creative. The exodus from Egypt is nothing less than a new creation.

While there may be no connection historically, canonically the symbiosis of creation and exodus that is suggested by the first and last poems of Torah, which share a common verb, comes to fruition in Isaiah 51:9–11, in which creation and exodus dovetail in the vision of an exilic voice:

Awake, awake, put on strength,
  O arm of the LORD!

Awake, as in days of old,
    the generations of long ago!
Was it not you who cut Rahab in pieces,
    who pierced the dragon?
Was it not you who dried up the sea,
    the waters of the great deep;
who made the depths of the sea a way
    for the redeemed to cross over?
So the ransomed of the LORD shall return,
    and come to Zion with singing;
everlasting joy shall be upon their heads;
    they shall obtain joy and gladness,
     and sorrow and sighing shall flee away.

This exilic poem, unlike Genesis 1, allows for foreign gods—Rahab, like Tiamat, is cut into pieces—and presents, therefore, an independent voice. What this poem allows us to see, nonetheless, is the relationship between creation and exodus, the parallel between the dark abyss of creation and the turgid waters of the Red Sea, the hope binding together otherwise distant experiences: creation, exodus, and, in the historical context of second Isaiah, return from exile as well. In short, the past yields hope, even hope against hope. The abyss, centuries of slavery, decades of exile—none of this can tamp down the hope of everlasting joy, gladness, and the flight of sorrow and sighing.

This may be the right moment to stop and consider the canonical method. I wrote to Rob Wall about Genesis 1:2, particularly the phrase, spirit of God, without letting him know that I would write an article for his Festschrift. He responded:

> . . . sequence is an important, purposeful element of the canon's aesthetic—its final (or canonical) form. Much like following the plot line of the biblical narrative, linguistic analysis of this phrase in context includes this diachronic aspect, so that its full or "canonical" meaning unfolds dynamically in a way that each mention brings with it all prior mentions, the one glossing the next. . . . Intertextual analysis within a canonical context enables readers to correct prior interpretations (or translations!) based upon subsequent uses.

I employed this method when I rejected the translation "wind." Later instances of the phrase "spirit of God" simply do not permit the interpretation of the first occurrence of that phrase to convey wind. That dimension of the canonical approach is straightforward. Yet Rob would continue:

> Within a canonical setting, first mentions are programmatic and as such linger on in the interpreter in working with each subsequent mention. In this sense, the use of *ruach elohim* in Genesis 1:2 is crucial, even central to the whole: *ruach elohim* is a creative, formative, life-giving agent of the Creator whose very presence is prospective of a future when what is now shrouded in darkness, chaotic, and covered in water—that is, incapable of life—is remade into what is alive and life-giving. So you bring that programmatic meaning forward with you to Genesis 41:38 and then into Torah and then 1 Samuel. This seems to me what you are implying in your post. What happened upon Balaam and Saul personifies what happened upon that formless, darkened, water-logged earth when Creator spoke those ten words to it and transformed it into a very good place.

This is a remarkable statement of method with enormous implications. I will not proceed in this direction to unpack subsequent references in light of Genesis 1:2, though that would be an interesting essay. Instead, I want to pause to imagine the significance of Rob Wall's statement.

All forms of inspiration in the canon, understood in the canonical perspective, must be seen through this opening lens: the spirit who indwells human beings is the creative spirit, which hovers in a protective, powerful neck-grasping posture over our "formless, darkened, water-logged" existence.

Current debates about the continuation of spiritual gifts must be set in the context of the spirit's powerful presence as creator; they are not merely matters of doctrine.

Current contentiousness about speaking in tongues must be set in the context of the spirit's powerful presence as liberator; they are not principally ecclesial markers or evidence of individuals' sanctification.

Current beliefs about the spirit as the one who gives meaning to life must be understood as part of the formative, forceful, foundational presence of God; the spirit is not meant primarily to give purpose to my hollow life.

The debut of the spirit in the Bible, therefore, is rife with meaning. When we first glimpse the spirit of God in the canon, the spirit who will liberate Israel from Egypt, we see sheer power—power exercised on behalf of the entire creation. Our ability to apprehend how spirit can mean so much, can evoke such rich images of God's presence in creation, exodus, and, as we will see, new exodus, provides the perfect starting-block for the human race by reminding us that God's spirit exists without us, before us, above us, around us—and not just *in* us.

The Spirit and Exodus

According to N. T. Wright, the indwelling of the spirit in the church can only mean—must only mean—some kind of identification of the divine spirit with the long-awaited returning *shekinah*. For the divine spirit to take up residence in the church is for Exodus 40 and Ezekiel 43 to find a radical, unexpected, and even shocking new fulfillment. But there can be no doubt that this is what Paul meant to say.[12] The words "some kind of" are suggestive but uncertain. Nonetheless, the possible identification of *shekinah* and spirit leads Wright to a crescendo:

> In context, both of Ephesians and of second-Temple expectations, this too can only mean one thing. The hope that one day YHWH would return to Zion, to dwell in the renewed Temple forever, has now been fulfilled— but in a radical, shocking and unexpected fashion. The role of God's living presence, the glorious Shekinah, is taken by the spirit. Once again, in second-Temple Jewish terms there cannot be a higher pneumatology than this. The spirit is incorporated within the divine identity, the identity which is shaped particularly by the eschatology of YHWH's return.[13]

Understanding the spirit in the context of Second Temple Jewish expectations of a new exodus, Wright contends, deepens the resonance of other Pauline texts as well. For instance, Romans 8, in which the spirit comes to the aid of believers and pleads on their behalf, "is accomplishing what was accomplished in the original story through the tabernacling presence of

---

12. Wright, *Paul and the Faithfulness of God*, 712.
13. Ibid., 716.

YHWH during the wilderness wanderings."[14] To put it bluntly, "What the one God of Israel had done in the exodus narrative, and had promised to do himself at the eschaton, Paul sees being accomplished by the spirit."[15] Similarly, in the familiar contrast of slavery and sonship, of spirit and Torah, Paul accuses the Galatians of "trying to sneak off back to Egypt, trying to return to the slavery from which they had been rescued."[16] This retreat is, for Paul, untenable because "the role both of Torah and of the tabernacling presence of God with his people has been taken, jointly, by the Messiah and the spirit."[17]

Underlying all of this, Wright is forced to admit that the spirit can be identified with the *shekinah* of the exodus story only in "some kind of" way. Wright's uncertainty, despite how boldly he goes on to make his case, is fueled by the absence of key biblical texts in Wright's pneumatology. Had he incorporated Isaiah 63:7–14 and Haggai 2:5, Wright would have been able to identify spirit and *shekinah* more compellingly. These two texts allow us to discover a rich vein of pneumatology that takes us far beyond the confines of an individualistic spirituality.

Isaiah 63:7–14
Set between visions of temple restoration (Isa 56:1–8) and recreation (65:17–25) in Isaiah 56–66, Isaiah 63:7–14 is a self-contained hymn of lament, in which the prophet promises to "recount the gracious deeds of the LORD" (Isa 63:7). The first several lines are unremarkable, with traditional references to "the praiseworthy acts of the LORD"; to God's favor, mercy, and steadfast love; and to an assurance that Israel is God's people (Isa 63:7–8).

The next lines turn abruptly from praise in general to the exodus, wilderness, and settlement traditions, laced with three references to God's spirit:

> It was no messenger or angel
>   but his presence that saved them . . .

14. Ibid., 720.
15. Ibid., 721 (italics removed from original).
16. Ibid., 718.
17. Ibid., 718 (italics removed from original).

But they rebelled
    and grieved his holy spirit;
therefore he became their enemy;
    he himself fought against them. . . .
Where is the one who put within them his holy spirit . . .
Like cattle that go down into the valley,
    The spirit of the LORD gave them rest. (Isa 63:9–14)

Though self-contained, this hymn is suffused with the exodus language that is characteristic of Isaiah 40–55:

Then they remembered the days of old,
    of Moses his servant.
Where is the one who brought them up out of the sea
    with the shepherds of his flock? . . .
Who divided the waters before them . . .
    who led them through the depths . . .
Like cattle that go down into the valley,
    The spirit of the LORD gave them rest. (Isa 63:11–14)

The prophet transforms ancient traditions to create an amalgamation of hope and warning.

At the center of this hope lies the spirit: God's presence saved Israel, yet "they rebelled and grieved his holy spirit." Presumably God's presence and spirit are identical. Still, the identification is not a simple one because the layering of traditions in Torah, which underlies this hymn, is complex.

Torah contains references to a tradition of *an angel* that led Israel. Prior to the parting of the sea, the angel of God and the pillar of cloud moved from in front of (that is, leading) Israel to a position behind Israel to protect them from Egypt (Exod 14:19). After the miraculous journey through the sea, God promises:

I am going to send an angel in front of you, to guard you on the way and to bring you to the place that I have prepared. Be attentive to him and listen to his voice; do not rebel against him, for he will not pardon your transgression; for my name is in him. But if you listen attentively to his voice and do all that I say, then I will be an enemy to your enemies and a foe to your foes. When my angel goes in front of you, and brings you to the Amorites, the Hittites . . . (Exod 23:20–23).[18]

Alongside this tradition of an angelic deliverer is another, according to which God's presence or face went with Israel. God promises Moses, "My presence will go with you, and I will give you rest" (Exod 33:14), to which Moses reacts, "If your presence will not go, do not carry us up from here" (33:15).[19]

These two traditions—God's angel and presence—overlap in the book of Exodus. As we just saw, in Exodus 33:14–15, God promises Moses God's *presence*. Just before this, God had promised Moses an *angel* to lead Israel: "But now go, lead the people to the place about which I have spoken to you; see, my angel shall go in front of you" (32:34). God then orders Moses to leave, repeating the promise of 32:34: "I will send an angel before you, and I will drive out the Canaanites, the Amorites . . ." (33:2).[20]

The traditions of God's angel and God's presence merge in Isaiah 63, where the holy spirit takes on their tangled roles. No longer against an appointed angel did Israel rebel (Exod 23:21); now it is the holy spirit against whom Israel rebelled (Isa 63:10). No longer did God's presence give Israel rest (Exod 33:14); now it is the spirit of the LORD who guides Israel and gives it rest (Isa 63:14). To put an accent on this: it is no longer the *shekinah* but God's holy spirit that God put within the people to accompany them through the wilderness (Isa 63:11). In short, in Isaiah 63:7–14, *the prerogatives of God's angel and presence devolve onto the holy spirit in a context that is replete with the theology of exodus.*

---

18. Moses refers to the angelic deliverer in a message sent to the king of Edom to request safe passage through Edom: "[A]nd when we cried to the LORD, he heard our voice, and sent an angel and brought us out of Egypt" (Num 20:16).

19. The Deuteronomist recalls a similar tradition: "And because he loved your ancestors, he chose their descendants after them. He brought you out of Egypt with his own presence, by his great power, driving out before you nations greater and mightier than yourselves . . ." (Deut 4:37–38).

20. In Exod 23:22, for instance, there is an explicit correlation between listening attentively to the voice of the *angel* and doing all that *God* says.

Haggai 2:5

Isaiah 63 contains the elements of spirit and exodus. Haggai 2 adds to these the elements of the temple and eschatological glory. In an oracle dated to 520 B.C.E, Haggai is commanded to say:

> Yet now take courage, O Zerubbabel, says the LORD; take courage, O Joshua, son of Jehozadak, the high priest; take courage, all you people of the land, says the LORD; work, for I am with you, says the LORD of hosts, according to the promise that I made you when you came out of Egypt: my spirit stands in your midst.[21] Do not fear. For thus says the LORD of hosts: once again, in a little while, I will shake the heavens and the earth and the sea and the dry land; and I will shake all the nations, so that the treasure of all nations shall come, and I will fill this house with splendor, says the LORD of hosts. The silver is mine, and the gold is mine, says the LORD of hosts. The latter splendor of this house shall be greater than the former, says the LORD of hosts; and in this place I will give prosperity, says the LORD of hosts. (Hag 2:4–9)

There is no promise in the exodus tradition of the spirit in Israel's midst. That is why the question in Isaiah 63:11, "Where is the one who put within them his holy spirit?" is so novel in Israelite literature. Haggai's affirmation that the spirit abides in Israel's midst is, along with Isaiah 63, equally an affirmation of the spirit in the exodus tradition.

This interpretation is borne out by the choice of the verb, עמד, "to stand," to depict the spirit's presence. The spirit's standing in Israel's midst evokes the image of the pillar of cloud which *stood* in the midst of the Israelites and which was closely associated with the angel of God. The first canonical reference to the angel of God, in fact, occurs in Exodus 14:19, in which both this angel and the cloud move from the front of the camp to the rear in order to separate the Israelites from the Egyptians. Both the noun, עמוד, "pillar," and the verb, עמד, "to stand," appear in this context. Subsequently, the cloud is said to take its stand at the tent of meeting (Exod 33:9–10; Num 12:5), and the presence of the pillars of cloud and fire are identified with the divine presence among the people (Exod 13:21–22; Num 14:14; Deut 1:33).

---

21. My translation.

The oracle of Haggai differs in significant ways from Isaiah 63. First, Isaiah 63, while set in the context of a future-oriented new exodus perspective, looks back to the exodus; the spirit is introduced into a hymn about the past. In contrast, the oracle in Haggai 2 looks exclusively to the future, probably the eschatological future. The shaking of the heavens and earth, the sea and dry land, even all the nations, portends eschatological hope rather than the decades after return from exile.

The expectation, too, that the latter glory will exceed the former glory, that the temple will be full of glory—silver, gold, prosperity—is also an indication that the *shekinah*, with its glory, will inhabit the temple. And what can this *shekinah* be, other than the spirit of the exodus which stands in Israel's midst?

Spirit and Exodus

Liberation, guidance, divine presence, a new temple, eschatological glory— and dire warning—gather like a thundercloud in easily neglected canonical texts composed in the crevice between exile and restoration. Overshadowed by the fire of Pentecost and the dazzle of glossolalia, these texts, once unearthed, offer dimensions of pneumatology that escape the potential for individualism. In Haggai, the spirit stands, like the pillar and angel of God, in the presence of a tattered, post-exilic community with the promise of eschatological glory. Like the ragtag exodus community, the post-exilic community cannot find its way forward; for this, it needs the pillar-angel-spirit to stand in its midst, moving to the front to proceed and to the rear to protect.

In Isaiah 63, God gives the spirit into Israel's midst; the spirit does not belong principally to individuals. Nor does that spirit allow for the preservation of the status quo; the spirit leads the people, just as the angel of God's presence had led a band of former slaves to a land flowing with milk and honey. The spirit, in short, inspires *movement* for a refugee *community* rather than meaning for an individual believer.

Even more startling is the threat that accompanies the spirit's presence in Isaiah 63. At the exodus, God warned the people not to rebel against the angel sent to lead them (Exod 23:21). Now it is the spirit whom the people of the new exodus are in danger of grieving. The old story is now theirs. The old blessings are now theirs. So too is the old warning now theirs.

That warning entailed not underestimating God's angel, God's spirit. This is no mealy-mouthed giver of gifts, no pleasant bestower of blessings, no purveyor of purpose to hapless individuals. The spirit is treacherous, capable, fierce in the face of enemies, and no less fierce in the face of fickle friends. To know this spirit, notwithstanding the peril, is to tread the path toward a new community, a new temple, a new land, and, beyond all of these, renewed glory.

The Spirit and Restoration

Haggai and the prophet of Isaiah 63 transform the exodus account by importing the spirit and allowing that spirit to take on the tangled roles of the pillars of cloud and fire and the angel of God's presence in the story of the exodus. The purpose of this transformation is to strengthen—and warn—the fledgling post-exilic community to remain faithful in the daunting tasks ahead. These prophets would find a noteworthy ally in another prophet, who would begin his work within two months of Haggai. Zechariah[22] would continue for about two years (Zech 1:1; 7:1), much longer than Haggai's half year of prophetic leadership. Both confront the blessing of Persian stability and the bane of realizing that there would be no imminent restoration of Davidic kingship; the fair but firm hand of Darius I had seen to that. Like Haggai, Zechariah is a political realist who directs his energies to forming a faithful little province—Jerusalem may only have been four or five acres with four or five hundred inhabitants—that will not raise the eyebrows of Persian power.

This is the context of Zechariah's renowned reference to the spirit: "This is the word of the LORD to Zerubbabel: Not by might, nor by power, but by my spirit, says the LORD of hosts" (Zech 4:6). Zechariah counsels the Davidic heir, Zerubbabel, governor of the province of Yehud (Judah), not to turn to violence to accomplish his ends. This statement is much more than a straightforward piece of advice.

The saying occurs at the center of visions in Zechariah 1–8. Zechariah sees a golden lampstand—a menorah from the temple—with two olive trees.

---

22. Chapters 1–8 only; chapters 9–14 are generally believed to be later and independent of the first eight chapters. See Carol L. Meyers and Eric M. Meyers, *Zechariah 9–14* (New York: Doubleday, 1993) 15–16.

Following a typically literary form, Zechariah asks what they are (4:1–6a); the angel asks if he knows, and Zechariah responds, "No, my lord." The angel who accompanies Zechariah does not explain the vision, however, until several lines later, when he reveals: "These seven are the eyes of the LORD" while the olive trees are "the two anointed ones," presumably Zechariah and Joshua (Zech 4:10b-14). Taken together, verses 1–6a and 10b-14 create a seamless vision.

This vision is interrupted by divine instructions to Zerubbabel, governor of Yehud. In this oracle, God promises that Zerubbabel will lay the first stone in the rebuilt temple, to the acclaim of the people, who shout, "Right! Right!" Not only this, Zerubbabel will complete the reconstruction of the temple.

There is a tension in this promise: In antiquity, temple-building was the responsibility of royalty. Solomon, Israel's third king, had built the temple in Jerusalem, at this same spot. Josiah, too, had brought reform to the temple cult. To promise Zerubbabel, an heir to the house of David and Solomon, that he would begin and complete the temple, is tantamount to bestowing royal prerogatives upon him. The stern geopolitical reality, however, made this possibility unthinkable for a province in the Persian Empire, which had appointed a governor and a high priest—but not a king. Zerubbabel may possess the prerogative of rebuilding the temple, promises Zechariah, but he may not consequently possess royal status. He does not, and will not, acquire royal power so long as Persia rules.

Therefore, Zechariah must preface this promise with an unequivocal word: Not by might, nor by power, but by my spirit, says the LORD of hosts. The words "might" and "power" taken in tandem comprise a show of force; "might" conjures images of physical power, military strength, and, quite frequently, refers to an "army."[23] Nothing of what Zerubbabel will accomplish as the governor of the province can be traced to armies, violence, or war. If he builds the temple, he does so peaceably and in the peaceful realization that he is no king. Zechariah, in fact, refers several times to Zerubbabel without reference to his Davidic lineage or his title;[24] this tendency differs drastically from Haggai[25] and underscores that Zerubbabel's status lies in his peaceful

---

23. For example, 2 Kgs 18:17; Jer 46:22; Ezek 17:17.
24. Zech 4:6–7, 9–10.
25. For example, Hag 1:14; 2:2; 2:21; see preface in 1:1.

accomplishments and not a building program or an aggressive stance toward Persia. His is a peaceable kingdom, a kingdom that belongs to Darius I.

Although the simple words "by my spirit" are too laconic to be easily unpacked, they may recall the images of the ideal ruler and the servant in Isaiah. The ideal ruler, a shoot from the stump of a humble Jesse, rules with the rod of his mouth, judges on behalf of the poor, and delights in the awesomeness of God when the spirit of the LORD rests upon him (Isa 11:1–5). The servant who is anointed with the spirit brings justice to the nations that await his torah, his teaching (42:1–4). This servant must do much more than restore the survivors of Israel; the servant is to be a light to the nations, liberation to the earth's ends (49:6).

Whether Zechariah's words tap into this rich reservoir we may never know, though he does seem to be acutely aware of Isaiah's depictions. Earlier, for example, he describes Zerubbabel as "my servant" (Zech 3:8) and "a man whose name is Branch; for he shall branch out in his place, and he shall build the temple of the LORD . . . he shall bear royal honor, and shall sit upon his throne and rule. There shall be a priest by his throne, with peaceful understanding between the two of them" (6:12–13). Whether the Branch is to be identified as Joshua or Zerubbabel—both, of course, as post-exilic leaders, have a hand in the restoration of the temple—a post-exilic leader is the branch or shoot from the stump of Jesse (Isa 11:1) who exercises his peaceful reign (Isa 11:1–6).[26] Haggai, too, depicts Zerubbabel in the indisputable garb of the servant of Isaiah 42:1, when he says, "On that day, says the LORD of hosts, I will take you, O Zerubbabel *my servant*, son of Shealtiel, says the LORD, and make you like a signet ring; for *I have chosen you*, says the LORD of hosts" (Hag 2:23).

It is likely, therefore, that the words "by my spirit" evoke the image of peaceful rule. Picking up from Isaiah 11 and Isaiah 42, Zechariah draws a clear line in the sand between military might and God's spirit. Zerubbabel will build the temple, though he must do so without taking on the prerogatives of kingship and, with them, a posture of rebellion toward Persia.

The promise and realities of Persian politics that confront Zechariah lead him ultimately to reject power, to eschew violence. There is no room

---

26. On the disputed identity of the Branch, see Ralph L. Smith, *Micah-Malachi* (Waco: Word, 1984) 200–201.

for a Deborah, Gideon, Jephthah, Samson, or Saul in Zechariah's purview. Persia is not an oppressor like Philistia, a despotic neighbor like Midian. Persia has restored a remnant of exiles to its homeland, appointed legitimate rulers, and liberated Israelites from exile. Therefore, the only appropriate course of action for a ruler, even a ruler in the lineage of David, is to reject military options, to accept Darius' decrees, and to acknowledge that ultimately the temple will be rebuilt by God's spirit.

With this oracle from the period of restoration, we have traipsed purposefully into a political minefield. The spirit has nothing to do here with personal fulfillment. The spirit has nothing to do with glossolalia or any other gift of the spirit exercised for the edification of the church. What is the realm of the spirit in Zechariah 4:6? Politics and political realism. Zechariah sets the spirit over against military options and aggressive rule that will bring its downfall. He sets the spirit instead within the sphere of the peaceful messiah and peaceable servant. To what end? So that the little province of Judah can survive under the powerful sway of the Persian Empire. Only by God's spirit can the builders of this small nation discover their niche among the geopolitical heavyweights of the Ancient Near East.

The spirit is, in brief, the ultimate political realist, who can rebuild without raising the hackles of larger nations, those vast empires that dominate the world. To reduce this spirit to anything less is to fail to grasp the breadth of the spirit, whose guidance is discernible, not now in an individual, nor even in the church, but in the fragile rebirth of a provincial and political community that is destined to survive in a world in which nations large and small rise and fall.

Conclusion

While my son Jeremy and I twice drove vehicles—our Honda Civic and Odyssey—from Seattle to Dallas, we listened only to country music and frequently to the testosterone-drenched music of Toby Keith. While I don't agree with his politics, I confess that I like many of his songs. When it's a hot day outside in Dallas (Rob warned me about the heat), I blast the air conditioner, roll down the car's windows, and turn up the volume to "Should've Been a Cowboy" and "How Do You Like Me Now?" There are times when I think Toby Keith captures the pulse of a wide swath of America, such as in his song, "I Wanna Talk About Me." The verses detail how Keith talks with his loved one about her work, family, toenail polish, etc., but the chorus repeats the words of the title: "I want to talk about me . . . I . . . number one. . . . What I think, what I like, what I know, what I want, what I see."[27] The song continues along this vein—quintessentially expressing American individualism on a popular note.

I am certain—here I think N. T. Wright is right—we have allowed this sort of individualism to co-opt our theology, our soteriology and, I would add, our pneumatology, at least on a popular level. It is possible, nonetheless, to counter this individualistic pneumatology by embracing the story so ably preserved by ancient Israel and its heirs. At climactic moments in Israel's story, the spirit appears: in creation, in liberation from slavery, and in restoration after the ravages of exile. By immersing ourselves in Israel's story, we can liberate a potentially solipsistic conception of the spirit by means of an experience of the spirit hovering with powerful pinions over a brooding abyss, leading a fledgling nation from treachery to rest, inspiring leaders in the muck and mire of fragile political alliances, lifting our eyes beyond pedestrian tasks to unbounded glory—and, along the way, threatening our inevitable recalcitrance.

27. For the music video, see https://www.youtube.com/watch?v=HxUuDPNbkJk.

Transformed Discipleship:
A Canonical Reading of Martha and Mary

Laura C. S. Holmes

A low groan spread over the class. One woman shifted uncomfortably in her seat. A man started looking at the ceiling, trying to make himself inconspicuous. Another woman's face started turning bright red with a combination of anger, guilt, and shame. These were the distressed reactions to my announcement that we would be discussing Luke 10:38–42, the Scripture text about Jesus visiting Martha and Mary.

These five verses generate intense emotional reactions and division in almost any setting. Women, in particular, are likely to react to this text in defensive ways, either justifying the need for *someone* to "be Martha" and take care of the details, or feeling guilty about the lack of time to "be Mary" and not be subjected to the constant "busyness" of everyday life. Male readers can be hesitant to see themselves in this text at all, relegating discussion about this passage to women only. These verses seem to encourage readers either to choose between the two characters, or split themselves into two, identifying an "external Martha" and an "internal Mary," thereby trying to validate Jesus' praise of Mary in the context of the necessary duties of everyday life.[1] Consequently, an isolated reading of the Lukan account yields characters that are often interpreted as static portraits of disciples: one is frantically busy with details, the other is calmly listening at Jesus' feet. On that reading, the message of this text seems obvious, if uncomfortable: sit and listen, regardless of what else needs to be done.

Yet this reading of the text falls short on two grounds: it does not account for details in the passage and its context in the Gospel of Luke, and it neglects the fact that Martha and Mary recur in the scriptural narrative

---

1. These descriptions are informed by my own teaching on the passage as well as reflections from Anne Thurston, *Knowing Her Place: Gender and the Gospels* (New York: Paulist, 1998) 10.

as sisters in John 11–12. When these passages are read together canonically, readers see the transformation of both of these sisters. They are portrayed as followers of Jesus as soon as they are introduced in Luke, but both Martha and Mary have room to grow by Luke 10:42. The Gospel of John narrates that growth in ways that elaborate on the Lukan account. We need both Luke and John to tell the whole story of Martha and Mary's transformational encounters with Jesus. Reading Luke or John alone may result in misunderstanding the portrayals of these characters, particularly of Martha, interpreting her discipleship in harmful ways. Canonically speaking, interpreting the accounts of Martha and Mary in Luke and then John together is beneficial, as this is how readers progress if they take the order of the Gospel canon seriously.[2] Furthermore, pairing these stories together has significant payoff for readers: not only does John resolve the cliff-hangers of Luke's account but together these Scripture texts offer a comprehensive picture of what the particular challenges of discipleship are in different contexts. A canonical reading of Jesus' encounters with Martha and Mary transforms readers' understanding of these characters and how they inform the life of discipleship.[3] This canonical approach does not harmonize these stories; instead, it respects how each account reflects the Gospel in which it is located, and yet can also speak across Gospel lines to shape readers' faith and life.

Luke or John Alone:
A Mistaken Martha and a Redundant Mary

Biblical scholars and pastors commonly try to determine the interpretations of Luke 10:38–42 and John 11:1–12:8 without recourse to the other text. While an important exercise, several trajectories emerge in the history of interpretation of these texts that illustrate the dangers of such a restrictive interpretation. Overall, the tendency with the Lukan passage about Martha and Mary is to

---

2. As Rob Wall claims: "The final arrangement of collections within the biblical canon is also suggestive of a logical pattern for engaging Scripture" ("Canonical Criticism," in *The New Interpreter's Dictionary of the Bible* [ed. Katharine Doob Sakenfeld; Nashville: Abingdon, 2006] 1.563). As we will see, even from a historical perspective, John's text seems to presuppose knowledge of these sisters, while Luke's does not, encouraging a reading of Luke's Gospel first and John's second.

3. This formative role of Scripture is essential to a canonical reading.

overinterpret the text, treating each sister as a static or allegorical example of how people—especially women—should or should not behave if they are to follow Jesus. This takes several forms: there is the "nagging Martha" edition, its cousin the "silent Mary" version, and the "defending Martha" interpretation.

Common in mid-twentieth century commentaries and repeated in many sermons, the "nagging Martha" version of Luke 10:38–42 claims that Martha's main problem is misplaced priorities. If she had known that Jesus would prefer a simpler meal rather than the multi-course production she was preparing, then she would not have been so distracted and would have had time to sit with Mary at Jesus' feet.[4] Furthermore, interpreters may hear Martha's statement as "nagging" Jesus to have Mary help her, thereby feminizing Martha's reaction to the situation and diminishing her complaint. These perspectives determine that Martha's service is "excessive preparations for a meal" or that if she had only taken the time to listen to Jesus first, then she would have had plenty of time to have been a good hostess.[5] If Martha is the unfortunate example, Mary is the fortunate one: called the "perfect disciple" and consistently praised by readers (and by Jesus: 10:42), Mary is the model.[6] In other words, "Martha should slow down and relax. The disciple should never be too busy to sit at Jesus' feet."[7]

However, emphasizing Mary's praiseworthy position at Jesus' feet neglects the fact that she says nothing throughout the entire story. Her inaction makes her a difficult figure to model one's life after. Indeed, some readers have found her silence oppressive: "[I]n the course of the narrative

---

4. Martha "wished to honor [Jesus] with an elaborate meal, but it was more important to listen to him (and therefore to be content with giving him a simpler meal). Thus, the story is not meant to exalt the contemplative life above the life of action but to indicate the proper way to serve Jesus; one serves him by listening to his word rather than by providing excessively for his needs" (I. Howard Marshall, *The Gospel of Luke: A Commentary on the Greek Text* [Grand Rapids: Eerdmans, 1978] 451). A similar version of this interpretation is articulated by Mikael C. Parsons, who says that hearing Jesus, not "providing for physical needs," is what is needed (*Luke* [Grand Rapids: Baker Academic, 2015] 183).

5. Marshall, *Luke*, 453–54; Ben Witherington III, *Women in the Ministry of Jesus* (Cambridge: Cambridge University Press, 1984) 101; Leonard Swidler, *Jesus Was a Feminist: What the Gospels Reveal about His Revolutionary Perspective* (Lanham: Sheed and Ward, 2007) 31–32.

6. Joseph A. Fitzmyer, *The Gospel According to Luke 10–24* (Garden City: Doubleday, 1985) 892.

7. Darrell L. Bock, *Luke 9:51–24:53* (Grand Rapids: Baker Books, 1996) 1042.

Martha, the independent and outspoken woman, is rejected in favor of the dependent Mary who chooses the posture of a subordinate student."[8] Even more, if Luke's definition of being part of Jesus' family is "hearing the word and doing it," Mary's characterization in Luke remains incomplete (8:21).

Finally, readers have a tendency to sympathize with Martha to such an extent that they want to protect her (and her readers) from Jesus' critique. Some claim that Jesus' critique is part of a broader effort to silence the voices of women in the early church.[9] Others validate Martha's "service" to such an extent that they struggle to articulate why Jesus would have critiqued it.[10] This becomes increasingly common in early Protestant interpretations of this passage that wished to valorize Martha's work over Mary's "speculative life."[11] Most often, modern interpretations that tend this direction make claims like "it is difficult to imagine that the authorial audience would understand Jesus' praise of Mary to be an implicit criticism of Martha's hospitality."[12] Without critiquing Martha's service or hospitality, commentators struggle to comprehend Jesus' comment.[13] As readers often

8. Elisabeth Schüssler Fiorenza, "A Feminist Critical Interpretation for Liberation: Martha and Mary: Luke 10:38–42," *Religion and Intellectual Life* 3 (1986) 29.

9. Schüssler Fiorenza, "A Feminist Critical Interpretation for Liberation" 30–31; Satoko Yamaguchi, *Mary and Martha: Women in the World of Jesus* (Maryknoll: Orbis, 2002) 122; Barbara E. Reid, *Choosing the Better Part? Women in the Gospel of Luke* (Collegeville: Liturgical, 1996), 158. Mary Ann Beavis notes that the feminist valorization of Martha comes at Mary's expense ("Mary of Bethany and the Hermeneutics of Remembrance," *Catholic Biblical Quarterly* 75 [2013] 743–44).

10. This challenge is highlighted in the explanation of Bart J. Koet and Wendy E. S. North, "The Image of Martha in Luke 10:38–42 and John 11:1–12:8," in *Miracles and Imagery in Luke and John: Festschrift for Ulrich Busse* (ed. J. Verheyden, G. van Belle, J. G. Van der Watt; Leuven: Peeters, 2008) 58.

11. John Calvin, *Calvin's Commentaries, vol. 2: A Harmony of the Gospels: Matthew, Mark, and Luke* (trans. T. H. L. Parker; ed. David W. Torrance and Thomas F. Torrance; Edinburgh: St. Andrews, 1972; repr. Grand Rapids: Eerdmans, 1979) 89; see also David Lyle Jeffrey, *Luke* (Grand Rapids: Brazos, 2012) 153; F. Scott Spencer, *Salty Wives, Spirited Mothers, and Savvy Widows: Capable Women of Purpose and Persistence in Luke's Gospel* (Grand Rapids: Eerdmans, 2012) 174–75. For more on the history of interpretation of this passage, see Giles Constable, "The Interpretation of Mary and Martha," *Three Studies in Medieval Religious and Social Thought* (Cambridge: Cambridge University Press, 1995) 1–141.

12. Parsons, *Luke*, 182.

13. The most creative version of this interpretation comes from Meister Eckhart (d. 1327), who claimed that Martha's request of Jesus for Mary's help was to ensure that Mary was actually listening to what Jesus said, and not just sitting by Jesus for selfish enjoyment.

find, however, the more we strive to redeem Martha from Luke's story alone, the more strained Jesus' praise of Mary may seem.

Luke's account of these sisters puts readers in a never-ending comparison between them, much as we see with other household disputes in Scripture (for example, Sarah and Hagar; Leah and Rachel).[14] The best options for reading Luke's account alone tend to see these sisters as representing different ideals, or ways to be a disciple, and that the claim of this passage (with an ironic nod to 10:42) is that we need both.[15] Interpreting these sisters as ideals or allegories has a long history of interpretation within the church, with the earliest evidence in the writings of Clement and Origen.[16] However, the downside of such abstraction is that it tends to read this account as a parable. Making the two women into ideals or static models prevents them from illustrating what true discipleship looks like: transformation of life and faith. Furthermore, such a reduction diminishes their unique qualities in the narrative.[17] There is no getting around the fact that Luke's account is set up to contrast these sisters, not to conflate them. Unlike many other

---

Eckhart thought that Mary's trajectory of discipleship was to grow into the service Martha was embodying. Martha did not need to sit at Jesus' feet because she already had done so previously (Constable, "Interpretation" 116). Alice Y. Yafeh-Deigh highlights how modern African theologians have continued to support, rather than critique, Martha, in the interpretive tradition of Eckhart ("The Liberative Power of Silent Agency: A Postcolonial Afro-Feminist-Womanist Reading of Luke 10:38–42," in *Postcolonial Perspectives in African Biblical Interpretations* [ed. Musa W. Dube, Andrew M. Mbuvi, and Dora Mbuwayesango; Atlanta: Society of Biblical Literature, 2012] 417–39).

14. Spencer, *Salty Wives, Spirited Mothers, and Savvy Widows*, 148–54.

15. In John T. Carroll's words: "The distinct roles of the two sisters seem almost a caricature, dividing labors that belong together in the disciple: receiving the Lord's teaching and serving, or hearing and doing" (*Luke: A Commentary* [Louisville: Westminster John Knox, 2012], 247). See also John Nolland, *Luke 9:21–18:34* (Dallas: Word, 1993) 602; Fitzmyer, *Luke 10–24*, 893. Schüssler Fiorenza also argues for these sisters to represent particular actions: service and proclamation (Martha); listening without proclamation (Mary). See "A Feminist Critical Hermeneutic for Liberation" 25.

16. Constable, "Interpretation" 5, 15.

17. This is similar to interpreting Martha and Mary as round, rather than flat, characters. See Dorothy A. Lee who argues for a round characterization of Martha in John 11. See "Martha and Mary: Levels of Characterization in Luke and John," in *Characters and Characterization in the Gospel of John* (ed. Christopher W. Skinner; London: Bloomsbury T & T Clark, 2013) 201–2.

accounts of household disputes in Scripture, however, we see these sisters again. Luke's account on its own begs for resolution.[18]

If readers consider the account of Martha and Mary in John 11–12 independent of Luke, readers are apt to forget these sisters and focus only on Jesus and Lazarus (and Judas in John 12:1–8). The passage is often described by the miraculous event ("The Raising of Lazarus"), which is narrated briefly at the conclusion of the account (11:43–44).[19] Since the raising of Lazarus serves as the catalyst for Jesus' arrest in the Gospel of John (11:47–53; 12:10–11), it would make sense to focus on it. Nevertheless, the narrative time is spent on Jesus' encounters with Martha and Mary.[20] The canonical characterization of these sisters offers insight into why their story is so extensive.

A further consequence of separating the Johannine narrative from the Lukan account is that interpretations tend to relegate Mary's role to a footnote. Because she repeats what Martha says (11:21, 32), she seems unnecessary for the story. Many interpreters claim that her place in John 11 is simply "to introduce her" for her primary role in anointing Jesus with perfume in John 12.[21] Or, interpreters tend to give particular actions too much weight that cannot be supported in light of the rest of the story (for example, claiming that Mary's kneeling posture makes her statement "somehow less assertive").[22] Alternatively, interpreters claim that based on the introduction (11:1–2), Mary is an extremely important character whom the reader must not forget—but whose name is not mentioned in the introduction in 11:5, and

18. Simply because a Scripture text seems to desire resolution does not mean the reader gets to experience it (for example, Luke 15:11–32). However, when canonical resolution (or at least a trajectory toward resolution) is provided, as with Martha and Mary, or even the ending of Mark, it is worth seeing how that trajectory affects the first story, while not diminishing the open-endedness of the first account.

19. While this statement refers more to popular usage, it is supported by English Bible translations. For example, the NRSV and ESV subheadings only refer to Lazarus and Jesus; they never mention Martha or Mary (NIV says "the sisters of Lazarus"; CEB says "Jesus with Martha and Mary").

20. Francis Taylor Gench, *Encounters with Jesus: Studies in the Gospel of John* (Louisville: Westminster John Knox, 2007) 87.

21. Sandra M. Schneiders, *Written that You May Believe: Encountering Jesus in the Fourth Gospel* (2nd edition; New York: Crossroad, 2003) 105.

22. Lee, "Martha and Mary" 202.

who is second to Martha by 11:19.[23] Even Mary's anointing of Jesus in which she takes center stage (12:1–8) is often subsumed under comments about its relationship to the other parallel accounts of an anonymous woman anointing Jesus (Matt 26:6–13; Mark 14:3–9; Luke 7:36–50) or other Marys in the NT (especially Mary Magdalene).[24] Alternately, scholars may continue to contrast the sisters in John, pitting them against each other.[25] Essentially, more narrative provides more decisive evidence for an interpretive trajectory.[26]

Seeing Martha and Mary in John 11–12 as continuing the path of discipleship established for their characters in Luke 10:38–42 provides a more robust framework through which readers can determine how these characters change based on their encounters with Jesus. Without both accounts in Luke and John, readers are left with a distorted view of the characters and the discipleship they embody. A canonical reading asks interpreters to use all of the resources available, not to pretend they are somehow the same story but to see the unity and the diversity of voices contributing to the portrayals of these women and the Jesus they follow, to better instruct the readers in their own life of discipleship.

Can Divided Gospels Be Reunited?

For many years in biblical studies, asking a question about the relationship between two Gospels was presumed to be a question about the historical relationship between them: did John know about Luke's traditions of Martha and Mary, or vice versa? There is no way to prove these relationships definitively, despite much effort.[27] While a consensus view notes the theological

---

23. Francis Moloney, "Can Everyone Be Wrong? A Reading of John 11:1–12:8," *New Testament Studies* 49 (2003) 510.

24. Beavis, "Mary of Bethany" 755.

25. Jo-Ann Brant claims about John 12: "Martha is doing what is socially subscribed; Mary chooses to do something more." While true in a sense, this assessment denigrates Martha's action in a way that a canonical approach corrects (*John* [Grand Rapids: Baker, 2011] 179).

26. Colleen M. Conway chronicles how diverse the perspectives are on Mary's actions, even just in 11:30–34 (*Men and Women in the Fourth Gospel: Gender and Johannine Characterization* [Atlanta: Society of Biblical Literature, 1999] 144).

27. Philip F. Esler and Ronald Piper, *Lazarus, Mary, and Martha: Social-Scientific Approaches to the Gospel of John* (Minneapolis: Fortress, 2006) 55; Fitzmyer, *Luke*, 891;

and literary similarities between Luke and John, this essay engages in reading these Gospels canonically.

Rob Wall's scholarship has long advocated for a canonical approach to reading Scripture. Components of this approach include a theological commitment to the scriptural interpretation being in line with Scripture's theological ends, namely the rule of faith, for the formation of faithful disciples in the church.[28] Furthermore, the final shape of Scripture, not just in its final textual form, but its canonical collections, is informative for the church's understanding of faith and life.[29] This formative telos and structural purpose inform the following arguments about the relationship between Luke 10:38–42 and John 11:1–12:8.

It is illuminating to read these texts about two sisters with the same names together; indeed, the Johannine passage seems to presuppose previous knowledge from the reader about these characters (11:1–2), thereby privileging the canonical reader who has read Luke 10. The accounts in Luke and John share similarities in setting (but not location), characterization, and relationship to Jesus. In terms of setting, both Luke and John portray the sisters inside or just outside their house (Luke 10:38; John 11:20, 30; 12:1–2). Both use the same term, κώμη, to describe the sisters' village (Luke 10:38; John 11:30). Martha is consistently described in terms of her service and hospitality (Luke 10:38, 40; John 12:2) while Mary is always found at Jesus' feet (Luke 10:39; John 11:32, 12:3). Martha is known more for speaking than Mary is. The same words are used to describe Jesus in both texts, namely, "teacher" and "Lord."[30]

Despite their similarities, there are differences between the narratives about these sisters in Luke and John. While these differences between Luke and John are important and remind us that these accounts are different stories with their own contexts and locations in their respective Gospels, these

---

D. Moody Smith, *John Among the Gospels* (2nd edition; Columbia: University of South Carolina Press, 2001) 85–110, 159–65, 210. About Mary and Martha, Smith concludes that it is one of the passages "in which John does not contradict the Synoptics so much as he seems to explain, or elaborate upon, their depiction" (212).

28. Robert W. Wall, "The Canonical View," in *Biblical Hermeneutics: Five Views* (ed. Stanley E. Porter and Beth M. Stovell; Downers Grove: IVP Academic, 2012) 111, 115.

29. Ibid., 119–20.

30. Koet and North, "The Image of Martha" 59–60; Lee, "Martha and Mary" 201–2.

differences do not negate the similarities.[31] Furthermore, there are benefits to reading these accounts of Martha and Mary canonically, particularly in terms of the church's understanding of worship and discipleship.

Canonical Payoff:
From Unfinished Action to Transforming Discipleship

As we have seen, reading Luke 10:38–42 and John 11:1–12:8 separately can lead to a distortion of Luke's characterization of the sisters. Often, readers conclude with an interpretation that reproaches Martha, praises Mary, and remains unfinished. However, it is worth considering how the best readings of Luke 10:38–42 interpret this text so that its incomplete story probes the reader's desires for transformation and resolution. These desires are satisfied by a canonical reading that turns to the Gospel of John.

When we encounter Martha and Mary for the first time in Scripture, we find Martha receiving (δέχομαι) Jesus.[32] Martha's reception of Jesus is both informed by cultural standards of hospitality to strangers and is in line with Jesus' description of how missionaries should hope to be received

---

31. These differences and similarities are chronicled by Wendy E. Spronston North, *The Lazarus Story within the Johannine Tradition* (Sheffield: Sheffield Academic Press, 2001) 118–19. There are three primary differences: Luke does not name the village the sisters live in, John knows of a brother named Lazarus, and John claims that the woman who anoints Jesus' feet is named Mary, the sister of Martha and Lazarus. The location of Bethany is sometimes accounted for by the Gospel of Luke's geographical organization (Marshall, *Luke*, 451; Bock, *Luke 9:51–24:53*, 104) or by John moving Martha and Mary from Galilee to Bethany because John knows a tradition about a woman anointing Jesus there (Mark 14:3–9; Esler and Piper, *Lazarus, Mary, and Martha*, 57). Luke's setting, with Jesus visiting only the sisters, is notably provocative (Richard B. Vinson, *Luke* [Macon: Smith & Helwys, 2008] 348; Fred B. Craddock, *Luke* [Louisville: John Knox Press, 1990] 152). While it is possible that John's Lazarus is connected to Luke's parabolic Lazarus (16:19–31), I find this unlikely. Moreover, as Mary's action is the occasion for Martha and Jesus' conversation in Luke, so Lazarus' death is the situation that provokes Jesus' encounter with the sisters in John. In this way, Lazarus *as a character* is not the primary focus of John's text. Lastly, while John's account names Mary as the woman who anoints Jesus' feet (12:1–8), this is in contrast to an anonymous "sinner" in Luke 7:36–50. Only later traditions conflate these women, often with Mary Magdalene; see Susan Haskins, *Mary Magdalene: Myth and Metaphor* (New York: Riverhead, 1993).

32. Many, but not all, of the oldest manuscripts specify that Martha receives Jesus into her home. Commentators are divided about the originality of "into her home," but the meaning remains the same. Martha takes on the responsibility of hospitality by welcoming Jesus.

(10:1–16). Therefore, Martha is introduced in a praiseworthy manner by her actions as a host. However, this description is interrupted by the narrative's introduction of Mary, citing her relationship to Martha (sister), her location (at Jesus' feet), and her actions (listening to Jesus' teaching; 10:39).

Although these introductions highlight the differences between the two sisters, it is clear that both embody aspects of discipleship that Jesus has commanded earlier in Luke 10. Martha exhibits hospitality; Mary positions herself as a listening disciple (10:1–16).[33] Given that the narrative focuses solely on Jesus and these women, it becomes clear that the responsibility for hosting Jesus falls on Martha, independent of slaves or servants.[34] In Luke, Jesus has often had the occasion to teach about hospitality, and to offer instruction during meals (7:36–46; 19:1–9; see also Acts 9:43–11:13).[35] Furthermore, this depiction of Martha is reiterated in 10:40, as she is busy with much διακονία, which could be translated as "service," or "ministry" (Luke 8:3; 12:37; 22:26–27; Acts 1:17, 25; 6:1, 4; 11:29; 12:25; 20:24; 21:19). Based on this broad usage, it is best to understand Martha's actions in light of these traditions both about hospitality and about supporting Jesus' ministry: Martha is sharing her belongings with Jesus for the service of God's kingdom.[36] To wit, "in receiving Jesus, Martha is a child of peace (Luke 10:6) who has encountered God's reign."[37]

This positive introduction is only a prelude to the household crisis at the center of this story: while Martha is serving, she does so as one who is "distracted" or "overburdened" (περισπάω).[38] While not used elsewhere in

33. Mary's position at Jesus' feet echoes that of a student with a rabbi/teacher; see Luke 8:35; Acts 22:3; *m. ʾAbot* 1.4 (Nolland, *Luke*, 603).

34. The absence of help in this scene has led some interpreters to argue that Martha and Mary were poor (Yamaguchi, *Mary and Martha*, 133), while other interpreters infer wealth, either based on the precedent of women financially backing Jesus' ministry (Luke 8:1–3) or on the basis of the cave-like tomb and dinner hosted in John 11–12 (Marianne Meye Thompson, *John* [Louisville: Westminster John Knox, 2015] 240).

35. Parsons, *Luke*, 182; Vinson, *Luke*, 348.

36. Koet and North, "The Image of Martha" 55; Spencer, *Salty Wives, Spirited Mothers, and Savvy Widows*, 170.

37. Warren Carter, "Getting Martha Out of the Kitchen: Luke 10:38–42 Again," in *The Feminist Companion to Luke* (ed. Amy-Jill Levine and Marianne Blickenstaff; Cleveland: Pilgrim, 2004) 217.

38. Grammatically and narratively speaking, the relationship between Martha and Jesus is the center of this account (see Loveday Alexander, "Sisters in Adversity: Retelling Martha's

the NT, this term is used in similar contexts in the *Similitudes* of the *Shepherd of Hermas*, describing a rich man who is "distracted" about his riches (2:5) and another who is busy with too many things, and therefore is sinning (4:5).[39] While these texts are primarily focused on individual actions ("distraction") and their consequences, the translation of being "overburdened" with responsibilities hints at something beyond Martha's choice to serve Jesus. Martha may well be "overburdened" by societal expectation of what should be expected of one who serves Jesus. Readers may share this burden after reading the parable of the Good Samaritan (10:25–37) immediately preceding this passage: who could live up to such a model of service?

Luke describes Martha's interaction with Jesus in three ways, all centering around this claim of Martha's distraction and burdens. First, the narrator tells us that Martha is carrying too much on her own. Second, she requests that the "Lord" would intervene to tell her sister to help her. Even though she is burdened by "many things," she highlights that this is because she is "alone" (10:40). Third, Jesus' response states that she is anxious (μεριμνάω) and troubled (θορυβάζω) by many things.[40] This triple-affirmation of Martha's situation at first seems to imply that her distraction is her only—or even her primary—problem. However, the narrator's comment sets the reader up to question Martha's ability to clearly assess her state of affairs, and Jesus' statement is in response to her comment. Therefore, Martha's comment becomes the central component of this exchange.

Notably, Martha's comment emphasizes her position in this scene. She asks Jesus if he cares that "*my* sister left *me* by *myself* to serve" (10:40).[41] Even though she calls Jesus "Lord," affirming that he has the authority to send his disciples—like Mary—where he wants to send them, she follows up her

---

Story," in *The Feminist Companion to Luke* [ed. Amy-Jill Levine and Marianne Blickenstaff; Cleveland: Pilgrim, 2004] 206).

39. Loveday Alexander notes that ἀπερισπάστως is used in 1 Cor 7:35 to described the "undistracted" (KJV) devotion exhorted of disciples. Yet the same word is also used in a 2nd century papyrus, noting that someone is "vexed" about tax collectors. As Alexander says, this is "hardly grounds for moral censure" ("Sisters in Adversity" 210 n. 22).

40. Being troubled about things, especially material things, is highlighted as a danger for disciples (Luke 12:22–31). See Nolland, *Luke*, 602 and Joel B. Green, *The Gospel of Luke* (Grand Rapids: Eerdmans, 1997) 437.

41. The Greek is repetitively alliterative, as I reflect in this translation. See also Vinson, *Luke*, 352.

self-concern with an idea of where he should send Mary! Assuming he cares that Mary has left her alone, she says, "tell her to help me!"

There are two types of conversations in the Gospel of Luke where characters tell Jesus what to do. Sometimes, characters acknowledge their own weakness or simply speak the truth about their circumstances (5:8; 7:6). At times, Jesus tells them what to ask (10:2; 11:1). But occasionally, their requests of Jesus stem from their own (sometimes potentially justifiable) agendas (4:1–13; 9:59, 61; 13:25). These requests are not honored or praised. Martha's comment to Jesus combines the first and last category. She is speaking the truth about her circumstances: she is juggling too many things, as the narrator and Jesus affirm. However, when she tells Jesus what he should do about it, her comment moves into the last category: telling Jesus how to advance her agenda is the root of her problem, and becomes the basis for Jesus' reproach (10:41–42).

Evaluating Martha's main problem means that we have to understand how Mary is portrayed as well. Unlike Martha, Mary never speaks in this narrative; she is notable for her position (at the Lord's feet) and her actions (listening to Jesus' teaching). While Martha desires her help, Jesus claims that Mary has chosen this position, and nothing or no one will take it from her (10:42). Jesus' claim seems to invite a comparison between the two women, as we have seen.[42] Mary's position should be praised: by listening she receives Jesus; by sitting at his feet she "acknowledges his authority."[43]

Nevertheless, interpreters who claim that Mary, by listening, is a "model disciple" have elaborated on this picture of the sisters.[44] A model disciple is one who hears the word of God and does it (10:37; 11:28).[45] Mary listens, but in this way, she has done what Martha has also done: she has received Jesus as a prophet. She has "begun the journey of discipleship," but we do not know if she follows it through.[46]

---

42. This comparative pattern is exacerbated by translations that render ἀγαθός as "better." It could simply be translated as "good" (Vinson, *Luke*, 353; Jeffrey, *Luke*, 152). Also, note Luke Johnson's comment: "Mary chose the good part. Or perhaps better, 'Mary made the right choice' of what was necessary. Luke uses *agathos* rather than *kalos* so there is a moral dimension to her choice: by her listening, she has received the person of the Prophet, for the Prophet is defined by his 'word'" (*The Gospel of Luke* [Collegeville: Liturgical, 1991] 174).

43. Johnson, *Luke*, 173.

44. Parsons, *Luke*, 183; Nolland, *Luke*, 603.

45. See also Carter, "Getting Martha Out of the Kitchen" 230.

46. Green, *Luke*, 434. See also Vinson, *Luke*, 352.

Both Lukan portraits of Martha and Mary highlight their positives and their negatives even when we consider the context of this account in the Gospel.[47] Given the broader context of Luke 10, it is clear that providing service to missionaries doing the work of God's kingdom is not a problem. Mary's listening might be "good," but that does not imply that Martha's service is necessarily "bad." After all, the good Samaritan has just demonstrated love of neighbor through service and not words (10:25–37).[48] Martha's exchange both highlights the missing components of Jesus' commands about receiving missionaries (for example, how much food should be served? How long will they stay?) and points to the fact that her speech, not her service, is her central fault.[49] Within Luke, Mary might illustrate the potential dangers of listening to Jesus' word: inaction or suffering reproach from others.

As noted above, the risks of solely interpreting Luke 10:38–42 within the Gospel of Luke are that these approaches tend to use Martha and Mary as models of discipleship, but they are abstracted to such an extent they are unable to be disciples themselves. When we read John's Gospel, we get a fuller narrative of discipleship with these women. In this way, we can see the transformation that takes place in their discipleship, rather than implying that Luke's static snapshot tells us all we need to know.

When we turn to the Fourth Gospel, we find the sisters' unity highlighted from the very beginning of the narrative. This is clear even in the introductions: Bethany is described as the village of "Mary and her sister Martha," reversing the expected introduction from Luke 10:38. This seems to be, in part, to highlight Mary's role of anointing Jesus in the second story about these sisters (John 12:1–8). It also indicates more parity between the sisters, as the second description of these characters is "Martha and her

47. Fitzmyer is in the minority of modern commentators who declares that Luke 10:38–42 is "unrelated to the preceding passages" (*Luke*, 891).

48. Craddock argues that Luke puts the parable of the Good Samaritan next to this story of Martha so that the audience can see that "one is to 'go and do;' the other is to 'sit down and listen.' Jesus' word is not the same to everyone in every situation of need" (*Luke*, 149).

49. Nolland sees "a deliberate contrast between Martha who *tells* Jesus what he *must* say and Mary who *listens* to what Jesus *wishes* to say" (*Luke*, 604). The lack of specifics about hospitality (Luke 10:1–16) is because Jesus gives the instructions to the missionaries, rather than to those who receive them, and then narrates this account from the perspective of the one who receives him (Carroll, *Luke*, 349).

sister and Lazarus" (11:5), and later, "Martha and Mary" (11:19). In other words, where Luke's account seems to divide and contrast the sisters, John's account unites them. This is even clearer in their message to Jesus, where both sisters send the same account (11:3), and despite Jesus's delay, the narrator affirms his love for both of them and Lazarus (11:5).[50]

By the time that Jesus does arrive in Bethany, Lazarus has been in the tomb for four days (11:17) and a number of people have come to comfort Martha and Mary in the loss of their brother (11:19).[51] Thus begins the narrative that focuses on the characterization of Martha, as she encounters Jesus alone. Read in light of Luke's account of these sisters, John's description of Martha's interactions with Jesus highlights the differences in location and spoken confession, underlining Martha's growth as a disciple.

The Fourth Gospel describes Martha meeting Jesus on the road, as she greets him before he arrives at their house.[52] Narratively, this allows readers to focus on Martha and Jesus with no distractions. It also highlights the privacy of this encounter, in contrast to Mary's (11:31). However, unlike Luke, it moves Martha out of the house, which has been and will be her "normal" sphere (Luke 10:38; John 12:2). On the road, she cannot serve as host, except as one who greets Jesus.

In this new setting, Martha's greeting is simple: "Lord, if you had been here, my brother would not have died" (11:21). This comment makes clear what the sisters' message (11:3) had left implicit: the sisters were confident that Jesus would have changed the course of Lazarus' illness. At the same

50. Koet and North claim that this delay shows how the community can be comforted in Jesus' absence ("The Image of Martha" 49), while Andrew T. Lincoln points up the pastoral ramifications of this text, showing that delay and absence can still be expressions of love (*The Gospel According to Saint John* [Peabody: Hendrickson, 2005] 319).

51. While "their" is only explicit in some, and likely not the most reliable, Greek manuscripts, on account of the introductions (11:1–5), it is implied. The people who join Martha and Mary are called "the Jews" (οἱ Ιουδαῖοι), those who are often described negatively in John's Gospel. However, in this passage, they function in a neutral way, as the crowd is divided in their assessment of Jesus and his ministry by the end of the passage (see also Thompson, *John*, 247).

52. This encounter is neutral—neither positive nor negative—with respect to Mary, as John typically narrates one-on-one conversations with Jesus (for example, 3:1–11; 4:7–26; 5:5–9; 9:35–39; 13:6–10).

time, Martha "does not specify what she wants Jesus to do,"[53] a significant
change from her action in Luke (10:40). Here, she laments.[54] Moreover,
before Jesus speaks, she offers an expression of faith: "[E]ven now, I know
that God will give you whatever you ask" (11:22).[55]

When Jesus enters this conversation with Martha, as in most of his
conversations in John, the content starts to take on more than one meaning,
with puns and wordplays. Much as in Jesus' conversation with the Samaritan
woman, however, these double meanings serve as further probes for revelation (4:7–26), not awestruck silence (3:1–11). When Jesus claims that her
brother "will rise again," Martha logically reflects Jesus' own teaching back
to him: "I know that he will rise again in the resurrection on the last day"
(11:24; compare with 6:39–40). The double meanings are created because
Martha is responding in light of her previous theological knowledge and
Jesus is describing who he is, enabling her to expand her knowledge.[56] Jesus
does not engage in this discussion as though it is a philosophical argument
about the timing of the resurrection of the dead; instead, he demonstrates
that resurrection is not a future event because he is not a future event. The
life that Jesus brings, embodies, and empowers is available here and now.[57]
Jesus claims, "I am the resurrection and the life" (11:25). While Jesus' comment that those who believe in him "will never die" seems to fly in the face
of Lazarus' death if his statement is taken literally,[58] Martha does not make
this mistake. In fact, she is the only character in the entire Fourth Gospel
who responds positively to a predicate nominative "I am" statement.[59]

53. Conway, *Men and Women in the Fourth Gospel*, 140.

54. Yamaguchi claims that Martha's statement "combines the first two elements of traditional Jewish lament, the address and the complaint" (*Mary and Martha*, 120).

55. Such confidence that Jesus would merit a good reception from God is valid, according to John's Gospel, but it is also too limiting. Jesus claims that disciples will receive what
they ask of him (14:13, 14); later in this account readers find that Martha has underestimated
Jesus' relationship with the Father, as Jesus does not even have to ask the Father to receive
what he wants (11:41–42).

56. Conway, *Men and Women in the Fourth Gospel*, 141.

57. Gench, *Encountering Jesus*, 87; Lincoln, *John*, 324.

58. Nicodemus, the Samaritan woman, the Jewish authorities, and Jesus' disciples have
already demonstrated the foibles of interpreting Jesus' statements literally (3:1–11; 4:7–15;
8:51–53; 11:11–16).

59. The only other positive responses to any "I am" statements in the Fourth Gospel
are the Samaritan woman (4:26) and the disciples (6:20).

When Jesus asks her if she believes what he has said ("this"), she says, "Yes, Lord." She follows this affirmation with one of the most profound christological confessions in the entire Gospel, confessing precisely what the evangelist wants the reader to be able to say by the conclusion of the narrative (20:31).[60] She says, "I believe that you are the Messiah, the son of God, the one coming into the world." This statement sums up the Gospel's claims about Jesus so far. From the prologue on, John's audience learns that Jesus has come from God and is God's son (1:9; 3:31; 6:51; 8:23; 18:37). While the fact that he is God's son and God's messianic agent (1:41, 49) may not immediately seem connected to Jesus' claims about resurrection, there is more here than meets the eye (compare with 5:19–30). Jesus' role as Messiah and as God's son who has come down from heaven is to bring life out of death (17:3). Martha's confession shows that testifying that Jesus is the Messiah also means claiming that he is "the one who has the power of life. This is the shape of [his] messianic mission."[61] Therefore, affirming Jesus' relationship with God confirms Martha's belief in what Jesus says about resurrection and life (11:25–27).[62]

Martha's confession comes at a mini-climax in this story about Lazarus. While the problem (Lazarus' death) has not been solved, Martha is portrayed in a very different light by the end of this conversation than she was in Luke 10. If speech was her primary problem in Luke, we can say that by this point in John 11, Martha's speech is redeemed. Martha's testimony proclaims God's grace and truth (1:16) rather than her self-preoccupation and demands for Jesus. Martha's interactions with Jesus are those of a disciple who has grown in her faith: she believes what Jesus says is true, and she speaks truth to him (11:21–22, 24, 27). From a Martha who was critiqued for what she said in Luke, we now have a Martha whose faithful speech is

---

60. Lincoln, *John*, 324.

61. Thompson, *John*, 247.

62. Martha's confession is introduced with a perfect tense, which could be translated "I have believed" (πεπίστευκα), indicating a past action with continuing results. Moloney claims that the use of a perfect tense here implies that Martha's belief does not change in light of Jesus' revelatory statement ("Can Everyone Be Wrong?" 509). Instead, it seems that many of John's pivotal confessions tend to use the perfect tense (for example, 1:15, 32, 34, 41, 45; 3:18; 6:69; 16:27), either implying the continuous validity of the testimony or the "firmness" of the individual's conviction (for the latter, see Conway, *Men and Women in the Fourth Gospel*, 141).

confirmed in John. In fact, she is the only character in John who converses with Jesus and who gets to conclude the conversation.[63]

At this point, the narrative moves to characterize Mary in her interactions with Jesus. However, Martha returns for two more scenes. In the first, she joins Mary and the mourners at Lazarus' tomb. Awkwardly, she is reintroduced as "the sister of the dead man" (11:39). This reminder serves to shift the focus to Lazarus (again), as well as to point to what becomes the growing edge of Martha's faith. John's readers learn that Martha's resurrection-confessing faith still has room to grow. In her previous conversation with Jesus, what she confesses is true, just as what Jesus says is true, but both mean more than she can know. Furthermore, this introduction points to the stakes: Lazarus, as Martha reiterates, is really, truly dead. This is confirmed when she objects to Jesus' command to remove the stone from the tomb, telling him that the smell of decay will be unpleasant. For Martha, the opening of the tomb is the movement from a confessed faith to an embodied one.[64]

Jesus' response is even more perplexing than Martha's statement, as he says: "Did I not tell you that if you believed, you would see the glory of God?" (11:40). As John tells the story, the answer is no, he did not tell Martha (you is singular, σου) anything about her belief and God's glory. Instead, he had told the disciples who were with him before he came to Bethany that Lazarus' illness leads to God's glory, not to death (11:4). Given that God's glory is another way to talk about God's presence in Jesus, particularly in Jesus' death, resurrection, and exaltation (1:14), then Martha's confession that she sees God's presence in Jesus has indeed affirmed this (11:28). The indirectness of Jesus' statement shows that it is not a critique of Martha (for example, there is no "Martha, Martha" address; Luke 10:41), but an encouragement to build on the theological knowledge she has. This is another revelatory moment; what will she do afterward?

John gives us one more scene with Martha: when Jesus returns to her family's house six days before Passover, "they gave a dinner for him," and

---

63. This pattern is similar to the Samaritan villagers' response to Jesus, but this is the only time where an individual character has the last word. See Conway, *Men and Women in the Fourth Gospel*, 143.

64. Gench, *Encountering Jesus*, 88. It is worth noting that the Fourth Gospel does not expect anyone, even the disciple Jesus loves, to understand the resurrection and its significance before it happens (20:9; compare with 2:22).

"Martha served" (διακονέω; 12:2). In this way, Martha's characterization comes full circle. Serving Jesus at home was her place in Luke 10:38–42, and she spoke poorly about it, focusing all attention on herself in the guise of hospitality. While she does not speak at all in John 12, that does not denigrate her power of speech. Instead, readers have witnessed the power of Martha's speech to confess who Jesus is and to show how even the best confession is refined in continued relationship with Jesus. Martha is silent in John 12 because there is no need for speech. She serves, or ministers, to Jesus (and apparently those with him) without need for reproach. Martha's characterization shows how her encounters with Jesus have transformed both her service and her speech, two central aspects of discipleship for all of Jesus' followers, in ways that are honoring to Jesus.

With the conclusion of Martha's story of transformative discipleship, we now turn to the trajectories of Mary's story in John 11–12. In these chapters, Mary speaks only once, in contrast to her sister, but her actions shape both other characters' and readers' responses to her. Mary's characterization is essential to the Fourth Gospel's portrait of discipleship because she embodies what it means to abide in Jesus (15:1–17): it looks like obedience, devotion, and service.[65]

Beyond Mary and Martha's initial introduction in John (11:2–3), Mary is only described by her location (she stays home; 11:20) and eventually, by her company (mourners, οἱ Ἰουδαῖοι) who are "with her in the house" (11:31). For our purposes, the central point here is that unlike Martha, Mary is never alone with Jesus in this story. Her actions and words are always on display for others, not "secretly" (λάθρᾳ), as Martha's can be. This is not a contrast in characterization of the sisters, as though acting in secret or in public was better. It simply affects the way that readers and other characters respond.[66] There is no reason to think that the mourners who are present are adversarial toward Jesus or this family (see Mark 5:38–40);[67] in fact, some of

---

65. As Lincoln notes: "Just as her sister, Martha, has been the first to anticipate the full Johannine confession of faith in Jesus' identity, so now Mary, another female follower of Jesus, is the first to anticipate the full Johannine model of costly, loving discipleship" (*John*, 338).

66. Another way to consider this is to see Martha as the representative of the reader (see Lincoln, *John*, 328) and Mary as the character who moves along the plot.

67. Conway, *Men and Women in the Fourth Gospel*, 139.

them believe in Jesus after seeing him raise Lazarus (11:45). Mary will bring them to Jesus, just as the Samaritan woman brings townspeople to him, though this is primarily so that they can serve as witnesses at the tomb.[68]

When Mary hears Martha's statement that Jesus is calling for her, she "gets up quickly" (ἠγέρθη ταχύ). This rapid reaction demonstrates Mary's obedience (see John 13:27; 20:4; Matt 28:7–8). She hears the voice of her Shepherd, even mediated through her sister, and she immediately responds (10:3–5).[69] While the mourners with her also respond quickly (11:31), they do so because they have seen her, not because they have heard from Jesus. Indeed, in classic Johannine irony, these mourners follow Mary to the tomb because they think she is going to weep there (11:31). She will go to the tomb, though that is not her purpose in leaving the house. She is not alone in weeping, as Jesus also will weep (11:33–35). This irony began when Jesus claimed that this illness will not end with Lazarus' death—he leaves unspoken that it will end with his own (11:4, 53).[70]

Mary leaves the house in obedience to Jesus' call. When she (and the mourners) encounter Jesus on the road, her reaction is two-fold: she speaks and she kneels at Jesus' feet. Mary only speaks one sentence in Scripture, and it replicates Martha's greeting to Jesus: "Lord, if you had been here, my brother would not have died" (11:32). The unity of the sisters' voices indicates further reclamation of Martha's voice: these women now speak together, and they speak truth that Jesus also affirms (11:4–6). Unlike Martha, Mary says nothing beyond this claim that the presence of Life, in Jesus, would have prevented Lazarus' death. In light of Martha and Jesus' conversation, the reader can see the devoted faith inherent in both sisters' reactions to the situation. Mary's statement is not simply a duplication of Martha's, however. As we have noted, Mary is accompanied by other Jews whom she has brought to Jesus. They hear her faithful lament and complaint of Jesus' absence, which shapes their reactions (11:33–34, 36–37, 45–46).[71]

Although we never hear Mary's individual voice in Scripture, her silence highlights the importance of her actions. Notably, Mary kneels at Jesus' feet

---

68. Ibid., 143; Lincoln *John*, 325.

69. The fact that Martha can accurately communicate the Shepherd's voice is another indication that her speech has been redeemed.

70. Lincoln, *John*, 319.

71. Conway, *Men and Women in the Fourth Gospel*, 145.

when she greets him (11:32). This posture echoes her position in Luke 10:39. Luke notes how she listens to Jesus from this position, but not how she responds. In John 11:32, she speaks, rather than acts. Her action is saved for the next chapter, where she is again at Jesus' feet (11:2; 12:3). The implication of her position at Jesus' feet is slightly different depending on the context. In Luke, Mary's position reflects a pupil learning from a rabbi (*m. 'Abot* 1.4; 2 Kings 4:38; Acts 22:3).[72] In John, kneeling at Jesus' feet connotes devotion, or a recognition of Jesus' identity (18:6; compare with 9:37–38).[73] Mary's posture differentiates herself from the crowd, as she is the only one who kneels before Jesus, demonstrating her devotion and acknowledgment of his authority.[74]

The next time we encounter Mary, she is once more at Jesus' feet. After some time has passed, Jesus again joins Martha, Lazarus, and Mary for dinner in Bethany, six days before Passover. While Martha and Lazarus are introduced based on their places at dinner (serving and at the table, respectively), Mary is not introduced until 12:3.[75] Without speaking, she anoints Jesus' feet with nard and wipes them with her hair, positioning herself at Jesus' feet for a third and final time.

Mary does not interpret her actions, but they are central to the Fourth Gospel's expression of discipleship. Mary's action of anointing Jesus' feet foreshadows his teaching about what following him truly looks like—rejecting

72. Nolland, *Luke*, 603.

73. Thompson, *John*, 247.

74. Jesus' reaction to Mary's statement and position, as well as the presence of the other mourners, is one of the most exegetically challenging parts of John 11:1–44. John 11:33 says that Jesus is "deeply disturbed in spirit and is troubled" (ἐνεβριμήσατο τῷ πνεύματι καὶ ἐτάραξεν ἑαυτὸν). Scholars differ as to whether this disruption is in anger (at lack of faith of bystanders: Gail O'Day, *The Gospel of John* [Nashville: Abingdon, 1995] 690; Craig S. Keener, *The Gospel of John: A Commentary*, volume 2 [Peabody: Hendrickson, 2003] 846; at death/evil: Raymond Brown, *The Gospel according to John* [Garden City: Doubleday, 1965] 435; Frederick Dale Bruner, *The Gospel of John: A Commentary* [Grand Rapids: Eerdmans, 2012] 676) or in compassion: Thompson, *John*, 248; D. Moody Smith, *John* [Nashville: Abingdon, 1999] 224). For our purposes, it is notable that the typical connotation of ἐμβριμάομαι, describing Jesus as angry, tends to reflect poorly on Mary (Conway, *Men and Women in the Fourth Gospel*, 147).

75. Jo-Ann Brant notes: "Lazarus' home is an abode of the dead. Rites of hospitality become funeral rites." This conflation of time and space informs Jesus' interpretation of Mary's action (*John*, 179).

(even rightful) claims of authority for those of service, humility, and love. Only in both Mary's anointing and Jesus' footwashing does the Fourth Gospel use the verb ἐκμάσσω, describing how Mary and Jesus wipe off the feet they care for (12:3; 13:5; compare with Luke 7:38, 44). Both accounts are set at a dinner (δεῖπνον, 12:2; 13:2, 4), and at both dinners, the narrator highlights the presence of a particular beloved friend (12:2; 13:23), as well as Judas' adversarial presence (12:4–6; 13:2).[76] Lastly, beyond the foreshadowing of the specific service of caring for another person's feet, both accounts are oriented around Jesus' death. The broader meaning of footwashing is sacrificial, pointing toward Jesus laying down his life and taking it up again, just as he does with his garments (13:4, 12; 10:11–18). In this way, Mary's actions are the embodiment of obedient discipleship to a command that Jesus has yet to give. While known for quiet listening in Luke 10 and devotion in John 11, we see Mary's characterization come full circle as she becomes most known for this action of service (11:2).

Listening for Harmonic Notes, not Harmonizing

A canonical reading of the stories of Martha and Mary offers several benefits beyond reading each Gospel account alone. The beginning of Martha's story in Luke 10 is complicated: while she is hosting and serving—actions that are praiseworthy—she is also reproached by Jesus when she tells him to have Mary serve with her. This active, yet poorly speaking, Martha changes by the time we see her in John 11. There, outside her house, she does not act in any particular way; she only speaks. This time, her speech is entirely laudatory: she articulates one of the most complete confessions of Jesus' identity in the Gospel of John. Like all disciples, Martha's transformation includes room for more growth, yet Scripture concludes her story by portraying her serving again, in John 12. This return to service shows that it is not her service itself that was the problem; it was her speech. The answer to problematic speech is not silence, but transformation. Martha's confession in John 11 is paired with her service in John 12 as a model for transformed discipleship.

---

76. See also Yamaguchi, *Mary and Martha*, 122.

Mary's story runs a different course. She begins with significant positive potential in Luke 10, listening attentively to Jesus and running aground of expected gender stereotypes. Yet, given the context of her story in Luke, it is striking that her listening to Jesus' word is not paired with proclamation or action. This changes in John 11–12. Her brief speech becomes a proclamation of faith to the witnesses of Jesus' miracle, and she becomes known for her action and service in anointing Jesus' feet.

Reading the portraits of these sisters from Luke and John together is important because it illustrates these characters' growth and transformation as Jesus' disciples. As canonical approaches to Scripture highlight, this becomes formative for ancient and modern disciples who seek to follow Jesus as Martha and Mary did.[77] The canonical harmony balances the voices such that speech is redeemed, the word is heard, proclaimed, and obeyed. Strangers and friends are welcomed, honored, and loved. This is discipleship worth emulating, as Jesus instructs (Luke 10:1–16; John 13:1–17).

At the same time, a canonical reading resists *harmonizing* Luke and John's voices such that they speak in unison. Part of the beauty of canonical approaches is that they recognize the diverse voices in the canon as integral to the proclamation of the gospel. In this particular case, it is helpful to see how these two texts create harmonic notes, or overtones, together, but they also fit as solos in their own Gospel contexts. The central point of a canonical reading is that it recognizes *both* the unity and the diversity of the Gospels' accounts.

In Luke, Jesus' reproach of Martha's speech occurs immediately after the parable of the Good Samaritan (10:25–37), where a surprising figure is praised for his neighborly service. Martha is a reminder that service by itself is not discipleship. How we speak about or evaluate our understanding of service matters. Martha highlights the tension between Jesus' calls for hospitality and service as discipleship (10:1–16, 25–37) and the need to listen to what Jesus says (10:39–42). This emphasis on hospitality, as we noted, is central to Luke's Gospel. In this way, Luke shows how service and hospitality,

---

77. One notable aspect of Martha and Mary's discipleship is that they do not leave their home in order to be Jesus' followers, unlike most male and female disciples in the Gospels. This nontransient portrait of discipleship is certainly helpful for modern disciples who are not often itinerant! See Vinson, *Luke*, 350.

even with the best of intentions, is essential to discipleship, but is not the only essential part of discipleship. Luke shows us Mary, who reminds readers that while listening to Jesus' word is good, action must follow, whether that action is prayer (Luke 11:1–4) or something like Martha's service. Luke's Gospel highlights these tensions, and does not resolve them. Like a parable, this story points out the dangers of discipleship without offering obvious solutions. This lack of resolution can be challenging to readers, which can produce thoughtful change. However, such a challenge can lead to incomplete resolution rather than life-giving instruction. If that should happen, it is up to the canonical interpreter to see what other resources Scripture offers.

In John, Martha's speech is redeemed from its self-oriented state in Luke. At the same time, much as hospitality is central to Luke, confession is central to John. Martha offers a witness to Jesus' identity that Gospel readers have been waiting for since the beginning of the narrative. While Peter claims this confessional role in the Synoptics (compare with John 6:69), Martha asserts it in John. Confession is such a central part of discipleship for the Fourth Gospel that it is part of the evangelist's own identity (19:35; 20:30–31; 21:24). In this way, John's account does not just redeem Martha's speech from Luke. Instead, it lifts up Martha's discipleship to the most admirable level—and shows how there's still growth beyond it. In John's narrative, discipleship always leaves room for more of the Spirit's transformative work.

Mary's portrayal in John can be summarized as a portrait of John's other primary component of discipleship: participating in the love shown by the Father and the Son (3:16; 13:1–2, 34–35). Mary embodies this love for others in her obedience, devotion, and service. In this way, the portrayals of these characters fit the individual Gospel's account of what it means to be a disciple of Jesus, but their overarching characterizations transcend the Gospel accounts to inform the church's life of discipleship.

There is one more shared aspect of Luke and John's accounts of Martha and Mary that illustrates the benefit of harmonic notes without harmonizing accounts. In each Gospel, the characters are asked to choose between good things: service or listening (Martha, Luke 10:38–42), and giving to the poor or giving to Jesus (Mary, John 12:3–8).[78] In both accounts, the presence of

---

78. Alexander, "Sisters in Adversity" 211.

Jesus is the decisive factor. The point of a canonical reading of these texts is to see the power of their combined witness: as the honoree has said, "for the current period of salvation history, to love God is to hear his messiah's Word."[79] For Martha, Mary, and Scripture's readers, the presence of Jesus shapes discipleship then and now.

79. In these passages, loving God is primarily John's focus, while listening to the messiah's Word is Luke's focus. See Robert W. Wall, "Martha and Mary [Luke 10:38–42] in the Context of a Christian Deuteronomy," *Journal for the Study of the New Testament* 35 (1989) 28.

The Place of the Johannine Canon within the New Testament Canon

John Painter

My contribution, in honor of my friend and colleague Robert Wall, draws attention to the complexity of the canon and some of the implications of its formation for interpretation. Recognition of distinctively "Christian" writings was an evolutionary process, and only retrospectively legitimately called Christian. The precanonical formation of the fourfold Gospels, the Pauline corpus, and the Catholic Epistles shaped the New Testament canon and its interpretation. The Acts of the Apostles and Hebrews intersperse the three collections, and for many reasons, including its early disputed status, Revelation comes last.[1] But if Genesis begins at the beginning, Revelation announces the end, appropriately closing the Christian canon East and West.[2]

Canonicity and the Significance of Order

The order of the fourfold Gospels separates Luke from Acts, which, in the Western canon, introduces the Pauline corpus.[3] Hebrews comes at the end of that corpus, probably implying its dubious authorship by Paul. Consequently, Hebrews separates the Pauline Epistles from the Catholic Epistles. They are followed by Revelation, which closes the New Testament canon and the Christian Bible. While the Johannine Epistles are kept together, they, the Gospel and Revelation, are separated from each other in both Eastern and Western canons. The Gospel and 1 John were attested as received books quite early, but 2, 3 John and Revelation remained disputed well into the fourth century. Though Irenaeus quotes words from 2 John 7, he does so as if they were part of 1 John (with which it overlaps in 2:18; 4:3) and refers explicitly to

1. Eusebius, *H.E.* 3.24.17–18; 25.2.
2. Eusebius, *H.E.* 3.24.17–18; 3.25.3–4.
3. The unity of Luke-Acts and the mutual illumination of reading each book in the light of the other is the fruit of the second half of the last century.

only one Johannine Epistle.[4] There is no clear early attestation of 2 or 3 John, which is why their authenticity was contested into the fourth century. What evidence there is suggests the close association of 2 and 3 John with 1 John.

The canon belongs to reception history. It reveals how the books were received and read rather than how and for what purpose they were written. The process of recognition and reception continued to the end of the fourth century. By this time the growing separation of East and West, the Greek-speaking and Latin-speaking churches, was hardening, revealing distinct Eastern and Western canons.[5] Differences of canonical order have not been negotiable between East and West, suggesting that there is something important in it. In this process, the weight of authority resting on reception history moves in the direction of making the church the authoritative definer and interpreter of Scripture. However, the church did not work arbitrarily. In defining Scripture, we see certain criteria at work. First evident in Acts 1:21–22, the criteria for the selection of a replacement for Judas clarify the nature of apostolicity. The replacement, like the "Twelve," was to be one of those who had been with Jesus from the time of his baptism by John, and who was also a witness of the risen Jesus. Apparently few qualified. Pauline apostleship does not conform to the former criterion, though his claim to be a witness of the risen Lord seeks to meet the latter, making, as he recognised, his claim to apostleship irregular (1 Cor 15:8–11). Direct historical connections with Jesus were crucial for apostolicity and canonicity. Failure to be able to trace a book back to the apostles left its reception in doubt, and works that lacked early attestation were disputed or rejected.[6]

The Significance of the Four Gospels

When Eusebius gave a rationale for the four Gospels he asserted that *Matthew* and *John* were the work of two apostles while the other two were the

---

4. See the discussion in John Painter, *1, 2, and 3 John* (Collegeville: Liturgical, 2002) 46–57, 337–41.

5. The Catholic Epistles follow Acts in the Eastern Canon. For a wider discussion of the shape and making of the canon, see John Painter, "James" in *James and Jude* (Grand Rapids: Baker Academic, 2012) 7–16. The Christian canon presumed the Jewish Scriptures. This aspect of the Western canon was disputed at the Reformation, with the Reformers choosing the Hebrew canon rather than the LXX, the Bible of the early church.

6. See Eusebius, *H.E.* 2.23.24–25; 3.24.17–25.7.

Gospels of the apostles Peter and Paul via their respective disciples Mark and
Luke.[7] This canonical establishment suggests that the four Gospels are exclusively and hermeneutically bound together, giving a sense of completeness,
a view held by Irenaeus. Certainly the first three Gospels belong together in a
special way and provide our best historical evidence concerning the mission
and message of Jesus. Their authors, however, were not simply channels of
the historical tradition. Each provides a distinctive selection, arrangement,
and reading of the tradition from the author's own distinctive perspective.
That is true regardless of the evidence of interdependence between the first
three Gospels. Nevertheless, in them the tradition remains close to the
surface. Even so, the Synoptics treat common material in different order
and in different ways. Those who, in the name of the historical accuracy of
each Gospel, insist that variations of order and detail between the Gospels
reveal repetitions of incidents, healings, miracles, and sayings, rather than
revealing different interpretative treatments of the same incidents, seem to
assume that modern standards of historicity determined these ancient Gospels, rather than the practices of *ancient* biographies. They ranged from the
fanciful to serious attempts to portray real people. But even the best of these
is more helpfully compared with an artist's painting than modern, precisely
documented historical accounts. Attempts to reconcile every difference in
chronology by insisting on repeated events strain credulity. The placement
of the cleansing of the temple toward the beginning of John and just prior
to the Synoptic passion story is taken to mean that the act was performed
twice, in spite of the failure of any one Gospel to offer two accounts.[8]

The Distinctiveness of the Fourth Gospel

The evidence of the conceptual categories, language, style, and narrative of
the Fourth Gospel differs from the Synoptics, suggesting that the tradition
has been subject to a more unified and thoroughgoing interpretation. Both
Irenaeus and Clement of Alexandria affirm, "Last of all John . . ." They do

---

7. *H.E.* 2.15.1–2; 3.39.14–16; 6.14.4–7; 6.25.3–6.
8. See C. H. Dodd, *The Interpretation of the Fourth Gospel* (Cambridge: Cambridge
University Press, 1953) 448, and *Historical Tradition in the Fourth Gospel* (Cambridge: Cambridge University Press, 1963) 157, including n. 2.

not mean simply fourth in the canon but last in the sense of the fourth of the Gospels to be written/published. Irenaeus makes Matthew first, then Mark as giving written form to Peter's oral gospel, and then Luke as the written form of Paul's oral gospel. Finally, last of all, John.[9] For Irenaeus, John provides the theological resources for the refutation of heresies. It is a theological Gospel. Alternatively, Clement makes the Gospels with genealogies first, then Mark as Peter's oral preaching in written form, and "finally John." Clement then contrasts the spiritual John with the "bodily factual" accounts of the first three Gospels. "John, last of all, conscious that the bodily facts had been set forth in the Gospels, urged by his disciples, and, divinely moved by the Spirit, composed a spiritual Gospel. This is Clement's account."[10] Placing John last recognizes time for reflection in the interpretative process of the "spiritual" as distinct from the "bodily factual" accounts of the other three. Dodd's work in *Historical Tradition* has done enough to show the difficulty of identifying historical tradition in John and that when it becomes evident, it is Synoptic-like. It is thus difficult to discern with any confidence whether John is making use of the Synoptics or Synoptic-like tradition.[11] What was clear to Dodd is the pervasive Johannine theological interpretation in contrast to the Synoptics, a point of view consistent with Clement's observation and with the later judgement of Augustine. In his work *The Harmony of the Gospels,* published circa 400 C.E., he adopts the canonical order of the Gospels, naming the first and fourth as apostolic compositions, without appealing to the apostolic links of the second and

9. See Irenaeus *A.H.* 3.1.1–2 (also in Eusebius *H.E.* 5.8.2–4). As Bruce Metzger notes, "It is not known when our four Gospels were collected into one codex and arranged in the order that now is common" (*The Canon of the New Testament: Its Origin, Development, and Significance* [Oxford: Clarendon, 1987] 296–97). The Muratorian Fragment on the canon "seems to imply" what became the canonical order. Metzger dates the "Fragment" at the end of the second century (191). The order of Irenaeus is at least as important, along with that of Origen, whose influence "was made popular by Eusebius," whose Canon Tables "were afterwards adopted by Jerome for his Latin Bible," and is supported by almost all manuscript evidence, with very minor support for eight variations of order (296).

10. See Clement *Stomateis* in *H.E.* 6.14.4–7. Quotations from Clement's lost work *Stomateis* have been preserved in the works of others such as this one by Eusebius.

11. See John Painter, "The Fourth Gospel and the Founder of Christianity," in *Engaging with C. H. Dodd on the Gospel of John* (ed. Tom Thatcher and Catrin H. Williams; Cambridge: Cambridge University Press, 2013) 257–84. For Dodd's classic work, see his *Historical Tradition and the Fourth Gospel* (Cambridge: Cambridge University Press, 1963).

third.[12] He argues that the first three Gospels deal with the human temporal life of Jesus, while John sets out the true divinity of the Lord as the Father's equal.[13] Thus for Augustine, like Clement, *John* is the theological or spiritual Gospel in contrast to the more historical Synoptics. The title of my 1975 book, *John: Witness and Theologian,* makes clear that this Gospel is *based on* good historical tradition that has undergone long, deep, and pervasive theological reflection and interpretation.[14]

This position has been the subject of an increasingly concerted challenge in the last twenty years or so. It is not that the challenge is new. Two different views of the relationship of John to the Synoptics are evident in the tradition of the early fourth century, prior to the fixing of the NT canon. What is new is the momentum the challenge has gained and the growing support it has gathered. What drives the challenge is already to be seen in the fourth century alongside and in conflict with the realization of the difference of John from the Synoptics. The renewed movement seeks to show that John provides the same kind of historical narrative and best historical practice as is said to be found in the Synoptics. It seems evident to me that John and the Synoptics *do things in different first-century ways.* I believe I am not alone in holding this view. Alternatively, some scholars engaged in the renewed movement: (1) attempt to find historical tradition from the early second century (Papias) to support their view of the early orthodox origin of John and complementary historicity of the four Gospels; and (2) aim to discredit scholars of the last generation who recognized the difference of John from the Synoptics in terms of its unified spiritual/theological interpretation of the Jesus tradition.

Charles Hill's Construction and Critique
of "The Orthodox Johannophobia Theory"

Looking back, it now seems that Charles E. Hill began his assault in his 1998 article, "What Papias Said about John (and Luke)."[15] Though not the first to

---

12. Augustine, "The Harmony of the Gospels," in Marcus Dobs, ed., *The Works of Aurelius Augustine*, volume 3 (Edinburgh: T & T Clark, 1873) 141.

13. See Augustine, "The Harmony of the Gospels" 144.

14. John Painter, *John: Witness and Theologian* (London: SPCK, 1975). I have no reason to change this view.

15. *Journal of Theological Studies* 49 (1998) 582–629.

note the possibility that a Papias testimony might underlie Eusebius' case for the historical accuracy of the four Gospels, his article mounted a full-scale attempt to show this to be the case.[16] The point of this identification is to establish the early second century attestation of the circumstances of the composition of the Gospel of John, showing it to be in complete harmony with the other Gospels and in the mainstream life of the church. The full significance of the article becomes clear only with Hill's 2004 book, *The Johannine Corpus in the Early Church*.[17] Here the identification of a hidden Papias testimony becomes crucial in the campaign to identify the Gospel of John in the Great church in the first half of the second century. Hill opposes a small group of scholars linked to misleading the biblical scholarly world into (1) accepting the emergence of the Gospel of John in the second half of the second century from a shadowy heretical/gnostic context and (2) believing that the Gospel of John was held with suspicion by the Great church until it was rescued by the defense of Irenaeus. Identification of the Papias testimony, therefore, serves two purposes. It locates the Gospel of John early in the second century in the context of the Great church, and it attests this Gospel's complementary historical accuracy along with the Synoptics.

In prosecuting his case, Hill created a rather melodramatic overall title/theory to identify the position he opposes, "The Orthodox Johannophobia Theory."[18] This is not accurately descriptive of the views he sets out to refute, nor is it helpful. It hardly encourages genuine scholarly engagement. Hill claims that the construction of this "theory" is based on "three major empirical bases": (1) "Johannophobia Proper," (2) "The Silence of the Early Orthodox Sources" about the Gospel of John; and (3) "The Gnostic Preference for John."[19] In the first of these "major empirical bases," he repeats the loaded, emotive language of his "theory," giving it a psychological explanation: "First, 'Johannophobia', as I am using it here, properly refers to an actual state of mind thought to have existed widely among the orthodox,

---

16. See T. Scott Manor, "Papias, Origen, and Eusebius: The Criticisms and Defense of the Gospel of John," *Vigiliae Christianae* 67 (2013) 1–21. Manor notes the earlier (1933) contribution on this issue by V. Bartlett (1 n. 1).

17. Oxford: Oxford University Press, 2004.

18. Hill, *The Johannine Corpus*, 11. See the *Review of Biblical Literature* review by Kyle Keefer (01/2005) of this book, where Keefer notes that this is an emotive and unhelpful title.

19. Hill, *The Johannine Corpus*, 63–65.

that is, a mental state of suspicion, prejudice, fear, or opposition as regards the Fourth Gospel."[20] If these states were complementary to fear, the title might be justified, but the final "or opposition" indicates that any one of them is enough for Hill to use the title "Johannophobia Proper." This is confirmed by his treatment of the offending scholars. As we shall see, C. K. Barrett nowhere *affirms* one of these categories and only "fear" justifies the use of *phobia*.

The actual case that Hill criticizes is built on the second and third evidence based arguments. Hill's attempt to refute them is far from convincing. A full critique of his book is not possible here. I have chosen to use his critique of Barrett as my test case in response to his critique. Part of my response involves an evaluation of the credibility of his attempt to identify a Papias testimony in *HE* 3.24.1–13. This is crucial for his attack on his second empirical basis. The third concerns the evidence of relatively early gnostic use of John, which he does not deny, though he tries to deflect the evidence by claiming that the gnostics misused the Gospel.[21] That is hardly the point. Sanders and Barrett also thought the gnostics misused the Gospel and did so quite early. Barrett found no convincing evidence for "the orthodox" use before 150 C.E. That Hill finds Barrett's criteria for recognizing use of the Gospel too rigorous shows that his identification of use is optimistic and unconvincing.

The Case of C. K. Barrett

Barrett's 1955 commentary, with a second edition in 1978,[22] is said to be the basis for the continued influence of the Bauer Sanders thesis in the English (and German) speaking worlds.[23] As friend and student of Barrett, I am sensitive to Hill's criticism, especially as he uses a single, one-fit-all critique, fashioned in Hill's terms. The critique lacks accurate attention to Barrett's

---

20. Hill, *The Johannine Corpus*, 63.

21. Ibid., 267.

22. C. K. Barrett, *The Gospel According to John* (1st edition, London: SPCK, 1955; and 2nd edition, Philadelphia: Westminster John Knox, 1978).

23. Hill, *Johannine Corpus*, 17–19, 30–31. The 1978 edition of Barrett's commentary was translated into German and appears in the Meyer Series alongside the Bultmann commentary.

careful weighing of evidence and overlooks the dubious nature of much of the evidence used straightforwardly to favor his case.

Barrett's 1955 Commentary

Hill commences his critique of Barrett's 1955 commentary by asserting that "His treatment of the place of the Gospel in the development of theology and in the church is strongly coloured by J. N. Sanders's research in *The Fourth Gospel in the Early Church*, to which he refers explicitly and repeatedly. Relying on Sanders, he writes . . ."[24] This strikes me as exaggeration/distortion, supporting his failure to acknowledge Barrett's independent and critical use, not only of Sanders, but also of the second century sources. At no time did Barrett adopt Sanders's Egyptian or later Syrian hypothesis of the origin of John.

Given that Hill attributes "Johannophobia" to Barrett, it is important for him to establish the evidence. He seeks to do so by quoting a passage about the reception of the Gospel before Irenaeus. "Orthodox Christian writers seem unaware, or scarcely aware, of the existence of the gospel, perhaps even suspicious of it; and this is true of those who might with greatest probability be expected to know and use it. Even Polycarp, according to Irenaeus the hearer of John, shows no knowledge of the gospel, though his epistle shows a possible allusion to 1 John. It is among gnostic heretics that John can first be proved to have been used."[25] First, Barrett says of the Orthodox, that they "seem unaware, or scarcely aware" of the Gospel, "perhaps even suspicious of it." The "perhaps even" introduces the least likely of the three possibilities arising from the Orthodox *silence*, which is one of two empirical bases. Second, note the careful distinctions made by Barrett. Silence in the sources does not *prove* the lack of knowledge; they "seem to be unaware, or scarcely aware, perhaps even suspicious." By contrast, when the sources *prove* earlier

---

24. Ibid., 17. In almost 150 pages, Barrett makes five or six references to J. N. Sanders, *The Fourth Gospel in the Early Church: Its Origin and Influence in Christian Theology up to Irenaeus* (Cambridge: Cambridge University Press, 1943). References to Sanders outside the Introduction are to the Sanders-Mastin 1968 Commentary.

25. Hill, *The Johannine Corpus,* 18; Barrett, *The Gospel According to John,* 1955:106 and 1978:124–25.

knowledge and use of the Gospel of John, "It is among gnostic heretics that John can first be proved to have been used."

Hill finds another place where Barrett uses the word "suspicion." He introduces the quotation by setting the context, "Without accepting the theory of an Alexandrian origin of the Fourth Gospel, Barrett still accepts Sanders's logic: 'since it seems that the church of Alexandria was not in its earliest days strictly orthodox, it is easy to understand that a gospel proceeding from such a source should at first be looked at with suspicion by orthodox Christians.'"[26] Hill fails to allow for Barrett's practice of setting out alternative views from the point of view of those who hold them, not setting them up for failure. Barrett did not hold the view of Alexandrian origin nor the logic flowing from it.[27] This is made clear in the next sentence, ignored by Hill: "Of these arguments only that derived from external evidence carries weight, and that less than has been supposed. Only in Egypt are climatic conditions favourable for the preservation of papyrus, and in consequence the great majority of the papyri known to scholars are of Egyptian origin."[28] Nevertheless, silence is negative evidence, and "suspicion" is hypothetical and unattested by external evidence. It carries no weight. So much for the evidence that "suspicion" bears the weight of "Johannophobia" in Barrett's treatment of the reception of the Gospel of John, even if it were adequate evidence for it, which I dispute.

Hill rightly sets out Barrett's conclusion concerning the double-sided evidence (silence about the Gospel of John in extant Orthodox sources before 150 C.E., with earlier evidence of gnostic use) upon which *his hypothesis* is based, but fails to acknowledge its hypothetical nature, which Barrett emphasizes, "It is certainly impossible to combine into one rational hypothesis all the data, internal and external, bearing on the question of authorship. It will do well to begin with the acceptance of *John* into the church's fourfold gospel canon." Hill's quotation follows: "There is no evidence that

---

26. Hill, *The Johannine Corpus*, 18; Barrett, *The Gospel According to John*, 1955:109 and 1978:129.

27. Indeed, Barrett regarded the evidence for all three proposed centers of Johannine activity to be weak. See *The Gospel According to John*, 1978:128–31. However, when he chose to develop a hypothesis, he chose to base it on Ephesus, emphasizing that the hypothesis was of course open to correction in the light of evidence (133).

28. Ibid., 1955:109 and 1978:129.

John was used by other than heretical Christians before the middle of the second century. . . . The fourfold canon, when it was made (perhaps principally as a counterstroke to Marcion), was an inclusive canon. . . . thus Luke and John were added to Matthew and Mark, for which we have the earlier authority of Papias. . . . [I]ts [*John's*] early disuse by orthodox writers and use by gnostics show that it originated in circles that were either gnostic or obscure. . . . [T]he gospel, though it uses gnostic terminology, is not gnostic in a heretical sense . . . it arose in quarters away from the main stream of the Church's life and activity, and did not at once become widely known."[29]

Barrett's 1978 Commentary

Hill concludes his critique of Barrett's 1955 commentary by introducing a quotation from the 1978 edition extending his 1955 hypothesis.[30] He first notes: "For Barrett, however, Irenaeus and others, though mistaken about the apostolic origins of the Gospel, were not mistaken in using it to forge an answer to heresy."[31] This is a misleading statement for a number of reasons. First, Barrett concludes that "[i]t is impossible to make out a satisfactory and conclusive case for any of the three great cities, Ephesus, Alexandria, and Antioch, as the place of origin of the Fourth Gospel," and finds it "impossible to combine into one hypothesis all the data, internal and external, bearing on the question of authorship." Nevertheless, he developed a hypothesis that "seemed to meet most of the known facts." It begins, "John the Apostle migrated from Palestine and lived in Ephesus." There he gathered a number of pupils. After his death, four of them were responsible for writing Revelation, the Epistles, and the Gospel. This is not a straightforward rejection of apostolic origins, though it modifies the view of Irenaeus. Given the end of John 21, the role of other hands in the final Gospel is commonly recognized.[32]

29. Hill, *The Johannine Corpus,* 18; Barrett, *The Gospel According to John,* 1955:111–12 and 1978:131–32.

30. Hill, *The Johannine Corpus,* 18–19; Barrett, *The Gospel According to John,* 1978:134.

31. Hill, *The Johannine Corpus,* 18. Hill's use of "forge" is ill-considered/unfortunate or devious in this context.

32. Barrett, *The Gospel According to John,* 1978:131, 133–34. This is partly quotation and summary using as far as possible Barrett's words.

Hill's introductory comments fail to note that, according to Barrett's hypothesis, the pupil who wrote the Gospel was not popular, somewhat reclusive, and died with the Gospel unpublished. All this is hypothetical, but not inconsistent with the facts. It explains the obscurity and isolation of the Gospel presupposed by the quotation, especially if the sentence prior to the quotation is included, "It was too original and daring a work for official backing." Hill's quotation flows from this:

> It was first seized upon by gnostic speculators, who saw the superficial contact which existed between it and their own work; they at least could recognize the language John spoke. Only gradually did the main body of the church come to perceive that, while John used (at times) the language of gnosticism, his work was in fact the strongest possible reply to the gnostic challenge; that he had beaten the gnostics with their own weapons, and vindicated the permanent validity of the primitive Gospel *by expressing it in new—and partly gnostic—terms.*[33]

The last nine words in italics were omitted by Hill without indicating a broken sentence. The omitted words are essential. They reveal Barrett's view of the significance of the evangelist's use of language uncharacteristic of the gospel tradition. But the gospel is not an apologetic work (as argued by C. H. Dodd). Rather, it is a theological work using gnostic language to better grasp/express the primitive gospel. According to Barrett, the Gospel was written in the theological context of the eschatological crisis of the failure of the *parousia* to eventuate, and in the milieu of gnostic thinking and language. The evangelist needed, for his own sake, to give new expression to the gospel using the new gnostic language.

> There are other considerations (see p. 132 *et al.*) that suggest the gospel had an obscure origin; it may not have been published during the author's lifetime; and it may be doubted whether he was very interested

33. Hill, *The Johannine Corpus,* 19; Barrett, *The Gospel According to John,* 1978:134 (italics mine, to indicate the omitted portion). It should be noted that, contrary to Hill's use and mine, Barrett uses a small "g" for the individual canonical gospels, but a capital for the primitive Gospel that finds expression in the gospels.

in its publication. It is easy, when we read the gospel, to believe that John, though doubtless aware of the necessity of strengthening Christians and converting the heathen, wrote primarily to satisfy himself. His gospel must be written: it was no concern of his whether it was also read. Again, it is by no means necessary to suppose that he was aware of the historical problems imposed on later students by his treatment of the traditional material. It cried aloud for rehandling; its true meaning had crystallized in his mind, and he simply conveyed this meaning to paper.[34]

His aim was to bring out the theological meaning of the story of Jesus in the context of the two urgent theological issues mentioned above. I have taken the opportunity of bringing out the credibility of Barrett's hypothesis because it is not generally known today, and Hill has not handled it adequately. He fails to distinguish what is known (fact) from what is hypothesis, and seems unaware of how much any view of the authorship and publication of the Gospel of John is hypothetical.

In the section dealing with the 1978 edition, Hill focuses on Barrett's additional treatment of the relationship of the Gospel of John to the gnostic writings, now known as the Nag Hammadi texts. These became accessible to scholars after the completion of the 1955 commentary. They revealed a greater complexity in gnosticism and revolutionized research on the subject. The texts range from those that exhibit little or no Christian influence to texts intimately related to the Christian movement. Barrett's comments relate the Gospel of John to this more complex reality. In his 1978 Preface he wrote "I believe that John does more to interpret the Nag Hammadi Texts than they do to interpret John."[35] I find the Preface provocative, as I think it was intended to be. This comment builds on his view of the evangelist's use of gnostic language to unlock the implicit theology of the Jesus story in a way that exposed the weakness of the gnostic challenge. But if the reclusive evangelist produced his theological reading simply because he needed to do it, nevertheless, Barrett notes, the church had urgent need of it.[36]

---

34. Barrett, *The Gospel According to John*, 1978:134–35, 139–40.
35. Ibid., 1978:viii.
36. See ibid., 1978:133, 135, 139, 141.

Barrett's Two Evidence-Based Arguments

Barrett's position is built on the double observation of Orthodox silence about the Gospel of John before 150 C.E.[37] and *evidence* of gnostic use of it. He assesses the evidence to indicate that the Gospel was not published before 90 or after 140 C.E. He argues that there is no evidence that the Apostolic Fathers knew the Gospel of John. In 1905, members of the committee of the Oxford society concluded that none of the Apostolic Fathers shows certain knowledge of John, though Ignatius probably knew it, and Polycarp may have known it.[38] On the whole, the 2005 work edited by Andrew Gregory and Christopher Tuckett reaffirmed the findings of the work whose centenary this publication marks.[39] Thus, they conclude that there is no evidence of dependence on the Gospel of John in the Didache, 1 Clement, the Epistle of Barnabas, 2 Clement, or the Shepherd of Hermas. They depart from the views of the 1905 volume in rejecting the probability that Ignatius knew and used the Gospel of John. In the volume, Paul Foster concludes, "Thus, it is necessary to conclude with Schoedel that Ignatius's use of the Fourth Gospel cannot be established with any degree of certainty,"[40] and Michael W. Holmes concludes, "There is no evidence that Polycarp did not know the Gospel of John, but neither is there evidence to demonstrate that he did."[41] Only the positive can be proved. The absence of any evidence that Polycarp knew the Gospel of John does not prove that he did not, but rules out affirming that he did. Despite the work of Charles Hill, the view that any of the Apostolic Fathers knew John remains rejected/disputed, as it was for Barrett.[42]

---

37. While silence does not *prove* ignorance, it needs to be explained.

38. See J. V. Bartlett et al., *The New Testament in the Apostolic Fathers* (Oxford: Clarendon, 1905). See the chart on page 137, which summarizes the main findings and is intelligible in the light of the book.

39. Gregory and Tuckett, *The Reception of the New Testament in the Apostolic Fathers* (Oxford: Oxford University Press, 2005).

40. "The Epistles of Ignatius of Antioch and the Writings that Later Formed the New Testament," in Gregory and Tuckett, *The Reception of the New Testament*, 184.

41. "Polycarp's *Letter to the Philippians* and the Writings that Later Formed the New Testament," in Gregory and Tuckett, *The Reception of the New Testament*, 198.

42. See *The Gospel According to John*, 1978:110–13.

Evidently aware of the disputed state of evidence concerning orthodox use of the Gospel of John before 150 C.E., Hill attempted to show that Eusebius preserved an unidentified testimony of Papias to the origin of *John* and *Luke*.

The Papias Testimony in *H.E.* 3.24.1–13?

In *H.E.* 3.24.1–13, Eusebius discusses the reception of the Johannine writings. He appeals to no testimonies but, though not yet quoted, the testimonies of Irenaeus (*H.E.* 5.8.2–4) and Clement (*H.E.* 6.14.4–7) discussed above are known and seem to be assumed. At the same time, his assertions, which go beyond those quotations, are unattested. They seem to be shaped from the quotations and other common knowledge in response to problems that emerged at a time somewhat later than Papias. In support, I note that Scott Manor asserts that "Origen is the earliest extant writer to claim that the chronology of Jesus' ministry recorded in the Gospel of John cannot be harmonized with that found in the Synoptics. Throughout the tenth book of his *Commentary of John*, Origen cites lengthy portions of all four gospels in order to highlight points of conflict that would eventually lead him to question their historical veracity."[43] My point is that it is with Origen, well known to Eusebius, that conflict between the Synoptics and John emerges and remains an issue for Eusebius. In *H.E.*3.24 he cobbles together a response in the context of setting out the received writings of John. Although Manor argues that a Papias testimony underlies this passage, he asserts that "Eusebius' argument found in *HE* 3.24.8–13 is a thinly veiled response to Origen's challenge to those who want to claim historical legitimacy to all four Gospel accounts. It is remarkably simple, but thorough enough to provide an explanation of the differences Origen has mentioned."[44]

That being the case, there is no need of Papias, who could hardly have devised a response to Origen. A creative use of Clement's testimony making use of other available tradition is enough. The general tone of this passage sounds like an appeal to common knowledge. Those who claim an

---

43. T. Scott Manor, *Epiphanius' alogi and the Johannine Controversy: A Reassessment of Early Ecclesial Opposition to the Johannine Corpus* (Leiden: Brill, 2016) 177.

44. Ibid., 211. I find incredible that Manor thinks Eusebius' explanation to be adequate.

unacknowledged use of an unknown testimony of Papias should note: There is no independent evidence of any testimony by Papias to the situation and composition of the fourth Gospel. Eusebius makes no claim to base what he says in 3.24.1–13 on any particular testimony. Rather he says, "Let the Gospel according to him (*John*) be first recognized, for it is read in all the churches under heaven." Here he is calling on common recognition, requiring no testimony. He continues calling only on what it is reasonable to assert. "Moreover, that it was reasonable for the ancients to reckon it in the fourth place can be explained thus." For this he has the order of the four Gospels, if taken chronologically, as Irenaeus, Clement and Origen did. Eusebius knew and later quoted the phrase "last of all John" found in the testimonies of Irenaeus and Clement of Alexandria, which could imply John's knowledge of the others. His quotation of Clement's words "John, last of all, conscious that the bodily facts had been set forth in the Gospels, . . . composed a spiritual Gospel," led Eusebius to the conclusion that: "The three gospels already written were in general circulation and copies had come into John's hands. He welcomed them, we are told, and confirmed their accuracy, but remarked that the narrative only lacked the story of what Christ had done first of all at the beginning of his mission" (*H.E.* 3.24.7). Eusebius appealed to no written testimony but to hearsay, to what "we are told." He goes on to claim the truth of what "we are told." It is confirmed, not by testimony, but by the first three evangelists restricting their accounts to the period after John's (the Baptist) arrest. He concludes, again calling on "We are told, then, for this reason the apostle John was urged to record in his gospel the period which the earlier evangelists had passed over in silence and the things done in that period by the Saviour, . . . before the Baptist's imprisonment. . . . Once this is grasped, there no longer appears to be a discrepancy between the gospels, because John's deals with the early stages of Christ's career and the others cover the last period of His story; and it will seem probable that John passed over the genealogy of our saviour according to the flesh because it had already been written by Matthew and Luke" (*H.E.* 3.24.8–13).

Eusebius appeals to no testimony.[45] The words "We are told" are used to introduce current explanations of the apparent chronological conflicts in

45. Manor (ibid., 179) says misleadingly, "Eusebius attributes to an unspecified source a similar account of John collecting and verifying earlier gospels (*HE* 3.24.7). That this original record most likely came from Papias will be discussed in the following chapter." This position

the Gospels. The reason for the omission of the genealogy from the Gospel of John is not based on anything but probability. At the same time, these conflicts/contradictions were made apparent by Origen.[46] Contrary to the identification of a Papias testimony underlying *H.E.* 3.24.1–13, the passage does not appear to be based on a single testimony but on the commonly known four Gospel order and other common hearsay. Certainly this explanation by Eusebius might have begun with encouragement from Clement's words, "conscious that the bodily facts had been set forth in the gospels. . . ." But, contrary to Clement, he takes the line of reconciling the historical narratives of the four Gospels to be the primary task. Thus he argues that John already knew the other Gospels, affirmed their accuracy, and set out to fill gaps, especially in the early period before the arrest of John the Baptist, a period not covered in them.[47] Eusebius asserts that *John* is historically as accurate as they are, but covers different periods and events. At this point Eusebius bypasses the evident different character of *John* from the other Gospels, something that is clear when he later deals with Clement's view in *H.E.* 6.14.5–7. Perhaps in deference to Clement, Eusebius goes on to say that it is natural that *John* should pass over in silence the genealogy and nativity of Jesus "and begin with the proclamation of His divinity, since the Holy Spirit had reserved this for him" (*H.E.* 3.24.13). All of this looks like Eusebius recognizing the obvious differences between *John* and the other Gospels and seeking for ways to reconcile them. That reconciliation is not found in the testimonies he records, though he works selectively from them to produce his desired outcome, even when that runs contrary to testimony.

Absence of a Papias testimony to Luke and John in Eusebius has led Hill and others to seek such testimony and to argue that we find that testimony in *H.E.* 3.24. Against this argument it needs to be said that, whatever Eusebius thought of the theological ability of Papias, there is no way he would fail to call on his early testimony, especially as this testimony (?) is so conveniently in agreement with his own views. Eusebius appeals to no testimony. Rather, unencumbered by known traditional testimonies, Eusebius

---

was argued by Hill in "What Papias said about John (and Luke)" 582–629 and is argued by Manor, *Epiphanius' alogi*, 200–211.

46. Manor, *Epiphanius' alogi*, 177–85, especially 177, 184–85.

47. Indeed, Mark 1:14 strongly implies that Jesus' ministry did not begin until John had been "arrested."

shaped his own synthesis to provide his response to a problem raised by the four Gospels and their apparently conflicting narratives, most obviously with the idiosyncratic narrative of *John*. Eusebius fails to see that conflicts cannot be avoided by consigning *John* to the ministry of Jesus prior to the imprisonment of John (the Baptist). Hill's attempt to enlist Papias here seems to be as desperate as Eusebius' attempt to reconcile chronological history of the four Gospels. Where Eusebius has significant earlier testimonies, he identifies them and quotes accurately. They were, after all, checkable in his day. He also draws selectively from these testimonies to construct his arguments. In these cases, he names no witnesses. That is what we find in 3.24. There Eusebius shapes commonly known details to form a response to problems made known commonly by Origen.

Gnostic Knowledge and Use of John

On the gnostic knowledge and use of *John*, there is the evidence of relatively early papyri, gnostic gospels making use of *John,* and Origen's preservation of the work of gnostic commentators on *John* from the second century. The evidence of early papyri, as Hill notes, strongly favours *John*.[48] Barrett notes that most surviving papyri were found in Egypt, as were Egerton Papyrus[2] and P[52]. But he makes no attempt to associate the Gospel of John with gnosticism simply on the basis of a supposed Egyptian gnostic milieu because "Only in Egypt are climatic conditions favourable for the preservation of papyrus, and in consequence the great majority of papyri known to scholars are of Egyptian origin."[49] He goes on to say that in 150 C.E. there may have been as many copies of *John* in Asia as Egypt. Further, we do not know the makers or users of the papyri. An exception may be the *Egerton Papyrus²*. It appears to be an otherwise unknown Valentinian Gospel, dependent on *John* and of similar date as P[52], which is considered to be our earliest Gospel evidence and is often dated to 125–150 C.E. However, in 2005 Brent Nongbri published an article dealing with P[52] and *Egerton Papyrus²*.[50] This became

48. Hill, *The Johannine Corpus*, 148–51.
49. Barrett, *The Gospel According to John*, 1978:129.
50. Brent Nongbri, "The Use and Abuse of P[52]: Papyrological Pitfalls and the Dating of the Fourth Gospel," *Harvard Theological Review* 98 (2005) 23–48.

the first in a series of articles on dating the papyri. He notes that "palaeography is not the most effective method of dating texts, particularly those written in a literary hand" and "the papyrological evidence should take second place to other forms of evidence in addressing debates about the dating of the Fourth Gospel." While not ruling out a date of 125–150 C.E., he says, "What I have done is to show that any serious consideration of possible dates of P[52] must include dates in the later second and early third centuries."[51] On the whole, Nongbri's conclusions have found support from scholars concerned with palaeography. What this means is that dating the papyri needs to allow a broader range than has commonly been the practice, that is, unless other evidence justifies narrowing the scope. Of course this also means that evidence of *Egerton Papyrus*[2] that makes use of *John* and appears to be Valentinian is from between 125 to 225 C.E. If the Valentinian connection were to be confirmed, a date in the mid-second century might be favoured.

It seems to be true to say that we have little or no evidence about the use of John in the first half of the second century, and that the first clear evidence we have of its use is in a relationship with Valentinian gnosticism. Circa 180 C.E., Irenaeus attributes to the Valentinians a recent work known as *The Gospel of Truth*, possibly the work of Valentinus: "But the followers of Valentinus, putting away all fear, bring forward their own compositions and boast that they have more Gospels than really exist. Indeed their audacity has gone so far that they entitle their recent composition the *Gospel of Truth*, though it agrees in nothing with the Gospels of the apostles, and so no Gospel of theirs is free from blasphemy."[52]

Amongst the Nag Hammadi texts is *The Gospel of Truth*, probably a Valentinian work that has become known by its incipit. The opening words

---

51. Ibid., 46. Given that Nongbri has formed his approach through a study of the Papyri over a lengthy period of time, it is not surprising that his approach has produced similar results in the study of P[66] and P[75]; see his "The Limits of Paleographic Dating of Literary Papyri: Some Observations on the Date and Provenance of P. Bodmer II (P[66])," *Museum Helveticum* 71 (2014) 1–35, and "Reconsidering the Place of Papyrus Bodmer 14–15 (P[75]) in the Textual Criticism of the New Testament," *Journal of Biblical Literature* 135 (2016) 405–37. He argues that secure dates can be found from the second into the fourth century for both P[66] and P[75] and favors a fourth-century date for each of them.

52. Ireneaus, *A.H.* 3.11.9. Reference to "more Gospels" of the Valentinians might include *Egerton Papyrus*[2].

are, "The Gospel of Truth. . . ." This could be the work identified by Irenaeus. If so, a date of between 140–180 C.E. seems likely. *The Gospel of Truth* shows marked signs of awareness of *John* and dependence on it.[53] If *Egerton Papyrus*[2] is also Valentinian, we have evidence of two gnostic gospels showing signs of dependence on John. Here the observation of Barrett on the relation of *John* to the *Gospel of Truth* is important. It is more a relationship of shared language than shared meaning. At the same time, it is important to note that the first known commentators on *John* were the Valentinian gnostics, Ptolemy, Heracleon, and Theodotus whose works are preserved by Origen, *In Evangelium Ioannis*.[54] These works belong to the early second half of the second century and support the view that, by that time, *John* had become a popular text for gnostics, at least among the Valentinians. This evidence is too late to throw light on the origin of the Gospel of John; rather they become the early users of it, as Barrett argues. I also take his provocative comment in his Preface to mean that *John* has influenced gnosticism but is not illuminated by the gnostic texts except in terms of the use of language.

By comparison there is a lack of evidence of the use and valuing of *John* by the Orthodox in the same period. Hill's attempt to overthrow Barrett's position is cavalier and unsuccessful. He obscured Barrett's careful, independent, and nuanced approach, which distinguishes what is actually known from the gaps in the evidence, and hypothetical solutions consistent with the evidence. Barrett's approach is credible and defensible.

Eusebius and the Other Johannine Books

Of the other Johannine books, Eusebius (circa 320 C.E.) considered that only 1 John was received, while 2 and 3 John and Revelation remained disputed (*H.E.* 3.24.17–18).[55] Yet Irenaeus had earlier asserted the common authorship of the Gospel, 1 John, and Revelation (circa 180 C.E. *Adv.haer.*5.33.4). He attributed these works to the apostle John and appealed to Papias,

---

53. Given that Irenaeus wrote circa 180 C.E., it cannot be later. Given what we know of Valentinus, it is not likely to be earlier than 140 C.E.

54. See also Elaine Pagels, *The Johannine Gospel in Gnostic Exegesis: Heracleon's Commentary on John* (Nashville: Abingdon, 1973).

55. Revelation is beyond the scope of this chapter.

Polycarp, and the elders of Asia Minor as the source of his view.[56] That view was contested by Eusebius (*H.E.* 3.39.1–17). He was anxious to distinguish the author of the Gospel from the author of Revelation and argued that, contrary to Irenaeus, Papias referred to two Johns, one the Apostle and the other the Elder, and knew only the Elder. Eusebius attributed the Gospel to the Apostle and Revelation to the Elder. Modern scholars have tended to identify John the Elder with the author of the Gospel, a view without support from ancient sources. More recently he has been identified as the author of 2 and 3 John.[57] The importance of this distinction becomes clear as we turn to the writings commonly associated with John. Three writings Irenaeus attributed to the Apostle John are commonly attributed to independent or different authors today. If these authors are thought to be members of a Johannine school, they are different but not independent.

The Relationship of the Epistles

Because early attestation is lacking for 2 and 3 John, their status remained disputed in the fourth century even though Polycarp and Irenaeus appear to have quoted 2 John as part of 1 John. Thus it is indirectly attested. Apart from 2 John, 1 John is anonymous and unaddressed. In 2 John the Elder addresses the elect Lady and her children, and the concluding verse expresses a farewell greeting, "the children of your elect sister salute you." Apparently the elect sisters represent related house churches of which the children are the members. Hence the greeting comes from the children. The sister of the elect Lady addressed by 2 John represents the church from which 2 John was sent. The elect Lady addressed by 2 John could be the *nom de plume* for any number of house churches in the circle now addressed by the Elder. 2 John is like a covering letter first known in that form. 1 John was likely composed and written first for use in the author's house church in which a schism

---

56. That view is complicated in that Irenaeus refers to 1 John 2:18–19, 21–22 in *A.H.* 3.16.5 and to 2 John 7–8 and 1 John 4:1–2; 5:1 in *A.H.* 3.16.8 as if from the same epistle. That Polycarp used both 1 and 2 John with no acknowledgment but was regarded as a witness to 1 John may support the view that 2 John was first known as an introductory attachment to 1 John. See John Painter, *1, 2, and 3 John* (Collegeville: Liturgical, 2002) 41–42.

57. See Georg Strecker, *Theology of the New Testament* (Louisville: Westminster John Knox, 2000).

occurred. In that context it needed no form of address, opening, or closing greeting. It was attested independently from the beginning, but 2 John was first known as part of 1 John, when it became a circular letter. It is plausible that some time after the local crisis, the issues addressed in 1 John became relevant to a wider circle of house churches as the schism spread. At this point 2 John was composed as a covering letter for the unaddressed 1 John. 2 John usefully introduces the issue of the schism and warns against providing hospitality to the schismatics and those who preach their message. 2 and 3 John are addressed by the Elder and each is addressed to a specific recipient. In the case of 2 John, the elect Lady and her children represent a circle of local house churches and their members. In the case of 3 John, Gaius, the addressee, was a supporter of the Elder who commends Gaius for his support. The Elder also raises the issue of Diotrephes, who refused hospitality to his supporters and threatened to excommunicate any who dared to do so. It is possible that the action of Diotrephes was a response to the Elder's policy of refusing hospitality to schismatics and their supporters, as urged in 2 John. If this reading is correct, it suggests that the canonical order of the Epistles is the chronological order.[58]

John: Gospel and Epistles

Because of similarities of language and motifs/themes between the Gospel and 1 John, there is good reason to examine their interrelationships.[59] Whether the Gospel and Epistles have one or up to four authors, a case can be made for some relationship between them. 2 and 3 John, as two examples of popular hellenistic papyri letters, are closer to each other than to either 1 John or the Gospel. 2 John is closer to 1 John than 3 John because 2 John shares the issue of the schism and its cause with 1 John. Given that 2 and 3 John are addressed by the Elder, the case for their common authorship is strong. When the difference of purpose of the more formal 1 John is taken into account, along with the overlapping issues with 2 John and the early evidence of 2 John as part of 1 John, the common authorship of the three Epistles is a strong hypothesis.

---

58. See Painter *1, 2, and 3 John*, 51–57, 331–59.

59. See ibid., 44–78, for a discussion of the evidence related to the relationship between the Gospel and Epistles.

Georg Strecker and the Johannine School: Docetic, Naïve Docetism, Antidocetic?

What of the relationship of the Gospel to the Epistles? Georg Strecker takes the corpus of diverse Johannine writings to be evidence of the Johannine school. Like other recent scholars, he takes the Papias reference to Elders preserved by Eusebius, and identifies John the Elder with the Elder of 2 and 3 John.[60] He names him the founder of the Johannine school and author of 2 and 3 John. These Epistles were written first, followed by 1 John, written by another member of the school who wanted his "letter-like homily" to be identified with the Elder's 2 and 3 John. Strecker argues that the threefold use of the aorist tense "I wrote" in 1 John 2:14, following a threefold use of "I write" in 2:12–13, is a reference to 2 and 3 John. I think this is unlikely. But the outcome for Strecker is the order 2 John, 3 John, 1 John, followed by the Gospel and then Revelation. Only 2 and 3 John come from the Elder and 1 John, the Gospel, and Revelation come from other members of the school. For the school, the Epistles come from the early phase, and the focus is on the docetic challenge faced by the Elder and the author of 1 John. By the time the Gospel was written, this threat lies in the past and mere traces of it are discernible there.[61] Here Strecker is in disagreement with his colleague Udo Schnelle.[62] Although Schnelle thinks the writings of the Johannine school followed the same order as proposed by Strecker, he argues that the Gospel is explicitly antidocetic, presupposing a docetic challenge and developing a comprehensive theological response "to docetic christology."[63]

The Fourth Gospel: Docetic or Antidocetic?

A detailed critique of Schnelle's position is not possible here, but a number of responses need to be made. The first is to note that his close colleague demurs at his proposal that the Gospel mounts a comprehensive, systematic, theological response to docetic Christology. Second, had *John* been explicitly antidocetic, Ernst Käsemann's famous argument that the Jesus of the fourth Gospel is "the God who walks the earth," an expression of naïve

60. See Eusebius *H.E.* 3.39.3–7.

61. See Strecker, *Theology of the New Testament*, 419–22, 465 n. 32.

62. Udo Schnelle, *Antidocetic Christology in the Gospel of John* (trans. Linda M. Maloney; Minneapolis: Fortress, 1992).

63. Ibid., 52–63, 228.

docetism, would have been ruled out. Instead, of the four Gospels, it is the one of which this charge is most possible. The position is naïve because the author has not conceived of the docetic possibility and innocently has left the text open to such a reading, something he would hardly have done had the Gospel been the product of the struggle with "docetic christology." Third, Käsemann rightly focused on the Prologue and John 17. Although the incarnation appears to be appropriate to the human reality, it is the divine *logos* that becomes flesh with the consequent revelation of divine glory, and the Jesus who announces his departure in John 17 announces his return to the glory he shared with the Father before the foundation of the world. If the presumption is the context of the docetic struggle, this is naïvely unguarded. Fourth, the Jesus of *John* nowhere defends himself against the charge he is not human. Everywhere his humanity is presupposed. The accusation against him is that, being a man he makes himself equal with God (5:17–18 and taken up again in 7:1, 25; 8:37, 40; 10:30–33). Fifth, Jesus' struggle in John is with the Jewish authorities, and the Jewish Scriptures are central and prominent in the case the Gospel makes for believers in Jesus. No strand of the Gospel suggests that it was shaped in the world outside Judaism. Much of the shaping must have gone on before the destruction of Jerusalem in 70 C.E. There is evidence of Judaean influence in the Gospel, including influence from Qumran. The tradition concerning Asia Minor cannot be excluded, though this becomes little more than conjecture. Wherever it was, there is no reason to think of a break away from Jewish community, and Jesus is proclaimed in that context. Thus it is now necessary to discern the relationship of the Epistles to the Gospel, the order in which they were written, and the hermeneutical implications of their relationship.

The Gospel and Epistles of John

Two things need to be said about the Gospel of John. First is the strong tradition that it is chronologically the fourth Gospel, when the author was old, perhaps even after his death. John 21:20–25 implies a response to the author's unexpected death. The Gospel bears the marks of a long period of "gestation," probably in oral and written stages leading to interpretative development and expansion. Much of this will have been in and around Jerusalem, but also in the Jewish diaspora. Second, the Gospel reflects a Jewish context. That does not preclude contact with Gentiles, even in Jerusalem. Such

Gentiles are likely to have been influenced by Judaism. The Gospel is deeply shaped by the Jewish Scriptures and is illuminated by the scriptural tradition of Qumran. It bears the marks of the situation evident in the Johannine Epistles only by presupposing and reading it back into the Gospel on the assumption that the Epistles are earlier than the Gospel.[64] But the Epistles make no direct reference to any Jewish Scripture and appear to reflect life remote from any Jewish community. The communities of the Epistles appear to be making their way in the Roman world, fashioning communities under the influence of the Johannine gospel tradition without appeal to its roots in Jewish Scripture, though that tradition is unthinkable without it.

The Breakup of the Johannine Corpus

The canonical breakup of the Johannine corpus might imply that the Gospel is to be understood in relation to the other Gospels rather than to the Epistles. Some recent developments have moved in this direction, asserting that *John*, like each of the Synoptics, should be treated as a source for our knowledge of the historical Jesus and that the failure to do so has led to the "dehistorification of John" and the "deJohnification of Jesus." Such a position sides with the unsupported view of Eusebius, who sought to show that the Synoptics and *John* provide accurate historical accounts covering different periods of Jesus' mission (*H.E.* 6.14.5–7). Here I side with the views of Clement and Augustine, who distinguish the nature and purpose of *John* from the other three Gospels, arguing that John, knowing the Synoptics, set out to write a spiritual/theological Gospel. The case for knowledge of Mark and Luke has long had supporters and is qualified by Barrett, who acknowledges that knowledge of the other Gospels does not imply use of them as Matthew and Luke used Mark. Nor does it exclude independent knowledge of the gospel tradition.[65] What makes *John* different is the intent to provide an interpretation drawing out the theological implications of the tradition for the time in which it was written. Westcott argued that John

---

64. See Painter, *1, 2, and 3 John*, 58–87.

65. See John Painter, "The Fourth Gospel and the Founder of Christianity," in *Engaging with C. H. Dodd on the Gospel of John* (ed. Tom Thatcher and Catrin H. Williams; Cambridge: Cambridge University Press, 2013) 257–84.

gave expression to the Gospel in terms of the theology of the last decade of the first century. This is not a matter of *John* being unhistorical. It is a matter of the degree and extent of theological interpretation of the tradition of *John*. The Synoptics tended more than John to preserve the Jesus tradition in their Gospels. Richard Burridge did much to show that the Gospels fit within the range of biographical writing of the first century. The trouble is that those who use this model quickly move to insist that the Gospels conform to modern standards of biography and historical writing. *John* might better be compared with Plato's account of Socrates, as Dodd suggests.[66] The point is that just as Plato and Socrates merge in the interpretation of Socrates, so *John* and Jesus merge in his interpretation of Jesus. This happens, to some extent, in every interpretation. The differences of *John* from the Synoptics support the recognition of a more comprehensive interpretative role in the Fourth Gospel. That role may be truer to Jesus than any other, just as Plato's thoroughly interpretative account may be truer to Socrates than of the other contemporary accounts.

Louis Martyn rightly made an impact on Johannine studies, highlighting the Jewish character of *John* and its historical context. I would prefer to say that, in *John*, aspects in the life of the author are *reflected* in the telling of the story of Jesus.[67] There is only one story, but it is natural that the telling of that story is coloured by points of contact between the story of Jesus and what was happening in the time in which the evangelist (John) was shaping the tradition that became the fourth Gospel. This position was already in my *The Quest for the Messiah* and was stated more concisely in my Louvain seminar paper for the English seminar on "The Death of Jesus in John" in 2005.[68]

---

66. Dodd, *Historical Tradition in the Fourth Gospel,* 17, 319.

67. J. Louis Martyn, *History and Theology in the Fourth Gospel* (New York: Westminster John Knox, 1968).

68. "The Death of Jesus in John: A Discussion of the Tradition, History, and Theology of John," in *The Death of Jesus in the Fourth Gospel* (ed. G. Van Belle; Leuven: Peeters, 2007) 336–37; *The Quest for the Messiah* (2nd edition; Nashville: Abingdon, 1993) 61, 65–68, 71–73, 79, 82, 96, 118, 120–24, 126, 130.

Bound and Unbounded Desire

STEPHEN E. FOWL

Rob Wall and I have known each other for so long now that I cannot be absolutely sure when we first met. I do know that our friendship was forged as we often found ourselves on the same side and in the distinct minority in many academic battles regarding theological interpretation of Scripture. One of my great academic pleasures was team teaching a course with Rob on interpreting Scripture. Over the course of that term it became very clear to me that to some of his colleagues and his students Rob could appear to be both very demanding and slightly intimidating.

The fact that several of his former students and current colleagues arranged to put this volume together to honor Rob is testimony to the fact that these people also know that, despite being demanding and somewhat intimidating, Rob is also their strongest supporter and advocate both within Seattle Pacific University and the academy more generally. A Festschrift such as this is well-deserved and ample testimony to his steadfast devotion to his colleagues and students. I am very grateful to have been asked to contribute to such an endeavor. The fact that my contribution will focus on greed has nothing to do with Rob, who is the very model of generosity. Rather, it stems from my current research.

Ephesians 5:5 indicates that a greedy person (πλεονέκτης) is an idolater. Similarly, Colossians 3:5 indicates that greed itself (πλεονεξία) is idolatry. Several questions and issues emerge from Paul's straightforward identification of greed with idolatry. First, although there are a number of texts in the OT and from the Second Temple period that indicate that greed is often a precursor or leads to idolatry, this is not what Paul says in Ephesians and Colossians.[1] He identifies greed (or the greedy person) with idolatry. This

---

1. Of course, Pauline authorship of both Ephesians and Colossians is disputed. I will use "Paul" to refer to the inscribed author of these texts.

needs some explanation.[2] In order to offer one explanation, I will look at the wider context of Ephesians 5 and Colossians 3 as a way of trying to be clear about the nature of greed and the connection Paul may see between greed and idolatry. It will become evident that although Paul seems to use the vocabulary of greed in fairly conventional ways, it is not at all clear how such conventional notions of greed can be identified with idolatry.[3] To make this identification clearer, I will explore greed in relation to a doctrine of creation out of nothing. In this light, I will argue two points. First, understanding greed in the light of a doctrine of creation makes better sense of Paul's identification of greed with idolatry than a more conventional notion of greed as grasping for more than one is due. Second, such an understanding will also clarify the dispositions and practices Christians might cultivate in order to avoid the greed that is idolatry. To that end, I will focus on gratitude and thanksgiving as the dispositions and practices best able to counter greed. These dispositions and practices are ways in which God through the Spirit helps to order and focus our desires properly. It may not come as a surprise, then, that it is in the contexts of Colossians 3 and Ephesians 5 that Paul displays in some detail the role of thanksgiving in the Christian life. Despite this close connection between the claims about greed and idolatry, on the one hand, and thanksgiving, on the other hand, my own reading

2. One explanation is that Paul is referring to all of the vices in these verses as idolatry and not simply greed. This seems to be the approach of Gregory K. Beale, *We Become What We Worship: A Biblical Theology of Idolatry* (Downers Grove: InterVarsity, 2008) 266. As I will indicate, particularly in Ephesians, there are strong grammatical reasons for limiting the identification of idolatry to just greed.

3. Brian Rosner, *Greed as Idolatry* (Grand Rapids: Eerdmans, 2007) offers a thorough survey of Christian interpretation of Eph 5:5 and Col 3:5. He also provides a detailed account of both greed and idolatry in hellenistic Jewish texts. He then employs a theory of metaphor to account for the clearly metaphorical identification Paul draws between greed and idolatry in these two passages. There is a great deal to learn from Rosner's work here. To the extent I differ from it, it primarily lies in the way he develops the metaphorical relationships between greed and idolatry. Too often he ends up making claims about greed that seem to me more properly made of wealth in order to forge connections to idolatry. Obviously, greed and wealth are connected to each other. It appears to me, however, that greed is fundamentally a disposition toward things—including but not limited to wealth. It displays how one views one's place in the world relative to others and to things. Keeping this idea front and center will result in a different set of connections to idolatry from those Rosner draws on pages 159–65.

is not driven by the assumption that this is precisely what Paul or his first readers thought when composing or hearing these epistles for the first time.

Context of Paul's Claims in Ephesians and Colossians

At the conclusion of a list of characteristics that are not fitting for those called to holiness and that Paul is eager for the Ephesians to avoid, he claims that no one who is greedy, that is, an idolater, will have a share in the kingdom of Christ and God. Further, in the context of Colossians 3 "greed, which is idolatry," is one of a list of vices, marking an "earthly" habit of life that Paul admonishes the Colossians to put away. Now that they are in Christ, their habit of life should lead them to focus on things "above." Although Colossians uses the more intense and even violent image of putting these "earthly" habits of life to death, Paul's point in Colossians is to stress the need for believers to make a comprehensive and decisive break with their pagan past. Although the Colossians passage is relatively clear, listing "greed" as one of several vices to be avoided and then asserting that "greed is idolatry," we are not told enough. In this respect, the context of Ephesians 5 is richer and certainly comprehends everything one would want to say about Colossians. Hence, I will focus on Ephesians 5:5 at this point and then return to Colossians 3 later.

Ephesians 5:3–5 is part of a longer discussion about the common life of the Ephesian congregation that runs from the beginning of chapter 4 through the end of the epistle. This overall section is guided by Paul's admonition to the Ephesians in 4:1 to "walk in a manner worthy of your calling." Paul invokes the image of walking worthily also in Philippians 1:27 and 1 Thessalonians 2:12. This idea always entails acts of judgment on the part of each congregation. Although Paul gives direct and concrete prescriptions to the Ephesians throughout chapters 4–6, the task of walking worthily always requires believers to discern the fit between their actions or possible actions on the one hand, and some set standard, on the other hand. To succeed in this task, the Ephesians and all other believers need to develop a set of habits and dispositions that will enable them to recognize that certain actions and not others will result in a common life that conforms to the standard to which they aspire, that is, their calling in Christ.

Specifically in 4:1–16, Paul discusses a number of habits, practices, and dispositions essential for the Ephesians if they are to walk in a manner worthy of their calling. These habits, practices, and dispositions are all directed toward maintaining the "unity of the Spirit in the bond of peace" (4:2). As Ephesians 4 develops, Paul shifts to address a number of things the Ephesians should avoid (4:17–24). These are practices, habits, and dispositions that would have been characteristic of the Ephesians prior to their incorporation into the body of Christ. In this respect, Paul indicates that walking worthily requires the Ephesians to make a clean break with their pagan past and to live in a manner that clearly distinguishes them from the surrounding culture. Paul uses the image of taking off an old set of clothes and putting on a new set tailored by Christ.

Being clothed with these new Christ-tailored garments entails a transformation in the common life of the Ephesian church. This will involve adopting some new practices and avoiding others. Paul describes these in 4:24–5:2. Although scholars have long recognized that the vocabulary here is fairly conventional, the Christological and ecclesiological context in which Paul deploys this vocabulary gives it a distinctively Christian tone.

Paul's identification of greed with idolatry appears in the following section, 5:3–14. Here Paul again uses fairly conventional vocabulary to articulate a number of vices the Ephesians should avoid. The vocabulary here describes practices that Jews and Christians would have typically used to castigate pagan culture.

As with Colossians, Ephesians 5:3–14 begins with a set of admonitions to the Ephesians to steer clear of a variety of activities. Paul initially names three of these activities: sexual misconduct (πορνεία), uncleanness (ἀκαθαρσία), and greed (πλεονεξία). The first of these terms is closely associated with a wide range of sexual misconduct. This may also be true of the second term, "uncleanness." At the same time, Paul understands that sex is never really a separate category of activity. Then as now, sex is bound up with issues of purity, identity, power, and desire, issues that implicate most aspects of life. Many versions translate the third term, πλεονεξία, as "covetousness." This is not an inaccurate translation, but it does obscure the fact that in 5:5 the greedy person (πλεονέκτης) is further identified as an idolater.[4] To retain this connection it might be better to translate this vice in 5:3 as "greed," also.

---

4. Although the neuter singular relative pronoun agrees with neither πλεονέκτης nor εἰδωλολάτρης, the fact that it is singular should limit its reference to the greedy person and

Greed 1.0

In hellenistic Jewish texts ranging from the LXX, the Pseudepigrapha, Josephus, Philo to the rest of the NT, πλεονεξία usually refers to that disposition of wanting, seeking, and holding onto more than one is due or more than one should have.[5] This overweening desire can be focused on money, but it need not be limited to money.[6] Sometimes that notion of what one is due or should have is presumed to have been set by nature or natural circumstances.[7] Other times it seems to depend on God.[8] In addition, Philo and Josephus both seem to assume that those with power are almost always greedy.[9] This combination of greed and power generally issues in violence and is thought to be the cause of most wars.[10] Even the poor, however, could be greedy. They would simply lack the power and means to act on that desire. On the face of things, and at this point in the discussion, we have little reason to think that Paul is using this term in any other than a completely conventional way to refer to the desire for more than one is due.

As I already noted, Paul aims to get the Ephesians, like the Colossians and his other primarily gentile congregations, to make a clean break with their pagan past. In addition to this, Paul remarks that none of these vices should be "noted" among the Ephesians. Most contemporary commentators take this as an admonition for the Ephesians to avoid even talking about

---

not to all three types of people mentioned in 5:5; see Harold Hoehner, *Ephesians: An Exegetical Commentary* (Grand Rapids: Baker, 2002) 660. The pronoun in Col 3:5 is also singular, although it does agree with its antecedent.

5. In certain military contexts, the word refers to a strategic advantage; see Josephus *Wars* 3.477; 4.43, 189, 358, 580; 5.66, 95, 143, 338, and 429.

6. For example, in 1 Thess 4:6, the verb πλεονεκτεῖν is associated with taking advantage of one's brother or sister in Christ with regard to sexual practices. In 2 Cor 2:11, the verb πλεονεκτηθῶμεν is used to describe being outfoxed by Satan. In 2 Macc 4:50, greed is focused on power. Josephus (*Ant* 3.29) and Philo (*Leg.All.* 3.166) both use greed to refer to over-gathering the manna that God sends in Exodus. In *Spec. leg.* 2.225, Philo contrasts greed with temperance in all matters, as also in *Aristeas*, 1.277.

7. In *Spec. leg.* 4.215, greed is associated with a failure to observe the natural rhythms established by the Sabbath year. In *De Jos.* 1.30, greed desires more than nature has apportioned to someone.

8. Josephus, *Ant* 4.225.

9. Josephus *Ant* 18.172; Philo, *Spec. leg.* 4.158, 213.

10. Josephus, *Ant* 13.225; *Contra Apionem* 2.272; T. Gad 5:1.

such practices.[11] This is a strange interpretation on several counts. First, it seems hard to imagine any sort of moral reasoning going on among the Ephesians if they cannot even talk about particular practices to avoid. Further, Paul mentions such practices himself in 1 Corinthians 5. In addition, it is hard to understand how mentioning a practice is, in itself, problematic. Most importantly, this is not the way the Greek verb ὀνομάζειν is used the two other times it appears in the epistle: In both 1:21 and 3:15, it refers much more precisely to naming something, to recognizing something and identifying it.

It seems better, therefore, to take this verse as not only admonishing the Ephesians to stay away from these practices but also to make sure that nobody outside the congregation can note the presence of these practices among them. Paul's concern here is primarily about how the Ephesians are perceived by those outside the congregation. Paul is reflecting both a concern for the integrity of the Ephesians' witness to their neighbors and a concern that the lives of the Ephesian Christians might bring God, Christ, and/or the gospel into disrepute needlessly.[12] This is consistent with Paul's concern throughout 5:3–14 with the ways in which the Ephesian church interacts with and is perceived by the wider culture.

The immediate reason Paul gives for avoiding all sorts of sexual misconduct, uncleanness, and greed is that such things are not "fitting" for those called to holiness. Paul has already established that God has called the Christians in Ephesus to holiness (1:4; 2:19–22). Moreover, he has just reminded the believers in Ephesus that they have been "sealed" by the Holy Spirit (1:13). Holiness is simply a constitutive part of Christian identity. In this light, certain ways of life can only be seen as inappropriate. Given Christian identity, particularly as narrated by Paul in Ephesians 2 and 3, certain practices are ruled out as fundamentally incompatible with that identity.

Paul then adds to this list of vices in verse 4 by noting that indecency, foolish talk, and coarse jesting are also inappropriate. The vices of verse 3 then reappear in verse 5. We read that no sexually immoral person,

---

11. See Andrew T. Lincoln, *Ephesians* (Waco: Word, 1990) 322; Ernest Best, *Ephesians* (Edinburgh: T & T Clark, 2001) 477; Hoehner, *Ephesians*, 653.

12. See the similar notion expressed in Ezek 36:22–24. Aquinas (*Ephesians*, 198) takes the verse this way.

no impure person, and no greedy person will have a share in the "kingdom of Christ and God." In verse 5, however, the nouns are altered so that they refer to people who engage in these vices rather than the vices themselves.

Although there are a few parallel texts that note that love of money or avarice leads to the abandonment of God and the worship of idols,[13] in Ephesians 5:5 and in Colossians 3:5 greed (πλεονεξία/ πλεονέκτης) is directly identified as idolatry. It is striking that Paul mentions greed, πλεονεξία, not love of money, φιλαργυρία (for example, 1 Tim 6:10). Further he does not make the point that greed is a precursor to idolatry; it is idolatry—or, in the case of Ephesians, the greedy person is an idolater. Given that Paul appears to use πλεονεξία/ πλεονέκτης in very conventional ways, the difficult question concerns how this might constitute idolatry.

By identifying greed as idolatry without explaining how this is so, Paul may be assuming that this identification was self-evident to his audience. If this is the case, however, we do not have much evidence for it. For example, much of the history of this verse's interpretation tends to treat greed as if it were the same as wealth and to treat wealth or abundance as a condition that disposes one toward idolatry much in the way Deuteronomy treats these matters (see Deut 6:11; 8:10–20; 11:13–17; 31:20; 32:15–18). In this light, Ephesians 5:5 is also often read alongside Matthew 6:24 where Jesus points out the impossibility of serving both God and Mamon.[14]

In that light, one might say that interpreting Ephesians 5:5 in the light of Deuteronomy or Matthew 6:24 certainly allows it to fit within other Scriptural patterns of thought. Nevertheless, reading Ephesians 5:5 in the light of either Matthew 6:24 or Deuteronomy does not take a full account of what Ephesians 5:5 actually claims. That is, that greed is idolatry.

As Rosner rightly notes, identifying greed as idolatry creates a metaphorical relation between the two terms. This may obviate the need to resolve the relationships between greed and idolatry in terms of strict identity. Alternatively, it still leaves readers with the puzzle of how to understand this relationship. Rosner offers us an admirable discussion of the semantic

13. In T. Judah 19:1, φιλαργυρία is mentioned as leading to idolatry because it mistakenly takes as God that which is not God. In T. Levi 17:11, love of money is listed with idolatry along with other vices.

14. Rosner, *Greed as Idolatry*, 160–66.

ranges of the two terms and some thoughts about which elements of each semantic field might intersect with each other to make this metaphor work.[15] To do this, however, he tends to fall into the traditional pattern of allowing notions of both wealth and love of money to bleed into and determine the notion of greed. Further, he says little about the prior convictions, beliefs, and assumptions that might lie behind Paul's novel identification of greed with idolatry. Moreover, in the context of Ephesians or Colossians, we do not really learn what lies behind the disposition to be greedy or to be a πλεονέκτης that, uniquely among these vices, ties it to idolatry. In short, there are still a number of conceptual and theological questions to answer with regard to Paul's assertion that greed is idolatry. What follows is one attempt to explain how this metaphor might work. I should say at the outset, there may be other explanations that work, too. This is not meant to rule out further thinking and reflection on this metaphor. Indeed, one might expect any live metaphor to generate further reflection.

Greed 2.0

If we are to make sense of Paul's claim that greed is idolatry, I suggest that it may be fruitful to begin by returning to look at the doctrine of creation, in particular, creation out of nothing. Of course, in Romans 4:17 Paul identifies God as "the one who brings to life those who were dead and calls into being that which was not." This claim is hardly a full blown account of creation *ex nihilo*. It does give us some reason to expect that later Christian reflection on the God who calls into being that which was not might be acceptable to Paul's way of thinking even if he did not articulate things this way himself.

Doctrinally, Christians want to assert that before God's creation there was nothing. This is because "[t]here could be no reality independent of, and potentially resistant to, the divine will, nor could it be supposed that that the world as we know it is a lower, inferior part of the divine being."[16] Such a

---

15. See Rosner, *Greed as Idolatry*, chapter 10.

16. Carol Harrison, "Taking Creation for the Creator: Use and Enjoyment in Augustine's Theological Aesthetics," in *Idolatry: False Worship in the Bible, Early Judaism, and Christianity* (ed. Steven C. Barton; London: T & T Clark, 2007) 180.

recognition establishes that divine being and human being are fundamentally distinct. "The divine is life, truth, goodness, beauty; created being *receives* life, truth, goodness, beauty from the divine, but is in itself, nothing."[17]

Although doctrinally crucial, neither Genesis 1–3 nor Romans 4:17 makes this precise point. Nevertheless, it should undergird Christian reflection on texts such as this. In the light of this relationship between God and humans, it is interesting to note that, immediately upon creating humans in the image of God, God blesses the humans. In particular, in blessing the humans, God addresses one of their most basic needs and desires—hunger. God's first words to the humans are: "See, I have given you every plant yielding seed that is upon the face of the earth, and every tree with seed in its fruit; you shall have them for food" (Gen 1:29). This offering of the material world typifies the relationship between God and humans in the garden. "All that exists is God's gift to man and it exists to make God known to man, to make man's life communion with God."[18] Moreover, to push this even further, it would seem that humans are created with desire (or hunger), both the desires particular to all creatures and a distinct desire for God that is tied to being created in the image of God.[19]

In the garden God's gift and human desire are in right relation to each other. This then enables communion with God. There is, in the conventional sense of πλεονεξία, no greed. It is important to note, however, that is not because human desiring is proportioned to what is due to each. Rather, it is that human desiring is properly ordered in relation to God's gracious provision. Strictly speaking, humans are due nothing from God. Nevertheless, they are graciously offered a share in fellowship with God (1 Pet 1:4).

---

17. Harrison, "Taking Creation for the Creator" 181. Harrison uses this as the basis for understanding Augustine's reading of Rom 1:20–25, arguing that for Augustine the foundation of all idolatry lies on the creature's refusal to recognize its total dependence on God.

18. Alexander Schmemann, *For the Life of the World* (2nd expanded edition; Crestwood: St. Vladimir's Seminary Press, 2002) 14. Schmemann further notes that although all creation depends on food, only humans can bless God for the food they receive.

19. See in particular here Gregory of Nyssa's *Commentary on the Song of Songs* (trans. Casimir McCambley; Brookline: Hellenic College Press, 1987) Homily 4, 119, 5–6. See also the comments of Morwenna Ludlow, *Universal Salvation: Eschatology in the Thought of Gregory of Nyssa and Karl Rahner* (Oxford: Oxford University Press, 2000) 56–58, and Martin Laird, "Under Solomon's Tutelage: The Education of Desire in the Homilies on the Song of Songs," *Modern Theology* 18 (2002) 517.

Moreover, this fellowship with God also enables and sustains one's proper relationships to others and to the rest of creation.

In the light of Schmemann's initial reflection on God's provision for human hunger, one can then see that the Fall is precipitated by humans eating what was not offered. They have grasped at something beyond the gifts God has given; their desire has outstripped God's gracious provision. In this light, greed breaks the communion between God and humans (as well as the communion between God, humans, and the rest of creation). If one thinks of the refusal of God's gift of fellowship as the most fundamental way in which humans turn from God or forget God, then we have a basis for understanding how greed can be idolatry in a way that might be distinct from the other vices Paul admonishes the Ephesians to avoid.

If there is some plausibility to this, it must lead us to return to Ephesians and Colossians to modify our earlier account of πλεονεξία in Paul. According to the conventional uses of this term in the Greek of Paul's day, πλεονεξία referred to desiring or grasping for more than one is due. In a world highly structured by social status and location, it was relatively easy to discern what is due to whom given their relative position in society. In this light, it is certainly possible to offer a coherent account of greed, but it remains difficult to account for how greed can be idolatry.

In the light of a doctrine of creation out of nothing, humans are strictly speaking due nothing but are offered communion with God. The God who wills communion with them graciously addresses their desires. They are thereby capable of remaining rightly and peaceably related to others and the rest of creation. In this context, greed is not primarily about wanting more than one is due. Rather, greed is the reflection of desire that is unbounded and unconcerned to live within and maintain God's gift of communion.[20]

Greed does not transgress a social standard of what is appropriate; it distorts and damages a relationship of communion by desiring something other than God or in subverting that desire for God. In effect it is the rejection of that communion and a turning away from God to attend to that which is not God—idolatry.

---

20. Although I cannot develop this claim here, it would seem that a properly bounded concern to live within and maintain God's gift of communion would require appropriate uses of the gifts of God's creation and the earth that sustains those gifts.

This specification should remind believers that idolatry at its root is a misdirection of love and attention away from God and toward something else that is not God. It is crucial to understand, however, that this is not a judgment that the created world is itself the problem. The material world as such, including such things as food, commodities, works of art, or even sex need not draw our attention and love away from God. Such things would appear to be given by God to address our hunger. When well-ordered and properly related to God, these desires can in many cases further sharpen our vision of God and enhance our devotion. Our desiring and engagements with the material world threaten to become idolatrous when and if they truncate or misdirect our attentions from God.[21] It is important to note here that desire does not need to be extinguished, but rightly directed.[22]

If greed is idolatry in the sense of unbounded desire that breaks the bounds of God's gift of communion, how might Christians avoid Paul's admonitions and judgments against πλεονεξία and the πλεονέκτης? At a general level, this must require a shaping or binding of our desires so that they are more properly proportioned and directed to God's gift of communion, so that we more fully desire that communion. Until that time when we will know just as fully as we have been known, when our communion with God is transformed by the reconciliation of all things in Christ, it would seem that, to avoid the idolatry that is greed, our desires should be subjected, shaped, directed, and healed by the work of the Spirit.

Given that this is where Paul's assertion that greed is idolatry has led so far, it may be useful to pause and recognize that there is a rich tradition of theological reflection on the training of desire. I do not have the space to rehearse that tradition here. What follows is merely an attempt to continue in the Pauline vein I began by following the course of Ephesians 5:3–5 and Colossians 3. In these passages, I will suggest that Paul offers a brief but particular course in the training of desire so that we avoid the idolatry which is greed.

---

21. Commenting on Nyssa's Homilies/Commentary on the Song of Song's, Laird notes, "The problem with desire, therefore is not that it is concerned with the body *per se* but that the soul seeks ultimacy in what is not God" ("Under Solomon's Tutelage" 508).

22. Laird, "Under Solomon's Tutelage" 509.

Thanksgiving

Recall that in 5:3 Paul rehearses a set of activities the Ephesians are to avoid. Among these is greed (πλεονεξία). By 5:5 these activities are touched on again. This time πλεονέκτης is used to speak of greedy people, and they are identified as idolaters. In between these series of vices which are inappropriate to those called to holiness, Paul says, "Let there be thanksgiving" (5:4). Against all of these, the single term "thanksgiving" stands as the sole counter weight to the six vices mentioned.

The introduction of thanksgiving injects an interesting twist into the discussion.[23] So far, the vices to be avoided in this passage are all related to interactions with others. The antidote to all of these destructive patterns of behavior and speech is not renewed focus on improving interpersonal relations but rather thanksgiving to God. There seem to be several respects in which this might be so.

I have argued that greed's identity with idolatry is tied to desire that is unbounded and unconcerned with what God has offered, that is, communion. The desires of the greedy become incorrectly or inappropriately focused on other people or on aspects of the material world. As we will see, for Paul, desires for others and for the material world are not wrong in and of themselves. Rather, such desire needs to be ordered in relation to our ultimate desire for God. Thanksgiving is a way of educating, reforming, and refocusing our desires toward God. Cultivating the habit of thanksgiving enables believers to love God properly and to love others and the rest of creation in ways that enhance rather than frustrate their communion with God.

We can see this by looking at the ways Paul uses the verb εὐχαριστέω and the noun εὐχαριστία. Typically, Paul's letters begin with expressions of thanks to God for the communities to which he is writing (see Rom 1:8; 1 Cor 1:4; 2 Cor 1:11; Eph 1:16; Phil 1:3; Col 1:3; 1 Thess 1:2; 2 Thess 1:3; Phlm 1:4). Paul's thanks is always directed to God and takes into account the work that God is doing in these congregations. In 1 and 2 Thessalonians, this general theme of Paul's greeting is extended into the body of the epistle as Paul repeatedly offers thanks for the community, their reception of the gospel,

---

23. See also Best, *Ephesians*, 479.

and the joy they have brought to Paul (1 Thess 2:13; 3:9; 2 Thess 2:13; see also 1 Cor 4:15). He even offers thanks for his co-workers Priscilla and Aquila (Rom 16:4). Those of us who read Paul's epistles regularly and have become familiar with his epistolary conventions can often treat these thanksgivings in too cursory a way. These thanksgivings reflect a deep love and desire for the people in these communities, and such desire leads him to thank God. Even when he is frustrated by and with these communities, this does not seem to diminish his longing for them or his gratitude to God.[24]

When it comes to the material world and food in particular, Paul holds the view that "all of God's creation is good and nothing is to be rejected if it is received with thanksgiving" (1 Tim 4:4). Paul expresses similar views in Romans 14:6 and, tellingly, with regard to being served meat that may have been sacrificed to an idol in 1 Corinthians 10:30.

Thanksgiving plays a central role in Paul's collection for famine relief in Jerusalem, too. In 2 Corinthians 9, Paul urges the Corinthians to be generous in giving money for this collection. Perhaps surprisingly their generosity does not result in Paul's gratitude to them, but in offerings of thanks to God. Although he does not use the term εὐχαριστία in Philippians 4:10–20, the same theme appears. The Philippians' generous gift to Paul results in thanks to God, who will then repay the Philippians. Moreover, earlier in Philippians 4:6, Paul has proposed that thanksgiving is the alternative to being anxious about one's needs.

It should be clear that throughout his letters, Paul extends thanks to God for his co-workers and his congregations. Further, he indicates that thanksgiving can properly sanctify believers' engagements with the material world, both the things they consume and the things they give away. These verses in themselves suggest that thanksgiving is a fundamental disposition and practice that will help believers rightly situate their desires for others and the rest of creation in a way that will short circuit the greed that is idolatry.

In Ephesians and Colossians, Paul offers an even fuller display of the role thanksgiving may play in educating, forming, and reforming the desires of believers. Indeed, one can argue that in these letters Paul suggests that

---

24. Galatians would be the exception to this general rule.

thanksgiving may be the summative act of the Christian life. Although the identification of greed with idolatry in Colossians 3:5 is not juxtaposed with thanksgiving as directly as it is in Ephesians 5, Colossians 3 does say a bit more about the role of thanksgiving in the Christian life. Hence, I will focus on Colossians, recognizing that what is said more directly in Colossians about thanksgiving could be inferred in Ephesians as well.

Colossians begins with Paul thanking God for the Colossians' reception and growth in the gospel. As Colossians 1 continues, Paul displays the focus of his prayers for the community. In particular he prays that God will strengthen the community to endure whatever may befall them. He further prays that such endurance will be a cause of joy for them, leading them to offer thanks to God for granting them a "share in the inheritance of the saints in the light" (1:12).[25] As Paul continues it becomes clear that this inheritance has been established through Christ's reconciling work on the cross. In 1:15–20, Paul describes this work as the restoration of communion with God, noting that Christ's role in creation makes him the fitting vehicle through which the Father restores communion with "all things."

The key passage for my purposes is Colossians 3:12–17. Here Paul continues the images of death and renewal that stood behind his admonition to put to death a range of earthly practices of which greed, which is idolatry, is one.[26] What follows is a series of imperative verbs that build on each other and which are intimately bound up with thanksgiving.[27] The first imperative enjoins the Colossians to clothe themselves with particular habits and practices. Having stripped off this old earthly self, the Colossians are urged to clothe themselves with a range of dispositions and practices (compassionate

---

25. Jerry L. Sumney (*Colossians: A Commentary* [Louisville: Westminster John Knox, 2008] 54) asserts that "in the light" must refer to the place where God dwells. This possibility might enhance the idea that Paul is speaking about the restoration of communion with God. The contrast between a believer's movement from darkness to light in passages such as Acts 26:18 or 1 Pet 2:9 probably indicates that "in the light" should not be taken as narrowly as Sumney does.

26. These images of taking off and putting on begin in 2:11–15, where they are connected to circumcision and baptism.

27. Marianne Thompson argues: "Thanksgiving is the vertical correlate of the horizontal virtues found in this section" (*Colossians and Philemon* [Grand Rapids: Eerdmans, 2005] 85). While affirming this, I also want to develop the role that thanksgiving plays in thwarting the greed that is idolatry.

hearts, kindness, humility, meekness, patience, and forbearance) so that they may properly forgive each other and live reconciled lives (3:12–13). Paul then goes on to say, "Above all, [clothe yourselves][28] in love, which binds everything together in perfect harmony" (3:14).

In the light of having done this, the Colossians are to let the peace of Christ be the ultimate arbiter over their hearts. Paul addressed the peace of Christ in 1:20 where the blood of the cross is the catalyst in reconciling all things to God, particularly in restoring communion with alienated humans.[29] Many English translations render the imperative in 3:15 as, "Let the peace of Christ rule in your hearts" [NRSV, ESV, NIV, KJV]. This is not strictly incorrect, but it does not quite bring out the idea that the Greek imperative βραβευέτω refers to acting as an arbiter or umpire in a contest.[30] The imperative here seems designed to impress on the Colossians and all believers that the desires of the heart need to be subjected to Christ's arbitration. This seems very similar to Paul's admonition in 2 Corinthians 10:5 to bring every thought captive to Christ. The idea in each case is not to obliterate thoughts or desires but to subject them to Christ's healing gaze.

In that light, there is little reason to think that allowing the peace of Christ to arbitrate the desires of one's heart will be peaceful. This is the hard work of spiritual transformation; this will not be quick, simple, or painless. Nevertheless, Paul indicates that the practice of allowing Christ to arbitrate the desires of their hearts is directed toward two particular ends. First,

---

28. The imperative verb is assumed here, and supplied in most English translations. It is not in the Greek.

29. Thompson (*Colossians and Philemon*, 85) argues, "This peace is not first a personal, subjective, inner peace, but rather the unity and wholeness, given by Christ to the community." Although it is the case that one of the aims of allowing the peace of Christ to arbitrate in their hearts is to enable the Colossians to embody the unity to which God calls them, it does seem that by allowing the peace of Christ to arbitrate in their hearts Paul is calling the Colossians to practices that relate to their inner life. Indeed, there is little reason to think that allowing the peace of Christ to arbitrate among the conflicting desires of one's heart will be anything but a difficult transformative experience of rooting out some desires and radically redirecting others.

30. The only other time this verb is used in the Bible is Wis 10:12. There wisdom is cast as the arbiter in the contest between Jacob and the angel (Gen 32:34). In addition, Paul used the cognate term καταβραβευέτω in 2:18 to mean "disqualify." Even when a term like "rule" might be appropriate, it is in the context of a conflict or unruliness. See Robert McL. Wilson, *Colossians and Philemon* (Edinburgh: T & T Clark, 2005) 264.

it enables the unity to which God has called the body of Christ (compare with Eph 2:14–16). Second, Paul goes further. He indicates that allowing the peace of Christ to arbitrate in their hearts will enable them to fulfill the imperative, "become thankful people" [εὐχάριστοι γίνεσθε] (3:15). The construction of this series of imperative verbs could indicate that when, or to the extent that, the peace of Christ arbitrates the desires of the Colossians' hearts, then they can and will become thankful people.

Thus far, I have suggested that Christians may avoid the greed that is idolatry to the extent their desires regarding all things are properly ordered toward communion with God. Cultivating the habits of thankfulness appears to be one of the ways Paul imagines Christians can maintain the proper ordering of their desires. Becoming thankful people, however, depends on the extent to which the peace of Christ arbitrates the desires of believers' hearts.

Before moving further in Colossians, it is important (but not surprising) to point out that, although Colossians is rarely invoked in most liturgies, this pattern regarding Christ's reformation of the desires of our hearts and its relationship to thanksgiving is deeply woven into the movements of the many Eucharistic liturgies. For example, in the *Book of Common Prayer* of the Episcopal Church, the service begins with people praying that the thoughts of our hearts might be cleansed by the Spirit so that we might worthily magnify God's holy name. Further, in more traditional forms of the initial penitential rite, the congregation confesses that "we have too much followed the devices and desires of our own hearts." Only in the light of confessing these and other sins and receiving forgiveness and absolution and sharing the peace of Christ are we then able to offer our sacrifice of thanks and praise. Participation in the Eucharist regularly places us in that position where we learn how to let the peace of Christ arbitrate the desires of our hearts so that we can become properly thankful people.

Such a scenario reminds us that becoming thankful people is not a one-time achievement but an ongoing work of a lifetime devoted to allowing the Spirit of Christ to arbitrate the desires of our hearts. This will no doubt involve rooting out and transforming distorted habits and affections and cultivating others as the Spirit invites us to ever more fully desire that which God desires for us. Further, although Paul uses imperative verbs here, they are in the third person. Neither the Colossians nor contemporary believers are the initiators of these activities.[31] The peace of Christ can arbitrate the desires of our hearts because God has called us back to God through Christ. God has moved to restore the communion that God desires with us.

Returning to Colossians, Paul concludes this passage by commanding the Colossians to let the word of Christ dwell [ἐνοικείτω] in them richly. This will enable them to help each other cultivate wisdom and to sing thankfully in their hearts to God.[32] If, as I have suggested, these imperative verbs build on each other, then to the extent that the peace of Christ arbitrates the desires of believers' hearts, the word of Christ[33] can dwell in them richly. The upshot of this indwelling is that the Colossians will be able to grow in wisdom and in their capacity for gratitude.

This would seem to be an important supplement to the notion that cultivating the habit of thanksgiving is the way to avoid the greed that is idolatry. This is because even though our desiring may be disordered, unbounded and unconcerned by God's desire for communion with us, people desire what is attractive to them. That is, we desire the good. As fallen humans, however, we are often mistaken about what the good is and where to find it. The vices listed earlier in Colossians or in Ephesians always confront people through their attractiveness, through their ability to appear to be virtuous or to play upon some aspect of virtue or beauty without actually resulting in beauty or virtue. Thus, they are able to distract believers' attentions and hearts away from God. The wisdom that results from the indwelling of the word of Christ is crucial for discerning the difference between those things worthy of our desire and things that only appear so, between desires ordered to enhance communion with God and those that will frustrate such communion.[34]

---

31. Wilson (*Colossians and Philemon*, 266) says of these imperatives, "this is not something the Colossians are to achieve, but something they are to allow to happen, and not hinder."

32. Both Thompson (*Colossians and Philemon*, 85) and Sumney (*Colossians*, 223) argue that wise teaching and thankful praise are the ways in which the Colossians show that the word of Christ is dwelling in them. The relationship between the participles and the main verb in this verse is ambiguous enough that it allows one to take wise teaching and thankful praise as both enabled by the indwelling of Christ's word (as above) and a sign of that indwelling.

33. There seems little reason to take the "word of Christ" as either Christ's word or a word about Christ, that is, the gospel. It can be both/and (see Wilson, *Colossians*, 266).

34. This seems to be similar to the wisdom needed to practice Augustine's distinction between use and enjoyment.

The culmination of all these imperative verbs is action. "Whatever you do in word or deed, do all of these things in the name of Jesus, thanking God the father through him" (3:17). Action in word or deed should be done in the name of Christ and in thankfulness to God. Although there is no imperative verb in the second clause of 3:17, one can assume it is based on the first clause. Moreover, the preceding series of imperatives have presumed a scenario that, if realized, will in the normal course of things result in all things being done in the name of Christ with thankfulness to God. It need not be commanded; it will be the unforced result of all the other imperatives.

Conclusion

In both Ephesians 5:3–5 and Colossians 3:5, Paul identifies greed with idolatry. It is not self-evident how this identification is supposed to work even granting that Paul is casting a new metaphor. One possible way of doing this is through attention to the doctrine of creation. Through this, one can see that God implants desire, including a desire for God, within humans. God meets that desire through offering humans communion with God. As long as their desire was rightly aligned with God's offer of communion, humans enjoyed fellowship with God. In Genesis 3, we read that humans desired something beyond what God had offered and, in effect, turned their back on God's offer of communion. This desire that is unbounded and unconcerned with communion with God is greed. Such greed rejects God's offer of communion and pursues other things which are not God. This observation sustains the claim that greed is idolatry. I should be clear at this point. I am not claiming that my reasoning that ties greed to idolatry through a doctrine of creation replicates Paul's reasoning or the reasoning of any member of the Ephesian or Colossian congregation. Given the cryptic nature of Paul's comments on this matter in both Ephesians and Colossians, I am not sure we could reconstruct his reasoning with any degree of confidence. Nevertheless, I will claim that this account does make sense of Paul's claims in ways that are consistent with Paul's views expressed elsewhere and with a whole network of Christian convictions and practices. Further, if one understands Paul's claims that greed is idolatry in the ways I have described, one can then move to read Paul's discussion of thanksgiving in these letters as that disposition and practice which works to counter the greed which is idolatry. Colossians 3 in particular offers a dense account of the ways in which growth in Christ both sustains and is sustained by habits of thanksgiving.

To the extent this case carries any weight, it provides Christians with ways of understanding Paul's claims about greed and idolatry. It suggests ways in which Christians might, with the Spirit's help, cultivate dispositions and practices that might counter the greed which is idolatry.

Bibliography

Albright, William F. "The Oracles of Balaam." *Journal of Biblical Literature* 63 (1944) 207–33.

Alexander, Loveday. "Sisters in Adversity: Retelling Martha's Story." Pp. 197–213 in *The Feminist Companion to Luke*. Edited by Amy-Jill Levine and Marianne Blickenstaff. Cleveland: Pilgrim, 2004.

Alter, Robert. *The Art of Biblical Narrative*. New York: Basic, 1981.

"The Articles of Religion of the Methodist Church." http://www.umc.org/what-we-believe /the-articles-of-religion-of-the-methodist-church. Accessed January 3, 2016.

Barr, James. *The Concept of Biblical Theology: An Old Testament Perspective*. Minneapolis: Fortress, 1999.

Barrett, C. K. *The Gospel According to John*. 1st edition, London: SPCK, 1955. 2nd edition, Philadelphia: Westminster John Knox, 1978.

Barth, Karl. *The Epistle to the Romans*. Translated by Edwyn C. Hoskyns. Oxford: Oxford University Press, 1933.

———. *Die Schrift und die Kirche*. Zollikon-Zürich: Evangelischen Verlag, 1947.

———. *Church Dogmatics*. Edited by Thomas F. Torrance. Translated by Geoffrey W. Bromiley. Edinburgh: T & T Clark, 1958.

———. *Gespräche*. Edited by Eberhard Busch. Gesamtausgabe IV. Zürich: Theologischer Verlag, 1959–62.

———. *Karl Barth's Table Talk*. Edited by John D. Godsey. Richmond: John Knox, 1963.

———. *God Here and Now*. Translated by Paul M. van Buren. New York: Routledge Classics, 2003.

Bartlett, J. V. et al. *The New Testament in the Apostolic Fathers*. Oxford: Clarendon, 1905.

Baskette, Molly P. *Standing Naked Before God: The Art of Public Confession*. Cleveland: Pilgrim, 2015.

Baskin, Judith R. "Origen on Balaam: The Dilemma of the Unworthy Prophet." *Vigiliae Christianae* 37 (1983) 22–35.

Beale, Gregory K. *We Become What We Worship: A Biblical Theology of Idolatry*. Downers Grove: InterVarsity, 2008.

Beavis, Mary Ann. "Mary of Bethany and the Hermeneutics of Remembrance." *Catholic Biblical Quarterly* 75 (2013) 739–55.

Bellah, Robert N., Richard Madsen, William M. Sullivan, Ann Swidler, and Steven M. Tipton. *Habits of the Heart: Individuals and Commitment in American Life*. Berkeley: University of California Press, 1985.

Best, Ernest. *Ephesians*. Edinburgh: T & T Clark, 2001.

Blenkinsopp, Joseph. *Judaism: The First Phase: The Place of Ezra and Nehemiah in the Origins of Judaism.* Grand Rapids: Eerdmans, 2009.

Bock, Darrell L. *Luke 9:51–24:53.* Grand Rapids: Baker, 1996.

The Book of Discipline of the United Methodist Church. Nashville: United Methodist Church, 2008.

Bosing, Walter. *Hieronymus Bosch, c. 1450–1516: Between Heaven and Hell.* Koln: Taschen, 1987.

Bowker, John W. "The Son of Man." *Journal of Theological Studies* 28 (1977) 19–48.

Boyarin, Daniel. *Border Lines: The Partition of Judaeo-Christianity.* Philadelphia: University of Pennsylvania Press, 2004.

———. *The Jewish Gospels: The Story of the Jewish Christ.* New York: The New Press, 2012.

Braaten, Carl E., and Robert W. Jensen. *Jews and Christians: People of God.* Grand Rapids: Erdmans, 2003.

Brant, Jo-Ann. *John.* Grand Rapids: Baker, 2011.

Brown, Raymond. *The Gospel according to John.* Garden City: Doubleday, 1965.

Brueggemann, Walter. *Theology of the Old Testament: Testimony, Dispute, Advocacy.* Minneapolis: Fortress, 1997.

Bruner, Frederick Dale. *The Gospel of John: A Commentary.* Grand Rapids: Eerdmans, 2012.

Bruns, Gerald. "Midrash and Allegory: The Beginnings of Scriptural Interpretation." Pp. 625–46 in *The Literary Guide to the Bible.* Edited by Robert Alter and Frank Kermode. Cambridge, MA: Belknap, 1990.

Bultmann, Rudolf. "Karl Barth's *Epistle to the Romans* in Its Second Edition." P. 119 in volume 1 of *The Beginnings of Dialectic Theology.* Edited by James M. Robinson. Translated by Keith R. Crim. Richmond: John Knox, 1962.

Burkett, Delbert. *The Son of Man Debate: A History and Evaluation.* Cambridge: Cambridge University Press, 1999.

Burnett, Richard E. *Karl Barth's Theological Exegesis: The Hermeneutical Principles of the Römerbrief Period.* Grand Rapids: Eerdmans, 2004.

Caird, George B. *The Revelation of St. John the Divine.* London: A & C Black, 1980.

———. *New Testament Theology.* Oxford: Clarendon, 1995.

Calvin, John. *Calvin's Commentaries, vol. 2: A Harmony of the Gospels: Matthew, Mark, and Luke.* Translated by T. H. L. Parker. Edited by David W. Torrance and Thomas F. Torrance. Edinburgh: St. Andrews, 1972; repr. Grand Rapids: Eerdmans, 1979.

Carroll, John T. *Luke: A Commentary.* Louisville: Westminster John Knox, 2012.

Carter, Warren. "Getting Martha Out of the Kitchen: Luke 10:38–42 Again." Pp. 214–31 in *The Feminist Companion to Luke.* Edited by Amy-Jill Levine and Marianne Blickenstaff. Cleveland: Pilgrim, 2004.

Castelo, Daniel, and Robert W. Wall. "Scripture and the Church: A Précis for an Alternative Analogy." *Journal of Theological Interpretation* 5 (2011) 197–207.

Childs, Brevard S. *Biblical Theology in Crisis.* Philadelphia: Westminster, 1970.

———. *Exodus.* OT Library; Philadelphia: Westminster, 1974.

———. *Introduction to the Old Testament as Scripture.* Philadelphia: Fortress, 1979.

———. *The New Testament as Canon: An Introduction.* Philadelphia: Fortress, 1984.

Clarke, Adam. *The Holy Bible Containing the Old and New Testaments with a Commentary and Critical Notes,* volume 3. New York: Abingdon-Cokesbury, n. d.

Collins, John J. *A Commentary on the Book of Daniel.* Minneapolis: Fortress, 1993.

———. *The Bible after Babel: Historical Criticism in a Postmodern Age*. Grand Rapids: Eerdmans, 2005.

Cone, James. *The Cross and the Lynching Tree*. Maryknoll: Orbis, 2011.

"The Confession of 1967." http://www.creeds.net/reformed/conf67.htm. Accessed January 3, 2016.

Congdon, Bruce W. "The Word as Event: Barth and Bultmann on Scripture." Pp. 241–65 in *The Sacred Text: Excavating the Texts, Exploring the Interpretations, and Engaging the Theologies of the Christian Scriptures*. Edited by Michael F. Bird and Michael W. Pahl. Piscataway: Gorgias, 2010.

———. "*Apokatastasis* and Apostolicity: A Response to Oliver Crisp on the Question of Barth's Universalism." *Scottish Journal of Theology* 67 (2014) 474.

———. *The Mission of Demythologizing: Rudolf Bultmann's Dialectical Theology*. Minneapolis: Fortress, 2015.

———. "Theology as Theanthropology: Barth's Theology of Existence in Its Existentialist Context." P. 34 in *Karl Barth and the Making of Evangelical Theology: A Fifty-Year Perspective*. Edited by Clifford B. Anderson and Bruce L. McCormack. Grand Rapids: Eerdmans, 2015.

———. *The God Who Saves: A Dogmatic Sketch*. Eugene: Cascade, 2016.

Constable, Giles. "The Interpretation of Mary and Martha." Pp. 1–141 in *Three Studies in Medieval Religious and Social Thought*. Cambridge: Cambridge University Press, 1995.

Conway, Colleen M. *Men and Women in the Fourth Gospel: Gender and Johannine Characterization*. Atlanta: Society of Biblical Literature, 1999.

Cox, Claude E. "Schaper's *Eschatology* Meets Kraus's *Theology of the Psalms*." Pp. 289–311 in *The Old Greek Psalter: Studies in Honour of Albert Pietersma*. Edited by R. J. V. Hiebert, C. E. Cox, and P. J. Gentry. Sheffield: Sheffield Academic Press, 2001.

Craddock, Fred B. *Luke*. Louisville: John Knox, 1990.

Cross, Frank Moore. "Yahweh and Ba'l." Pp. 147–94 in *Canaanite Myth and Hebrew Epic*. Edited by Frank M. Cross. Cambridge, MA: Harvard University Press, 1973.

"*Dabru Emet*: A Jewish Statement on Christians and Christianity." *Jews and Christians: People of God*. Edited by Carl E. Braaten and Robert W. Jenson. Grand Rapids: Eerdmans, 2003.

Dickinson, Emily. "Tell All the Truth, but Tell It Slant." No. 1129 in *The Norton Anthology of Modern Poetry*. Edited by Richard Ellmann and Robert O'Clair. New York: W. W. Norton, 1973.

Dobs, Marcus, ed. *The Works of Aurelius Augustine*, volume 3. Edinburgh: T & T Clark, 1873.

Dodd, C. H. *According to the Scriptures: The Substructure of New Testament Theology*. New York: Scribners, 1953.

———. *The Interpretation of the Fourth Gospel*. Cambridge: Cambridge University Press, 1953.

———. *Historical Tradition in the Fourth Gospel*. Cambridge: Cambridge University Press, 1963.

Dunn, James D. G. *The Partings of the Ways*, 2nd edition. London: SCM, 2006.

Eissfeldt, Otto. "Die Komposition der Bileam-Erzahlung." *Zeitschrift für die alttestamentliche Wissenschaft* 57 (1939) 212–44.

———. "Psalm 80." Pp. 65–78 in *Geschichte und Altes Testament*. Edited by W. F. Albright et al. Tübingen: Mohr, 1953.

———. "Psalm 80 und Psalm 89." *Die Welt des Orients* 3 (1965) 27–31.

Enns, Peter. *Inspiration and Incarnation: Evangelicals and the Problem of the Old Testament.* Grand Rapids: Baker, 2005.

Esler, Philip F., and Ronald Piper. *Lazarus, Mary, and Martha: Social-Scientific Approaches to the Gospel of John.* Minneapolis: Fortress, 2006.

Fabry, Heinz-Josef. "Messianism in the Septuagint." Pp. 192–205 in *Septuagint Research: Issues and Challenges in the Study of the Greek Jewish Scriptures.* Edited by W. G. Kraus and R. G. Wooden. Atlanta: Society of Biblical Literature, 2006.

Fitzmyer, Joseph A. *The Gospel According to Luke 10–24.* Garden City: Doubleday, 1985.

Fowl, Stephen E. "Selections from Thomas Aquinas's Commentary on Romans." Pp. 320–27 in *The Theological Interpretation of Scripture: Classic and Contemporary Readings.* Edited by Stephen E. Fowl. Cambridge, MA: Blackwell, 1997.

Frankel, David. "The Deuteronomic Portrayal of Balaam." *Vetus Testamentum* 46 (1996) 30–42.

Frey, Rudolf, et al. *Antwort: Karl Barth zum siebzigsten Geburtstag.* Zürich: Evangelischer Verlag, 1956.

Friedman, Edwin H. *A Failure of Nerve: Leadership in the Age of a Quick Fix.* Church Publishing, 2007.

Geissen, A., ed. *Der Septuaginta-Text des Buches Daniel.* Bonn: Rudolf Habelt Verlag, 1968.

Gench, Francis Taylor. *Encounters with Jesus: Studies in the Gospel of John.* Louisville: Westminster John Knox, 2007.

Goldingay, John. *Psalms 42–89.* Grand Rapids: Baker, 2007.

———. *Do We Need the New Testament? Letting the Old Testament Speak for Itself.* Downers Grove: InterVarsity, 2015.

Green, Joel B. *The Gospel of Luke.* Grand Rapids: Eerdmans, 1997.

———. "The (Re-)Turn to Theology." *Journal of Theological Interpretation* 1 (2007) 2.

Gregory, Andrew, and Christopher Tuckett. *The Reception of the New Testament in the Apostolic Fathers.* Oxford: Oxford University Press, 2005.

Gregory of Nyssa. *Commentary on the Song of Songs.* Translated by Casimir McCambley. Brookline: Hellenic College, 1987.

Gross, Walter. *Bileam: Literar- und Formkritische Untersuchung der Prosa in Numbers 22–24.* München: Kisel Verlag, 1974.

Hadas-Lebel, Mireille. "Rome 'Quatrième Empire' et le symbole du porc." Pp. 297–312 in *Hellenica et Judaica: Hommage à Valentin Nikiprowetzky.* Edited by A. Caquot, M. Hadas-Lebel, and J. Riaud. Leuven: Peeters, 1986.

Hagin, Kenneth E. *The Holy Spirit and His Gifts.* Broken Arrow: Kenneth Hagin Ministries, 1991.

Hamilton, James M., Jr. *With the Clouds of Heaven: The Book of Daniel in Biblical Theology.* Downers Grove: InterVarsity, 2014.

Harrington, Daniel J. *Interpreting the Old Testament: A Practical Guide.* Collegeville: Liturgical, 1991.

Harrison, Carol. "Taking Creation for the Creator: Use and Enjoyment in Augustine's Theological Aesthetics." Pp. 179–97 in *Idolatry: False Worship in the Bible, Early Judaism, and Christianity.* Edited by Steven C. Barton. London: T & T Clark, 2007.

Haskins, Susan. *Mary Magdalene: Myth and Metaphor.* New York: Riverhead, 1993.

Hatch, Nathan. *The Democratization of American Christianity.* New Haven: Yale University Press, 1989.

Hays, Christopher B. *Hidden Riches: A Sourcebook for the Comparative Study of the Hebrew Bible and Ancient Near East.* Louisville: Westminster John Knox, 2014.

Hays, Christopher M., and Christopher B. Ansberry, eds. *Evangelical Faith and the Challenge of Historical Criticism.* Grand Rapids: Baker, 2013.

Hays, Richard B. *Echoes of Scripture in the Letters of Paul.* New Haven: Yale University Press, 1989.

———. "Reading Scripture in the Light of the Resurrection." Pp. 216–38 in *The Art of Reading Scripture.* Edited by Ellen Davis and Richard Hays. Grand Rapids: Eerdmans, 2003.

———. *The Conversion of the Imagination: Paul as Interpreter of Israel's Scripture.* Grand Rapids: Eerdmans, 2005.

———. *Reading Backwards: Figural Christology and the Fourfold Gospel Witness.* Waco: Baylor University Press, 2014.

Heifetz, Ronald A. *Leadership Without Easy Answers.* Cambridge, MA: Belknap, 2003.

———. *Leadership on the Line: Staying Alive through the Dangers of Leading.* Boston: Harvard Business School Press, 2017.

Hill, Charles E. "What Papias said about John (and Luke)." *Journal of Theological Studies* 49 (1998) 582–629.

———. *The Johannine Corpus in the Early Church.* Oxford: Oxford University Press, 2004.

Hoehner, Harold W. *Ephesians: An Exegetical Commentary.* Grand Rapids: Baker Academic, 2002.

Holmes, Christopher R. J. "Revelation in the Present Tense: On Rethinking Theological Interpretation in the Light of the Prophetic Office of Jesus Christ." *Journal of Theological Interpretation* 6 (2012) 23–42.

Hunsinger, George. *How to Read Karl Barth: The Shape of His Theology.* Oxford: Oxford University Press, 1991.

———., ed. *Thy Word is Truth: Barth on Scripture.* Grand Rapids: Eerdmans, 2012.

Hurst, L. D. *New Testament Theology.* Oxford: Clarendon, 1995.

Jeffrey, David Lyle. *Luke.* Grand Rapids: Brazos, 2012.

Jobes, Karen H., and Moisés Silva. *Invitation to the Septuagint*, 2nd edition. Grand Rapids: Baker, 2015.

Johnson, Luke Timothy. *The Gospel of Luke.* Collegeville: Liturgical, 1991.

Jones, Scott J. *John Wesley's Conception and Use of Scripture.* Nashville: Abingdon, 1995.

Josephus. Translated by H. St. J. Thackeray et al. 10 vols. Loeb Classical Library. Cambridge: Harvard University Press, 1926–1965.

Junior, Nyasha. "Re/Use of Texts" in http://www.atthispoint.net/editor-notes/reuse-of-texts/265/.

Kaminsky, Joel S. *Yet I Loved Jacob: Reclaiming the Biblical Conception of Election.* Nashville: Abingdon, 2007.

Käsemann, Ernst. *New Testament Questions of Today.* Translated by W. J. Montague. London: SCM, 1969.

Keener, Craig S. *The Gospel of John: A Commentary*, volume 2. Peabody: Hendrickson, 2003.

Kenyon, Frederic G., ed. *The Chester Beatty Biblical Papyri. Descriptions and Texts of the Twelve Manuscripts on Papyrus of the Greek Bible.* Fasc. VII: *Ezekiel, Daniel, Esther*; London: Emery Walker, 1937.

Kingsolver, Barbara. *The Poisonwood Bible.* New York: HarperPerennial, 1999.

Knibb, M. A., ed. *The Septuagint and Messianism.* Leuven: Peeters, 2006.

Koet, Bart J., and Wendy E. S. North. "The Image of Martha in Luke 10:38–42 and John 11:1–12:8." Pp. 47–66 in *Miracles and Imagery in Luke and John: Festschrift for Ulrich Busse*. Edited by J. Verheyden, G. van Belle, J. G. Van der Watt. Leuven: Peeters, 2008.

Koskie, Steven Joe, Jr. *Reading the Way to Heaven: A Wesleyan Theological Hermeneutic of Scripture*. Winona Lake: Eisenbrauns, 2014.

Kugel, James. *The Bible As it Was*. Cambridge, MA: Belknap, 1999.

Laird, Martin. "Under Solomon's Tutelage: The Education of Desire in the Homilies on the Song of Songs." *Modern Theology* 18 (2002) 507–25.

Lancaster, Sarah Heaner. "Scripture and Revelation." Pp. 489–504 in *The Oxford Handbook of Methodist Studies*. Edited by William J. Abraham and James E. Kirby. Oxford: Oxford University Press, 2009.

Law, Timothy Michael. *When God Spoke Greek. The Septuagint and the Making of the Christian Bible*. Oxford: Oxford University Press, 2013.

Lee, Dorothy A. "Martha and Mary: Levels of Characterization in Luke and John." Pp. 197–220 in *Characters and Characterization in the Gospel of John*. Edited by Christopher W. Skinner. London: Bloomsbury T & T Clark, 2013.

Lemcio, Eugene E. *The Past of Jesus in the Gospels*. Cambridge: Cambridge University Press, 1991.

———. "*Kerygmatic* Centrality and Unity in the First Testament?" Pp. 357–73 in *The Quest for Context and Meaning. Studies in Biblical Intertexuality in Honor of James A. Sanders*. Edited by Craig A. Evans and Shemaryahu Talmon. Leiden: Brill, 1997.

———. "Images of the Church in 1 Corinthians and 1 Timothy: An Exercise in Canonical Hermeneutics." *Asbury Journal* 56 (2001) 45–59.

———. "The Synoptics and John: The Two So Long Divided. Hearing Canonical Voices for Ecclesial Conversations." *Horizons in Biblical Theology* 26 (2004) 50–96.

———. "'Son of Man,' 'Pitiable Man,' 'Rejected Man': Equivalent Expressions in the Old Greek of Daniel." *Tyndale Bulletin* 56 (2005) 43–60.

———. "Daniel: an 'Historical' Sign of the Eschatological Ancient of Days/God Most High? Reading Bel et Draco in Eschatological Contexts: Apocalyptic (Daniel 2 and 7), Prophetic (Esaias 27:1), and Sapiential (Wisdom of Salomon 14:11–14)." In *Orthodoxy and Orthopraxis: Essays in Tribute to Paul Livermore*. Edited by Doug Cullum and J. Richard Middleton. Toronto: Clements, forthcoming 2017.

Lester, G. Brooke. *Daniel Evokes Isaiah: Allusive Characterization of Foreign Rule in the Hebrew-Aramaic Book of Daniel*. London: Bloomsbury T & T Clark, 2015.

Leveen, Adriane. *Memory and Tradition in the Book of Numbers*. Cambridge: Cambridge University Press, 2008.

Levenson, Jon D. *The Hebrew Bible, the Old Testament, and Historical Criticism*. Louisville: Westminster John Knox, 1993.

———. "Did God Forgive Adam? An Exercise in Comparative Midrash." Pp. 148–70 in *Jews and Christians: People of God*. Edited by Carl E. Braaten and Robert W. Jenson. Grand Rapids: Eerdmans, 2003.

———. "The Perils of Engaged Scholarship: A Rejoinder to Jorge Pixley." Pp. 239–46 in *Jews, Christians, and the Theology of the Hebrew Scriptures*. Edited by Alice O. Bellis and Joel Kaminsky. Atlanta: Society of Biblical Literature, 2006.

Levine, Baruch. *Numbers 21–36*. New York: Doubleday, 2000.

———. "The Deir 'Alla Plaster Inscriptions (2.27)." Pp. 140–45 in *The Context of Scripture*, volume 2. Edited by William W. Hallo and K. Lawson Younger, Jr. Leiden: Brill, 2000.

Levison, John R. (Jack). *Filled with the Spirit*. Grand Rapids: Eerdmans, 2009.

———. "The Spirit in Its Second Temple Context. An Exegetical Analysis of the Pneumatology of N. T. Wright." Pp. 439–62 in *God and the Faithfulness of Paul: A Critical Examination of the Pauline Theology of N.T. Wright*. Edited by Michael F. Bird, Christoph Heilig, and J. Thomas Hewitt. Tübingen: Mohr Siebeck, 2016.

Lieu, Judith. *Neither Jew Nor Greek: Constructing Early Christianity*, 2nd edition. London: Bloomsbury T & T Clark, 2016.

Limburg, James. "Psalm 29." P. 123 in *Psalms for Preaching and Worship*. Edited by Roger E. Van Harn and Brent A. Strawn. Grand Rapids: Eerdmans, 2009.

Lincoln, Andrew T. *Ephesians*. Waco: Word, 1990.

———. *The Gospel According to Saint John*. Peabody: Hendrickson, 2005.

Lindbeck, George. "The Church." Pp. 179–208 in *Keeping the Faith: Essays to Mark the Centenary of Lux Mundi*. Edited by Geoffrey Wainwright. Philadelphia: Fortress, 1988.

———. "The Church as Israel: Ecclesiology and Ecumenism." Pp. 78–94 in *Jews and Christians: People of God*. Edited by Carl E. Braaten and Robert W. Jenson. Grand Rapids: Eerdmans, 2003.

———. "What of the Future? A Christian Response." Pp. 357–66 in *Christianity in Jewish Terms*. Edited by Tikva Frymer-Kensky, David Novak, Peter Ochs, David Fox Sandmel, and Michael A. Signer. Boulder: Westview, 2000.

Ludlow, Morwenna. *Universal Salvation: Eschatology in the Thought of Gregory of Nyssa and Karl Rahner*. Oxford: Oxford University Press, 2000.

Lust, J. *Messianism and the Septuagint*. Leuven: Peeters, 2004.

Manor, T. Scott. *Epiphanius' alogi and the Johannine Controversy: A Reassessment of Early Ecclesial Opposition to the Johannine Corpus*. Leiden: Brill, 2016.

Margoliot, M. "The Connection of the Balaam Narrative with the Pentateuch." Pp. 279–90 in *Proceedings of the Sixth World Congress of Jewish Studies*. Edited by A. Shinan. Jerusalem: World Union of Jewish Studies, 1977.

Marsden, George. *Fundamentalism and American Culture*, 2nd edition. Oxford: Oxford University Press, 2006.

Marshall, I. Howard. *The Gospel of Luke: A Commentary on the Greek Text*. Grand Rapids: Eerdmans, 1978.

Martyn, J. Louis. *History and Theology in the Fourth Gospel*. New York: Westminster John Knox, 1968.

McCormack, Bruce L. *Orthodox and Modern: Studies in the Theology of Karl Barth*. Grand Rapids: Baker, 2008.

———. "The Being of Holy Scripture is in Becoming: Karl Barth in Conversation with American Evangelical Criticism." Pp. 55–75 in *Evangelicals & Scripture: Tradition, Authority and Hermeneutics*. Edited by Vincent Bacote, Laura C. Miguelez, and Dennis L. Okholm. Downers Grove: InterVarsity, 2009.

Metzger, Bruce. *The Canon of the New Testament: Its Origin, Development, and Significance*. Oxford: Clarendon, 1987.

Meyers, Carol L., and Eric M. Meyers. *Zechariah 9–14*. New York: Doubleday, 1993.

Midrash Rabbah Numbers, 3rd edition. Translated by Judah Slotki. London: Soncino, 1983.

Miller, Patrick D. "Rethinking the First Article of the Creed." *Theology Today* 61 (2005) 499–508.

Moloney, Francis. "Can Everyone Be Wrong? A Reading of John 11:1–12:8." *New Testament Studies* 49 (2003) 505–27.

Moore, Michael S. *The Balaam Traditions: Their Character and Development*. Atlanta: Scholars, 1990.

Moule, C. F. D. *An Idiom-Book of New Testament Greek*, 2nd edition. Cambridge: Cambridge University Press, 1963.

——. *The Origin [sic] of Christology*. Cambridge: Cambridge University Press, 2007.

Mowinckel, Sigmund. "Die Ursprung der Bileamsage." *Zeitschrift für die alttestamentliche Wissenschaft* 48 (1930) 233–71.

Müller, Mogens. *The First Bible of the Church: A Plea for the Septuagint*. Sheffield: Sheffield Academic Press, 1996.

——. *The Expression "Son of Man" and the Development of Christology. A History of Interpretation*. New York: Routledge, 2008.

Neusner, Jacob. "Was Rabbinic Judaism Really 'Ethnic'?" *Catholic Biblical Quarterly* 57 (1995) 281–305.

Nimmo, Paul T. "Actualism" Pp. 1–2 in *The Westminster Handbook to Karl Barth*. Edited by Richard E. Burnett. Louisville: Westminster John Knox, 2013.

Nolland, John. *Luke 9:21–18:34*. Dallas: Word, 1993.

Nongbri, Brent. "The Use and Abuse of P^{52}: Papyrological Pitfalls and the Dating of the Fourth Gospel." *Harvard Theological Review* 98 (2005) 23–48.

——. "The Limits of Paleographic Dating of Literary Papyri: Some Observations on the Date and Provenance of P. Bodmer II (P^{66})." *Museum Helveticum* 71 (2014) 1–35.

——. "Reconsidering the Place of Papyrus Bodmer 14–15 (P^{75}) in the Textual Criticism of the New Testament." *Journal of Biblical Literature* 135 (2016) 405–37.

North, Wendy E. Spronston. *The Lazarus Story within the Johannine Tradition*. Sheffield: Sheffield Academic Press, 2001.

Novak, David. "From Supersessionism to Parallelism in Jewish-Christian Dialogue." Pp. 95–113 in *Jews and Christians: People of God*. Edited by Carl E. Braaten and Robert W. Jenson. Grand Rapids: Eerdmans, 2003.

O'Day, Gail. *The Gospel of John*. Nashville: Abingdon, 1995.

Olson, Dennis. "Biblical Theology as Provisional Monologization: A Dialogue with Childs, Brueggemann and Bakhtin." *Biblical Interpretation* 6 (1998) 162–80.

——. *The Death of the Old and the Birth of the New: The Framework of the Book of Numbers and the Pentateuch*. Chico: Scholars, 1985.

Origen. *Homily* 14.3 (PG 12). *Patrologia Graeca*. Edited by J.-P. Migne. 162 vols. Paris, 1857–1886.

——. *Homily* 15.4 (PG 12). *Patrologia Graeca*. Edited by J.-P. Migne. 162 vols. Paris, 1857–1886.

Orthodox Study Bible. Nashville: Thomas Nelson, 2008.

Pagels, Elaine. *The Johannine Gospel in Gnostic Exegesis: Heracleon's Commentary on John*. Nashville: Abingdon, 1973.

Painter, John. *John: Witness and Theologian*. London: SPCK, 1975.

——. *The Quest for the Messiah*, 2nd edition. Nashville: Abingdon, 1993.

——. *1, 2, and 3 John*. Collegeville: Liturgical, 2002.

———. "The Death of Jesus in John: A Discussion of the Tradition, History, and Theology of John." Pp. 327–61 in *The Death of Jesus in the Fourth Gospel*. Edited by G. Van Belle. Leuven: Peeters, 2007.

———. *James and Jude*. Grand Rapids: Baker Academic, 2012.

———. "The Fourth Gospel and the Founder of Christianity." Pp. 257–84 in *Engaging with C. H. Dodd on the Gospel of John*. Edited by Tom Thatcher and Catrin H. Williams. Cambridge: Cambridge University Press, 2013.

Parsons, Mikeal C. *Luke*. Grand Rapids: Baker Academic, 2015.

Pietersma, Albert. "Exegesis and Liturgy in the Superscriptions of the Greek Psalter." Pp. 99–137 in *X Congress of the International Organization for Septuagint and Cognate Studies, Oslo 1998*. Edited by B. A. Taylor. Atlanta: Society of Biblical Literature, 2001.

———. "Septuagintal Exegesis and the Superscriptions of the Greek Psalter." Pp. 443–75 in *The Book of Psalms: Composition and Reception*. Edited by Peter W. Flint and Patrick. D. Miller, Jr. Boston: Brill, 2005.

———, and Benjamin G. Wright, eds. *A New English Translation of the Septuagint*. Oxford: Oxford University Press, 2007.

Pittman, Bill. *Prayers for the Twelve Steps: A Spiritual Journey*. San Diego: RPI, 1993.

Pontifical Biblical Commission. "The Interpretation of the Bible in the Church." Presented March 18, 1994. http://www.ewtn.com/library/curia/pbcinter.htm#8. Accessed January 3, 2016.

Radner, Ephraim. *The End of the Church: A Pneumatology of Christian Division in the West*. Grand Rapids: Eerdmans, 1998.

———. *Leviticus*. Grand Rapids: Brazos, 2008.

———. *Time and the Word: Figural Reading of the Christian Scriptures*. Grand Rapids: Eerdmans, 2016.

Rahlfs, Alfred, ed. *Septuaginta*, 7th edition. Stuttgart: Württembergische Bibelanstalt, 1962.

———. *Psalmi cum Odis*, 2nd edition. Göttingen: Vandenhoeck & Ruprecht, 1967.

Reid, Barbara E. *Choosing the Better Part? Women in the Gospel of Luke*. Collegeville: Liturgical, 1996.

Reynolds, Benjamin R. "The 'One Like a Son of Man' According to the Old Greek of Daniel 7:13–14." *Biblica* (2008) 70–80.

Robinson, Anthony B., and Robert W. Wall. *Called to Lead: Paul's Letters to Timothy for a New Day*. Grand Rapids: Eerdmans, 2012.

Roiullard, Hedwige. *La Pericope de Balaam*. Paris: J. Gabalda, 1985.

Rösel, Martin. "Towards a 'Theology of the Septuagint.'" Pp. 239–52 in *Septuagint Research. Issues and Challenges in the Study of the Greek Jewish Scriptures*. Edited by Wolfgang Kraus and R. Glenn Wooden. Atlanta: Society of Biblical Literature, 2006.

Rosner, Brian. *Greed as Idolatry*. Grand Rapids: Eerdmans, 2007.

Rowland, Christopher. *The Open Heaven: A Study of Jewish Apocalyptic in Judaism and Christianity*. New York: Crossroad, 1982.

———. "Revelation," in *The New Interpreters Bible Commentary*, volume 12. Nashville: Abingdon, 1998.

Rudolph, W., and H. P. Rüger, eds. *Biblia Hebraica Stuttgartensia*, 2nd edition. Stuttgart: Deutsche Bibelgesellschaft, 1984.

Sacks, Jonathan. "Faith in the Future: The Promise and Perils of Religion in the 21st Century." http://www.rabbisacks.org/faith-future-promise-perils-religion/. Accessed 12/8/2016.

Sanders, James. *Torah and Canon.* Philadelphia: Westminster, 1972.

Schaper, Joachim. *Eschatology in the Greek Psalter.* Tübingen: Mohr-Siebeck, 1995.

Scheetz, Jordan. *The Concept of Canonical Textuality and the Book of Daniel.* Eugene: Wipf and Stock, 2011.

Schmemann, Alexander. *For the Life of the World*, 2nd expanded edition. Crestwood: St. Vladimir's Seminary Press, 2002.

Schneiders, Sandra M. *Written that You May Believe: Encountering Jesus in the Fourth Gospel*, 2nd edition. New York: Crossroad, 2003.

Schnelle, Udo. *Antidocetic Christology in the Gospel of John.* Translated by Linda M. Maloney. Minneapolis: Fortress, 1992.

Schüssler Fiorenza, Elisabeth. "A Feminist Critical Interpretation for Liberation: Martha and Mary: Luke 10:38–42." *Religion and Intellectual Life* 3 (1986) 21–36.

Schwöbel, Christoph. *Gott in Beziehung: Studien zur Dogmatik.* Tübingen: Mohr Siebeck, 2002.

Sherwood, Yvonne. *The Prostitute and the Prophet: Hosea's Marriage in Literary-Theoretical Perspective.* Sheffield: Sheffield Academic Press, 1996.

Smith, D. Moody. *John.* Nashville: Abingdon, 1999.

———. *John Among the Gospels*, 2nd edition. Columbia: University of South Carolina Press, 2001.

Smith, Ralph L. *Micah-Malachi.* Waco: Word, 1984.

Soulen, R. Kendall. *The God of Israel and Christian Theology.* Minneapolis: Fortress, 1996.

Spencer, F. Scott. *Salty Wives, Spirited Mothers, and Savvy Widows: Capable Women of Purpose and Persistence in Luke's Gospel.* Grand Rapids: Eerdmans, 2012.

Spina, Frank Anthony. "Canonical Criticism: Childs Versus Sanders." Pp. 165–94 in *Hermeneutics: Interpreting God's Word for Today.* Edited by Wayne McCown and James E. Massey. Anderson: Warner, 1982.

———. "Wesleyan Faith Seeking Biblical Understanding." *Wesleyan Theological Journal* 30 (1995) 26–49.

———. "Canon." Pp. 81–84 in *Handbook of Christian Theology.* Edited by Donald W. Musser and Joseph L. Price. Nashville: Abingdon, 2003.

———. *The Faith of the Outsider: Exclusion and Inclusion in the Biblical Story.* Grand Rapids: Eerdmans, 2005.

Stebbins, R. P. "The Story of Balaam." *The Old Testament Student* 4 (1885) 385–95.

Steinke, Peter L. *Congregational Leadership in Anxious Times: Staying Calm and Courageous No Matter What.* Lanham: Rowan & Littlefield, 2014.

Stendhal, Krister. "Biblical Theology, Contemporary." Pp. 418–32 in vol. 1 of *The Interpreter's Dictionary of the Bible.* Edited by George A. Buttrick. 5 vols. Nashville: Abingdon, 1962.

Strawn, Brent A. "Docetism, Käsemann, and Christology: Can Historical Criticism Help Christological Orthodoxy (and Other Theology) After All?" *Journal of Theological Interpretation* 2 (2008) 161–80.

Strecker, Georg. *Theology of the New Testament.* Louisville: Westminster John Knox, 2000.

Sumney, Jerry L. *Colossians: A Commentary.* Louisville: Westminster John Knox, 2008.

Swindler, Leonard. *Jesus Was a Feminist: What the Gospels Reveal about his Revolutionary Perspective.* Lanham: Sheed and Ward, 2007.

Tapie, Matthew A. *Aquinas on Israel and the Church: The Question of Supersessionism in the Theology of Thomas Aquinas*. Eugene: Pickwick, 2014.

Thompson, Marianne Meye. *Colossians and Philemon*. Grand Rapids: Eerdmans, 2005.

———. *John*. Louisville: Westminster John Knox, 2015.

Thurneysen, Eduard. *Revolutionary Theology in the Making*. Translated by James D. Smart. Richmond: John Knox, 1964.

Thurston, Anne. *Knowing Her Place: Gender and the Gospels*. New York: Paulist, 1998.

Treier, Daniel J. *Introducing Theological Interpretation of Scripture: Recovering a Christian Practice*. Grand Rapids: Baker, 2008.

Trible, Phyllis. *Texts of Terror: Literary-Feminist Readings of Biblical Narratives*. Minneapolis: Fortress, 1984.

Tyson, John R. *The Way of the Wesleys*. Grand Rapids: Eerdmans, 2014.

Vanhoozer, Kevin J., ed. "What Is Theological Interpretation of the Bible?" Pp. 19–23 in *Dictionary for Theological Interpretation of the Bible*. Edited by Kevin J. Vanhoozer. Grand Rapids: Baker, 2005.

Vinson, Richard B. *Luke*. Macon: Smith & Helwys, 2008.

Vlach, Michael J. *Has the Church Replaced Israel? A Theological Evaluation*. Nashville: B & H, 2010.

Wall, Robert W. "Martha and Mary (Luke 10.38–42) in the Context of a Christian Deuteronomy." *Journal for the Study of the New Testament* 35 (1989) 19–35.

———. *Revelation*. Peabody: Hendrickson, 1991.

———, and Eugene E. Lemcio, eds. *The New Testament as Canon: Readings in Canonical Criticism*. Sheffield: Sheffield Academic Press, 1992.

———. "Toward a Wesleyan Hermeneutics of Scripture." *Wesleyan Theological Journal* 30 (1995) 50–67.

———. "The Future of Wesleyan Biblical Studies." *Wesleyan Theological Journal* 33 (1998) 101–15.

———. "Canonical Contexts and Canonical Conversations." Pp. 165–82 in *Between Two Horizons: Spanning New Testament Studies & Systematic Theology*. Edited by Joel B. Green and Max Turner. Grand Rapids: Eerdmans, 2000.

———. "Reading the Bible from within Our Traditions: The 'Rule of Faith' in Theological Hermeneutics." Pp. 88–107 in *Between Two Horizons*. Edited by Joel B. Green and Max Turner. Grand Rapids: Eerdmans, 2000.

———. "Facilitating Scripture's Future Role among Wesleyans." Pp. 107–20 in *Reading the Bible in Wesleyan Ways: Some Constructive Proposals*. Edited by Barry L. Callen and Richard P. Thompson. Kansas City, MO: Beacon Hill, 2004.

———. "Toward a Wesleyan Hermeneutic of Scripture." Pp. 39–55 in *Reading the Bible in Wesleyan Ways: Some Constructive Proposals*. Edited by Barry L. Callen and Richard P. Thompson. Kansas City, MO: Beacon Hill, 2004.

———. "Canonical Criticism." Pp. 563–64 in vol. 1 of *The New Interpreter's Dictionary of the Bible*. Edited by Katharine Doob Sakenfeld, et. al. Nashville: Abingdon, 2006.

———. "Wesley as Biblical Interpreter." Pp. 113–28 in *The Cambridge Companion to John Wesley*. Edited by Randy Maddox and Jason Vickers. Cambridge: Cambridge University Press, 2010.

———. "John's John: A Wesleyan Theological Reading of 1 John." *Wesleyan Theological Journal* 46 (2011) 105–41.

———. "Participatory Holiness: A New Testament Perspective." Pp. 40–49 in *Holiness as a Liberal Art*. Edited by Daniel Castelo. Eugene: Pickwick, 2012.

———. "The Canonical View." Pp. 111–30 in *Biblical Hermeneutics: Five Views*. Edited by Stanley E. Porter and Beth M. Stovell. Downers Grove: IVP Academic, 2012.

———, with Richard B. Steele. *1 & 2 Timothy and Titus*. Grand Rapids: Eerdmans, 2012.

———, and Daniel Castelo. "Reading the Bible as Scripture" Pp. 11–25 in *A Compact Guide to the Whole Bible*. Edited by Robert W. Wall and David R. Nienhuis. Grand Rapids: Baker Academic, 2015.

———. *Why the Church?* Nashville: Abingdon, 2015.

Wallis, Jim. *America's Original Sin: Racism, White Privilege and the Bridge to a New America*. Grand Rapids: Brazos, 2016.

Weber, Robert, ed., *Biblia Sacra. Iuxta Vulgatam Versionem*, 5th edition. Stuttgart: Deutsche Bibelgesellschaft, 2007.

Webster, John. *Holy Scripture: A Dogmatic Sketch*. Cambridge: Cambridge University Press, 2003.

Weippert, Manfred. "The Balaam Text from Deir ʿAllā and the Study of the Old Testament." Pp. 168–69 in *The Balaam Text from Deir ʿAllā Re-evaluated: Proceedings of the International Symposium Held at Leiden 21–24 August 1989*. Edited by J. Hoftijzer and G. Van Der Kooij. Leiden: Brill, 1991.

Wellhausen, Julius. *Die Composition des Hexateuchs und der historischen Bücher des Alten Testaments*, 3rd edition. Berlin: Goschen'sche, 1899.

Westerholm, Stephen, and Martin Westerholm. *Reading Sacred Scripture: Voices from the History of Biblical Interpretation*. Grand Rapids: Eerdmans, 2016.

Westermann, Claus. *The Living Psalms*. Translated by J. R. Porter. Grand Rapids: Eerdmans, 1989.

Wharton, James A. "Karl Barth and His Influence on Biblical Interpretation." *Union Seminary Quarterly Review* 28 (1972) 5–13.

Wilson, Robert McL. *Colossians and Philemon*. Edinburgh. T & T Clark, 2005.

Witherington, Ben, III. *Women in the Ministry of Jesus*. Cambridge: Cambridge University Press, 1984.

Wright, N. T. *Justification: God's Plan and Paul's Vision*. Downers Grove: IVP Academic, 2009.

———. *Paul and the Faithfulness of God*. Minneapolis: Fortress, 2013.

Yafeh-Deigh, Alice Y. "The Liberative Power of Silent Agency: A Postcolonial Afro-Feminist-Womanist Reading of Luke 10:38–42." Pp. 417–39 in *Postcolonial Perspectives in African Biblical Interpretations*. Edited by Musa W. Dube, Andrew M. Mbuvi, and Dora Mbuwayesango. Atlanta: Society of Biblical Literature, 2012.

Yamaguchi, Satoko. *Mary and Martha: Women in the World of Jesus*. Maryknoll: Orbis, 2002.

Zenger, Erich. *A Commentary on Psalms 51–100*. Minneapolis: Fortress, 2005.

Ziegler, J., and O. Munnich, eds., *Septuaginta. Vetus Testamentum Graecum. Susanna, Daniel, Bel et Draco*, 2nd edition. Göttingen: Vandenhoeck & Ruprecht, 1999.

Contributors

DANIEL CASTELO is Professor of Dogmatic and Constructive Theology at Seattle Pacific University and Seminary, Seattle, Washington.

STEPHEN E. FOWL is Chair of the Department of Theology at Loyola College in Baltimore, Maryland.

LAURA C. S. HOLMES is Associate Professor of New Testament, and Associate Dean of Seattle Pacific Seminary, at Seattle Pacific University and Seminary, Seattle, Washington.

ANDREW KNAPP is a Development Editor in Biblical Studies for Wm. B. Eerdmans Publishing Company, Grand Rapids, Michigan.

SARA M. KOENIG is Associate Professor of Biblical Studies at Seattle Pacific University and Seminary, Seattle, Washington.

EUGENE E. LEMCIO is Professor Emeritus of New Testament at Seattle Pacific University and Seminary, Seattle, Washington.

JOHN R. (JACK) LEVISON is W.J.A. Power Professor of Old Testament Interpretation and Biblical Hebrew at Perkins School of Theology, Dallas, Texas.

DAVID R. NIENHUIS is Professor of New Testament Studies, Seattle Pacific University and Seminary, Seattle, Washington.

JOHN PAINTER is Professor of Theology at Charles Sturt University, Canberra, ACT, Australia.

STEPHEN Z. PERISHO is University Librarian for Theology and Philosophy at Seattle Pacific University and Seminary, Seattle, Washington.

ANTHONY B. ROBINSON is an ordained minister of the United Church of Christ, author, speaker, and adjunct faculty at multiple universities, including Seattle Pacific University and Seminary, Seattle, Washington.

SHANNON NICOLE SMYTHE is Assistant Professor of Theological Studies at Seattle Pacific University and Seminary, Seattle, Washington.

FRANK ANTHONY SPINA is Professor of Old Testament at Seattle Pacific University and Seminary, Seattle, Washington.

Index of Authors

North, W. E., 157, 161, 163, 167
Nyssa, 213

O'Day, G., 173
Olson, D., 130, 131, 132, 133
Origen, 128, 129, 130, 131, 158, 191, 192, 193, 194, 196

Pagels, E., 196
Painter, J., 179, 181, 182, 197, 198, 201
Papias, 197
Parsons, M. C., 156, 157, 163, 165
Philo, 207
Pietersma, A., 104, 109, 111
Piper, R., 160, 162
Pittman, B., 91
Polycarp, 185, 190, 197

Rad, G. von, 36, 37
Radner, E., 8, 20, 21
Rahlfs, A., 99, 104, 106
Rashi, 123
Reid, B. E., 157
Reynolds, B., 105, 106
Robinson, A. B., 84
Roiullard, H., 114
Rösel, M., 98
Rosner, B., 204, 209, 210
Rowland, C., 118
Rudolph, W., 100
Rüger, H. P., 100

Sacks, J., 134
Sanders, B., 184
Sanders, J., 3
Sanders, J. N., 185
Schaper, J., 103
Scheetz, J., 104
Schmemann, A., 211, 212
Schneiders, S. M., 159
Schnelle, U., 199
Schüssler Fiorenza, E., 157, 158
Schwöbel, C., 15
Sherwood, Y., 32, 33
Silva, M., 99

Simpson, B. F., 126
Smith, D. M., 161, 173
Smith, R. L., 151
Soulen, R. K., 10
Spencer, F. S., 157, 158, 163
Spina, F. A., 3, 6, 7, 15, 27, 34, 35, 39
Spronston North, W. E. S., 162
Stebbins, R. P., 121, 122, 124
Steele, R. B., 77
Steinke, P., 87, 88
Stendahl, K., 53, 68
Strawn, B. A., 31
Strecker, G., 197, 199
Sumney, J. L., 216, 219
Swindler, L., 156

Tapie, M. A., 9
Thompson, M., 216, 217, 219
Thompson, M. M., 163, 167, 169, 173
Thurneysen, E., 52
Thurston, A., 154
Treier, D. J., 48
Trible, P., 113
Tuckett, C., 190
Tyson, J. R., 38

Vanhoozer, K. J., 26
Vaticanus, C., 104
Vinson, R. B., 162, 163, 164, 165, 175
Vlach, M. J., 10

Wallis, J., 18
Wall, R. W., 3, 15, 24, 28, 31, 33, 34, 35, 36, 37, 39, 42, 44, 46, 47, 64, 69, 70, 71, 72, 73, 74, 75, 76, 77, 78, 79, 80, 81, 84, 97, 113, 133, 135, 136, 141, 142, 152, 155, 161, 177, 178, 203
Webster, J., 76
Weippert, M., 125
Wellhausen, J., 114
Wesley, J., 25, 37, 38, 39, 41, 43, 44, 79
Westcott, B. F., 201
Westerholm, M., 38
Westerholm, S., 38
Westermann, C., 42, 44

Index of Scripture